Outlaws Inc.

Outlaws Inc.

UNDER THE RADAR AND ON THE BLACK
MARKET WITH THE WORLD'S MOST
DANGEROUS SMUGGLERS

Matt Potter

B L O O M S B U R Y

New York   Berlin   London   Sydney

Published by Bloomsbury USA, New York

All papers used by Bloomsbury USA are natural, recyclable products
made from wood grown in well-managed forests.
The manufacturing processes conform to the environmental regulations
of the country of origin.

LIBRARY OF CONGRESS CATALOGING-IN-PUBLICATION DATA

Potter, Matt.
Outlaws Inc. : under the radar and on the black market with the world's
most dangerous smugglers / Matt Potter. — 1st U.S. ed.
p. cm.
Includes bibliographical references.
ISBN-13: 978-1-60819-530-5
ISBN-10: 1-60819-530-9
1. Smuggling. 2. Black market. I. Title.
HJ6619.P68 2011
364.1'336—dc22
2011016132

First U.S. Edition 2011

1   3   5   7   9   10   8   6   4   2

Typeset by Westchester Book Group
Printed in the U.S.A. by Quad/Graphics, Fairfield, Pennsylvania

To Mikhail

&

Sergei

The last of the independents

Contents

**PART IV HIGH AND WILD:
AFGHANISTAN TO IRAQ**

**PART V BACK TO THE JUNGLE: CENTRAL
AMERICA AND THE HORN OF AFRICA**

**PART VI THE JOURNEY HOME:
EAST AFRICA AND RUSSIA**

It was hunted for the sake of its arms and accoutrements
from hill to hill, from ravine to ravine, up and down the dried beds of
rivers and round the shoulders of bluffs, till it disappeared as water
sinks in the sand—this officerless, rebel regiment.

RUDYARD KIPLING, "THE LOST LEGION"

But would you kindly ponder this question. What would
your good do if evil didn't exist, and what would the
earth look like if all the shadows disappeared?

MIKHAIL BULGAKOV, *THE MASTER AND MARGARITA*

Prologue

The Russian pilot throws his paper cup onto the tarmac and walks across the pitted runway. The giant plane's Soviet military decals are still faintly visible under gray paint.

That's the signal. There are no words, no checks, no IDs: just a long walk in the last rays of the afternoon toward a tattered Soviet warplane so big it plays tricks with the eyes. As the engines rise to a deafening whine, I climb the ramp and twist my body into position inside the cavernous Ilyushin Il-76, code name Candid. Bathed in the bright light of the cockpit glass, the skipper kicks off his shoes, takes his seat, and flips the switches. Seconds later we're airborne, heading into the Afghan night.

From Afghanistan to Chechnya, the giant Il-76 was the USSR's ultimate warhorse. It saw action on every front, in every capacity, from commando missions to reconnaissance, military intelligence, explosives drops, arms transport, and even cosmonaut training.

At more than forty-six meters long and forty meters wide, it is one of the biggest planes on the planet. Weighing 210 tons, this superplane can fly in Arctic ice storms and African heat. It can operate from shorter, more bomb-damaged and unprepared runways than planes half its size. It can carry a staggering sixty tons of guns, soldiers, tanks, bombs, or anything else halfway around the world. And these days, for half a million dollars, anyone can have one.

But the Il-76 also carries a secret.

Beneath the floor of the cargo hold, deep in the belly of the plane, its Soviet creators added a number of extra spaces. Originally designed for escape equipment, armaments, and classified payloads, they can be hollowed out to create secret chambers. These chambers don't appear on any cargo paperwork; they won't be checked by customs; officially, they don't even exist. But they are there.

And if you're determined enough to fill them—and foolhardy enough to fly—then your plane will carry anything up to fifteen extra tons of "phantom" cargo. Cargo for which some men are willing to die and others are prepared to kill.

I had heard all about these mercenary aviators—mercs, as they're often known in Africa. I had read the CIA dossiers and seen the crash reports. But now as the plane took off with me on it, I was about to see an operation from the inside.

The men's names, their life stories, and even their appearances and flight patterns have been changed to protect them and me. But this is their world. From the lawless streets of Russia's Wild East to the pirate-controlled coast of Somalia, from rogue states and rebel "'stans" to the shadow world of drug traffickers and black markets, this is the story of those fifteen extra tons.

PART I

Good Men Are Hard to Find: The Crew

CHAPTER ONE

The Devil's Greatest Trick

Over Kabul

THERE IS NO WARNING, just a sickening upward lurch as we abandon our flight path. A red light goes on in the cockpit. The instruments say we're over Kabul, but that we're suddenly climbing, not landing, and that we're doing it too fast and too steep.

"What's going on?" I ask in Russian, but Sergei, one of the seven-man crew, can no longer hear me over the scream of the four engines tearing our dangerously overloaded giant up and out of what should have been our runway approach and almost vertically into the night. In the dim light of the freight hold, his face is a mask. Under my feet the greasy, gaffer-taped, twenty-year-old, 176-ton metal tube shakes, groans, and pops.

Then he looks at me and leans in close. "Missiles," he shouts, as if pointing out a house where he once lived, or a roadside bar. "Here's where they start shooting." For the first time I notice he stinks, not just of the usual sweat and oil, but of booze. I've seen the news stories: vague one-liners about unexplained cargo-plane crashes in Africa, Russia, the Balkans. Blamed on RPG launchers on the ground, vodka in the air.

"Jesus! Who?"

He shrugs. "Mujahideen. Rebels. Soldiers. You never know. But always somebody." He closes one eye, an imagined potshot. Then he grins.

"Mikhail is a top pilot, though. He knows the airstrip from the war. He's got this method where he lands by climbing up high over the airport, then sort of dive-bombing the runway like a corkscrew."

Sergei laughs. "You don't get shot down that way. His trick is knowing when to pull up out of the dive. Incredible! You watch."

But suddenly we are at peace. The plane levels off. The engines are almost hushed now, and despite the pressure, bursting ears, fear, and humpback-bridge dizziness, an odd feeling of almost euphoric weightlessness washes up from the soles of my feet.

It takes a moment for me to register the sudden downward tilt, to see the lights of Kabul in the cockpit glass. The ground is laid out like a map, dead ahead, where seconds ago there were stars.

The Soviets used the Il-76 in cosmonaut weightlessness training—the infamous "Vomit Comet" flights. It would execute a series of parabolic climbs and dives in which the descent was marked by an upward anti-gravitational push in the cabin. Extremely dangerous to execute—in a Candid, at an approach angle of 20 percent or more, stalling is a real risk—these dives from high altitudes in which the pilot would attempt to pull up just before the nose hit the tarmac are said to have resulted in a number of messy deaths and the spontaneous redecoration of many more flight decks. As we plummet earthward and my stomach passes upward, not just through my mouth but through the top of my skull, it's unclear which of these things will happen first.

Against my better judgment, I lean out to look over the pilot's shoulder. Mikhail is hunched forward like a man reading on the toilet, or praying. Either way, I'm with him. The ground is more than very close now; it's just yards from the nose. Pull up. For God's sake, pull up. But it's too late. Involuntarily, my fists clench, legs kick out, eyes shut. Fuck. This is it. We're going down.

"SOME PEOPLE DELIVER letters for the post. That's me—just a postman. Only the parcels are heavier."

I don't really know how I'd expected an outlaw aviator and international gunrunner to look, but Mikhail is definitely—almost comically—not it.

Heavy-boned, gray, and stooping, he looks fifty, maybe more. His gaunt, ashen face carries a permanent expression of mild disappointment more suited to anti-smoking ads in hospital waiting rooms than wanted posters at the UN. His enormous hands are cracked, filthy, and horn-nailed; he's wearing a gray boilersuit, battered cap, and army-surplus boots. Sitting on the parched earth of another third world airstrip after an aid run, cadged cigarette already on the go, he looks for all the world like a car-factory worker on his break. It's just gone seven in the morning, but already the hot dust is, he grumbles, making him thirsty for a Baltika.

Not, on appearances, quite the Han Solo–style maverick I've fantasized about riding the skies with.

But if Mikhail—whom I soon take to calling Mickey, first to his good-humored annoyance, then his resignation—makes an odd outlaw, he makes an even odder businessman. An Il-76 pilot all his adult life and a product of the Soviet military—via a childhood in the Urals, his local air force training base back in Russia, then the massive Vitebsk military base in Belarus and the Military Air Transport Regiment to which it was attached, then Central Asia—this squinting, chain-smoking veteran of the bloody, desperate last days of the Soviets' Afghan war is blue-collar right down to the sloping shoulders and alcoholic sweat. Yet here he is, he says: partner in a highly profitable air-transport business spanning the Emirates, Asia, Africa, and Eastern Europe, whose operations in the world's worst trouble spots put them beyond the sharp end of the global free market.

Mickey (not his real name—it's understood that his real identity, his past, even the details of his plane, will remain a secret) and the crew have flown together for more than a quarter of a century. As Soviet air force pilots, navigators, gunners, engineers, and loadmasters, they flew more than three hundred hostile missions over the same Afghan mountains, villages, plains, and cities they specialize in navigating today—and in the same plane.

"When the USSR started to break apart," Mickey explains, "well, some of us saw the weather change and took our chance to do something different." That something was a dramatic escape from the military and a bid for a piece of the private-enterprise pie. "It wasn't difficult. We knew some people, and when they 'acquired' a military plane, we flew it down to Kazakhstan and, you might say, rebranded." He suddenly looks embarrassed at this corporate-sounding phrase. "Naturally, not a word we used, but it turns out that's what it was."

Good-bye, Red Army star and CCCP livery; hello, anonymous, no-logo gray paint and primer. "We were," he smiles awkwardly, "suddenly *biznesmeny*"—to Russian speakers, the word is full of the carpetbagging mafioso connotations of those wild times. "And today we are the A-Team."

Call them and the twenty-four-hour, no-questions-asked elite crew will fly whatever you've got to wherever you want it in one of the largest planes on earth, danger no object—if the price is right.

"We operate as private transport for all sorts of things," says Mickey. "We fly a lot of freight. Military things. And a lot of aid."

Which has had the effect of turning Mickey, his men, and their "partners"—a shadowy group of men Mickey is reluctant to discuss and whom it will take me nearly a decade to pin down—into rather reluctant saints, too. Because from Pakistan to Somalia and from famines to tsunamis, Mickey's crew and their battered, twenty-year-old Ilyushin are the first into disaster areas with lifesaving humanitarian relief. Chartered by everyone from NGOs to Western governments, they are regarded as agile, responsive, and—largely thanks to their background in commando drops—able to get more aid closer to more hazardous, harder-to-access disaster zones than anyone else. If the money is right.

Their unorthodox methods, guts, and sheer chutzpah have made these aircrews legendary, and made them the men to call when—in the words of the A-Team themselves—you've got a problem and no one else can help.

John MacDonald is a Surrey-based chartering agent, one of the middlemen who take the initial job specs from armies, aid organizations, importer/exporters, and private individuals and find the planes and the aircrews to do them. Despite coming from a long line of aviation specialists and having "seen it all," he laughs as he recounts one wildcat Il-76 team job that left the American military command in southern Afghanistan breathless with admiration, knowing they'd been hoodwinked by a five-man crew of Russians and their shadowy network.

"The U.S. military had this huge generator they needed to get to an airfield site they were planning in the south. This was a remote area, and aside from a few pockets of U.S. troops, it was completely under bandit control. There was no fuel available for miles around the landing spot, and none of the outfits we approached would touch it with a barge pole. They all kept saying, 'We'll never get out again, how can we take off from an unprepared airfield with no fuel?'

"The job was priced at between $60,000 and $70,000, but one day there's a phone call from these Russian guys. They said, 'We'll do it, but it'll cost you $2 million, in advance.' The Americans didn't really have a choice by this stage, so they paid. And sure enough, right on time, this ex-Soviet air force crew flew in, with the generator, in this battered old Il-76, unloaded the generator, then sat down for a leisurely smoke.

"Just as all the Americans were wondering how on earth they were going to fly out again, there's a cloud of dust and up clatters this old minibus driven by some Afghan bloke—and these airmen just get in and drive off. The Yanks were all going, 'Hey, how will you get the plane back?' And the crew just said, 'We won't. It's an old one—we only bought it for this job, and we're ditching it here.' Half a million dollars it cost them, and they held it together with string just long enough to land, then cleared off $1.5 million in profit and left it to rust. It's still there.

"Everyone just applauded them—the U.S. guys in command, us, and charterers the world over. Not just for the flying, but for the incredibly sharp business mind that could hatch this. It was truly beautiful."

Mickey laughs when I tell him this story, but points out that flying dangerous missions, under fire, into hostile lands where the airports may or may not have been destroyed is "more or less what we were brought up to do." Still, like the potential rewards, casualties are high—together, maverick Il-76 and Antonov transport outfits court one of the highest civilian fatality rates since the dawn of aviation history.

And for anyone even thinking about shadowing these guys on their missions as I am, the roll call of death makes for especially sobering reading. In 2009 alone, two Russian-manned Il-76s collided above Makhachkala, near the Chechen border; an entire ex-Soviet crew and all passengers were killed when an Il-76 blew up midair over Uganda; a Ukrainian Antonov-12 bound for Entebbe crashed on takeoff in Luxor, killing all on board; and another crew was wiped out attempting a crash landing in the Congo. As I write this, in November 2010, another An-12 has just crashed with all hands dead in Sudan, and Pakistan's news network is showing a mysterious Georgian-registered Il-76 on an aid run to Sudan bursting into flames over Karachi, killing all eight Russian and Ukrainian crew. And that's comparatively good going: Of all the world's Antonov-12s—the Soviet military's second-most popular cargo plane—just under one in seven have been destroyed by accidents and disasters.

Mickey stops me. "Yes, of course there are risks, just like any job—don't make too much of them." He ranks the dangers, counting them off on his fingers like a man remembering ex-girlfriends—"Tiredness, enemy fire, stupid errors, overloading, mechanical failure, bad conditions, bad cargo, bad luck"—but adds that "alcohol and bad living have killed just as many men in the business as flying."

Over the years, he says, they've learned what not to do. They never approach an airport in Afghanistan or Africa on a standard landing approach, for example, having been attacked too many times by rocket launchers on the perimeter, so they climb and either corkscrew down over the runway or dive steeply onto the tarmac. "There are things you don't forget once you've done them in a war."

A recent United Nations report compared the crews to swallows: migrating great distances guided by mysterious commands and principles, rarely landing, and whenever possible avoiding contact with others. Missions are rumors, routes and stopovers often remaining unconfirmed until you're already in the air, cargo arrangements and contents kept deliberately fuzzy to preserve deniability on all sides.

"In Kabul," explains Sergei, "we know we're picking up mail and fruit for South America. When we get there, who knows? Maybe we'll collect washing machines for Morocco, and there someone will tell us to pick up humanitarian aid for Congo, then fish for Europe or bricks for Iraq."

This keeps turnaround and "ground time" to a minimum, and profits high. But it also has the effect of keeping their visibility and contact with the authorities low.

It seems insane, I tell Mickey: Why risk their lives on missions like this, in aircraft that were made before most of today's Red Army recruits were even born, aircraft held together with rust, for nothing more than the standard $120 per hour (for pilots) and $55 per hour (crew) plus per diems and board?

Mickey enjoys the life, he says. "I became a pilot because I love flying. So that's my life. I can choose most of what I do. The people are nice. It's a job." He does that modest Mickey shrug thing again. "*Zhizn harasho.*" It's all good.

I believe Mickey. He comes across as a decent, reliable man trying, like all of us, to carve something out for himself. But I also know a couple of things that he's omitting to mention in what, at this stage, is just a casual conversation.

Because as they line up anonymously on runways, jungle tracks, and military air bases across the world beside the hundreds of aboveboard, legitimate operators with their own liveried ex-Soviet warhorses, there's a shadier side to some of these crews, to a fair few of the outfits they fly for, and to their missions. Theirs is work that means big money—millions upon millions of dollars—changing hands, often through elaborate networks of bank accounts in places like Cyprus, Sierra Leone, Kosovo, and Dubai. And this money doesn't come from aid organizations, the U.S. military, the UN, or anyone else whose real name appears on the receipts.

Because, according to recent reports by the United Nations and monitoring groups like the Stockholm International Peace Research Institute, Amnesty International, and the International Peace Information Service—the world's elite trafficking detectives—many of these phantom pilots, in their "untraceable, migrating flocks of Ilyushin Il-76 planes," are also the key channel for the illicit transport of "destabilizing commodities" like narcotics, banned weapons, mysterious diamonds, arms to illegal or terrorist armies, and secret supply lines to rogue regimes looking to bust sanctions. They, and their even more elusive network of business partners, have over the past two decades fueled the growth of the global black market, the rule of warlords, and the rise of the mafia, in Eastern Europe and far beyond.

It's a tantalizing glimpse of the other world these men inhabit—a world in which nothing is as it seems. One in which a hold full of blankets bound for a disaster zone can apparently transform, midair, into fifteen tons of land mines for the local rebel militia or bootleg goods for the local mafia. One in which a man can be savior and warmonger at the same time, and the very flight that's full to capacity with doctors and medicine can also magically conjure up the Kalashnikovs that will, within days, be used to execute the patients. A world in which the words *mercenary*, *pilot*, *aid worker*, and *trafficker* have become dangerously interchangeable.

"The greatest trick the devil ever pulled was convincing the world he didn't exist." The tagline and refrain of the 1995 Bryan Singer film *The Usual Suspects* describes the methods of fictitious Hungarian trafficker, murderer, and crime lord Keyser Söze—a shape-shifting master of disguise whose murderous wake is obscured by rumor, myth, and the failure of the authorities to grasp his endless subtlety, resourcefulness, and determination. To this day in Italy and the United States, Mafia trial juries are flummoxed into making acquittals at the highest level by defense attorneys' arguments that there really is no such thing as the Mafia—that it's just a fantasy projected by Hollywood and a few overzealous and deluded prosecutors onto what really are discrete, one-off crimes unworthy of further investigation.

Even the existence of the most talked-about movement of the twenty-first century is in dispute. Many investigators contend that the very idea of a formal organization called al-Qaeda is primarily an American invention; that the phrase *al-Qaeda* was first brought to the attention of the public in the 2001 trial of Osama bin Laden and the four men accused of the 1998 U.S. Embassy bombings in East Africa, although there "was no organization," wrote BBC documentary journalist Adam Curtis for his series documenting neocon policy, *The Power of Nightmares*. "These were militants who mostly planned their own operations and looked to bin Laden for funding and assistance. He was not their commander." He points to evidence that bin Laden had not used the term al-Qaeda to refer to the name of a group itself until after September 11th, "when he realized that this was the term the Americans had given it."

In fact, these investigators claim that the idea of the organization was promoted by the U.S. Department of Justice post–9/11 because in order to charge bin Laden in absentia, they needed to use the existing Racketeer Influenced and Corrupt Organizations Act, which in turn meant they needed to demonstrate he was the head of an organization that could be commanded. Because if he commanded it, it could be uncovered, monitored, disrupted, and stopped. In the words of one senior U.S. State Department official, "When all you've got is a hammer, the whole world looks like a bag of nails."

To U.S. prosecutors and public officials of all stripes, whose very existence hinges on structures of affiliation, allegiance, command, transparency, and accountability, the alternative—that people, goods, and historical forces are conducted by a motive power over which they have no influence or oversight—verges on the literally unthinkable. Because without control and command, any movement becomes diffuse, shape-shifting, threatening, and fundamentally unassailable: Al-Qaeda becomes a state of mind.

The Mafia becomes a series of unfortunate coincidences. Osama bin Laden becomes Keyser Söze. And, like Mickey says, "I'm just a postman."

To most of us—from you and me right up to the charities themselves, the Pentagon, international law enforcement, and the UN—this twilight world of migratory cargo and global networks of rootless, unaccountable, nonunionized, go-anywhere-carry-anything airmen, each with a briefcase full of different life stories and enough ID to prove every single one beyond doubt, simply does not exist. We put a coin into a charity jar or sign a direct debit form, and we trust that what we send gets to where we're told it will go. In our world, what goes into a container at one end of a journey is what comes out at the other. Hammer it in, see the same nail come through.

So the idea of airmen declared dead after a crash apparently rising to take control of a plane in a different part of the world, or massive cargo aircraft disappearing midair, only to turn up at the same instant thousands of miles away a different color, and with a different life story and owner, is the stuff of spine-chilling bedtime stories and David Copperfield Vegas TV spectaculars. And like the ships that carried the Black Death along with their grain, any connection between the goods we knowingly send and the growth of black markets, terrorism, the mafia, the narcotics trade, brutal regimes, civil wars, and global instability is, for most of us, so obscure, so off the radar, that it doesn't even register until it's too late.

Luckily, there are some men and women, at the UN and international monitoring organizations, who've put cause and effect together and are tasked with tracking, disrupting, and halting the underground movement of contraband. But even for dedicated trafficking monitors and plane spotters, these countless Ilyushins and the outfits and men who fly them are ghosts, drifting in and out of sight—almost unstoppable, untraceable, and unpunishable. Meanwhile, to the rest of us, these ghosts don't even exist.

That is, until we see them for ourselves. I only became aware of these phantom aircrews, clandestine flights, and deadly cargo by accident—or rather, by a series of accidents—that led me from the last days of Soviet collapse, through a job advertising arms deals, to the mafia heartland of Milošević's Serbia.

As a young journalist, filing freelance reports from around the world for the BBC while holding down a day job on business magazines about Eastern Europe, I'd already seen the implosion of the old Soviet Union up close. While in Moscow and St. Petersburg in 1992, I'd watched spellbound the everyday effect on people's lives as the system, the rule of law, the economy, the whole Soviet dream went into meltdown, seemingly almost overnight.

Suddenly, the wide, classical *prospekts* of St. Petersburg became dark and dangerous places. Office workers and factory hands began stripping lightbulbs, chairs, fittings, ornaments, and cables from their workplaces and heading out into the squares to sell them alongside the householders hawking their belongings. I witnessed one waiter stealing his own restaurant's cutlery while serving guests.

But if it looked like chaos, there were also tantalizing hints of new, more organized forces at work. The mafia groups were already all-powerful—a well-intended clampdown on alcohol by President Gorbachev between 1985 and 1987, culminating in partial prohibition, had both sunk the state coffers in a country where alcohol is often more a career than a pastime and allowed a countrywide black market for smuggled, stolen, and homemade vodka, wine, and other booze to take root and grow out of control. Now, even amid the masses of patched-up vans and backfiring Ladas, one could see here and there conspicuously shiny Japanese-made jeeps with tinted glass, guarded or ridden shotgun by hulking, shaven-headed, ex-military types.

The Chechen mafia took over Moscow's exclusive, thirty-two-hundred-room "foreigners-only" Hotel Rossiya next to St. Basil's Cathedral, and I watched as they shook down guests and directed their army of bruised, overcoat-clad prostitutes to work the filthy lifts and hammer on guest rooms, attempting to sell sex, heroin, and amphetamines they called cocaine.

Meanwhile, on Moscow's lively Arbat Street, bony AWOL soldiers sold off liberated army gear—their uniforms, supplies, live bullets on the roll. Western defense analysts were already hurriedly trying to place and trace the last known locations of the billions of tons of explosives, bullets, nuclear and biochemical material, and military technology now lying loose and unguarded and very much for sale.

A lifelong Russophile, I was horrified. But in a funny way, I was fascinated too. This dangerous, dirty place on the verge of anarchy, full of the dark antiglamour of desperation and violence, was everything my middle-class home wasn't. And most of all, I was curious. What will these people do now? In a place this powerful and this unstable, what happens next?

Back in London and struggling in journalism, I worked briefly in a dead-end job at a journal publisher, whose titles included a defense trade magazine and several Russian business titles. Though the publishers can't have known it and ran them in good faith, I couldn't help noticing how occasional ad pages seemed to function as discreet clearinghouses for any MiG-29 fighter planes or bits of other hardware that Russian, Kazakh, Ukrainian, or Byelorussian *biznesmeny* or impoverished state concern had acquired and wished to convert into currency. Taking copy of the "We are your ideal partner in Russia for sell top military plane" variety, dictated by a man who only ever referred to himself as "The Contact" over a crackly phone line from a dacha* in the Caucasus seemed to fit, somehow, with what I'd seen myself a year or so earlier. None of them ever paid for their ads.

But with their dachas and deals, these men were clearly at the top of the tree: the winners from the big shake-up. I couldn't help wondering about where that money was going. About who could possibly have a use for all these Soviet planes. And about who was going to fly them. What ever happened to all those regular Joes down below?

Then in 1998, I found myself in what was left of a rapidly disintegrating Yugoslavia—the war in Bosnia over, the NATO intervention in Kosovo imminent—on what I hoped would become a freelance piece for the *Sunday Telegraph*. And with the currency collapsing and the Serb mafia and regime cronies holding court in the hotels of Belgrade, I considered myself pretty well versed in Eastern European anarchy. I thought I'd seen it all before.

What I hadn't prepared myself for was the first glimmering of an answer to the questions I'd been asking myself all along.

---

* We became quite friendly eventually, and he posted me a photo of the interior, log-clad with huge animal skins stretched out on the walls and rifles above the door.

CHAPTER TWO

What Am I Doing Here?

Serbia, 1998

THE FREEZING NIGHT RAIN COMES IN DRIFTS, smashing onto the driveway of the Hyatt Regency Belgrade with the force of an airborne tsunami. There's no point pulling my collar up against the roaring night, but I'm relieved to have made it out of the boozy, pistol-packing driver's cab. For a few seconds, the universe is chaos. Then the glass moves and I cross into the bubble of warm-blown air and light music.

Inside, cops are everywhere, flashing sidearms, smoking cigarettes, and drinking with mobsters. The atrium is crawling with "security": some state, some private, some mafia, some uniformed, some not. Packing the lobbies, restaurants, and business centers, press, diplomats, and NGOs bide their time, flipping between CNN and BBC World and swapping stories about how close we are to the inevitable backlash against Milošević's campaign of ethnic cleansing in Kosovo, his increasingly flagrant disregard for international diplomatic efforts to defuse the crisis, and his mafia-sponsored grip on Serbia itself.

Right now, this hotel is the branded international heart of Belgrade: a relatively safe environment where diplomats and anchormen stay and work, and where Serbia's own VIPs play. The once-proud Hapsburg city and former capital of Yugoslavia has by 1998 become the tattered gangland capital of a state now consisting solely of Serbia, its tiny mountainous neighbor Montenegro, and whatever claims on Kosovo it could make stick. Even now, it's obvious to everyone but the regime itself that these are its final days. Just like the Moscow I'd left in 1992, this freewheeling, broken Belgrade is a honeypot for the new rich, the scene of almost daily mafia assassinations, and home to an honest, increasingly desperate majority still grimly holding on for better days.

It's also the playground of the Milošević regime's cultivated army of cronies, mobsters, and mercenaries, and the black-market heart of the remaining economy: the town's official structures are ruled by "Red Businessmen"—gangsters given carte blanche by the regime to kill and traffic to their hearts' content, in return for their loyalty to Milošević when it's head-cracking time. Only now, they are falling too—blown up in cars, machine-gunned by ski-masked assailants, stamping desperately on sabotaged brake pedals, having outlived their usefulness to the regime or simply aroused the paranoid suspicions of an ever-shifting inner circle around the president. Even the most feared aren't safe: Before long, regime favorite, Serb militia commander, color-supplement pinup, and war criminal Arkan will be gunned down in the lobby of the InterContinental next door.

"One of theirs got assassinated upstairs," nods my young, slick-coiffed, and Italian-shoed fixer Sasha (not his real name) across the room at a smart young *American Psycho* look-alike. "A man called Knele in room 331. Checked in, left strictest instructions that nobody was to be allowed up to his room without the front desk calling to announce the visitor. Then a visitor walks straight into his room and blows his brains out." His hands trace an imaginary room layout on the table. "Think too much about *that* and you will become very paranoid. Because if somebody let the killer up to do his work, then you know nothing is forbidden."

It's a while before I figure out just why his phrase is nagging at me so badly.

Serbia is, to all appearances, isolated in the world. The government is careering into its last madness, ordering hit after hit, crackdown after crackdown. Someone on the hotel TV is talking about the latest arms embargo passed against Belgrade by UN Security Council resolution 1160, aimed at forcing what was still officially Yugoslavia to open a dialogue with Kosovo Albanians. Amid the economic collapse and stop-start hyperinflation at home come varying degrees of sanctions, downgrades, embargoes, and censures applied over the past few years by the EU, the United Nations, the United States, and other individual states and organizations in a list as long as your arm.

On paper, Belgrade is a city in which a great many things are forbidden. Outside the glass bubble, ordinary Serbs pick through rubbish, sell off their last belongings, teeter between poverty and desperation. Yet among the chosen out here in New Belgrade's luxury palaces, champagne corks pop. International news teams eat fresh fusion cuisine and get whatever protection, transport, and kit they need at the click of a finger. Cash is showered about with ostentatious largesse—no weak Yugoslav dinar here, just fresh deutsche marks and U.S. dollars. All over Belgrade, for the favored few, cocaine is freely available. Guns, luxury goods, and substances that should be scarce are ubiquitous. Where's it all coming from?

"If you can't beat 'em, join 'em," smiles one local businessman over lunchtime drinks at the Hyatt the next day. "Some stuff you can theoretically get legally, but it's too difficult and costs too much to do it. I can tell you one thing: If anyone in this city tells you their business, their government ministry, their shop, their restaurant, whatever, could survive for a single week without some benefit, directly or indirectly, knowing or unknowing, from the smuggling pipeline, you can tell them from me they're talking bullshit."

Food and fuel, he confides, are smuggled by land on a nightly basis across the border from Romania and Hungary. Other more specialist items for shops arrive on unpoliceable successions of plain container barges up the Danube, where New Belgrade gets first shout. Some basics designated as "humanitarian aid" get diverted, either en route or upon delivery into the hands of black marketeers. Meanwhile Yugoslav- or Soviet-made arms and other goods are sold for hard currency abroad: dollars, marks.

"All that sort of thing comes and goes by plane," he tells me, laughing at how cloak-and-dagger he sounds. "The dealers have their delivery men."

Soviet planes have been coming and going with noticeable regularity for a couple of years now, says the businessman. This has opened up a black-market wormhole through which anything—guns, people, cash, black-market goods, drugs—can appear or disappear. It makes sense. When you drive through impromptu barricades all day, these mysterious giant Soviet-era planes begin to sound like no-brainers—no stickups, shakedowns, or quasi-military roadblocks at thirty thousand feet. But they also sounded expensive. The fuel for a journey from anywhere outside the Balkans would cost hundreds of thousands of (theoretically unavailable) U.S. dollars. Someone has to be flush.

It turns out that a man named Rade Markovic, one of Milošević's most trusted secret-police chiefs and a regime assassin implicated in a series of unsolved gangland murders across Belgrade—for which he will later be sentenced to forty years in jail—is now liaising extremely closely with a man called Mihalj Kertes, head of customs at Belgrade's Nikola Tesla Airport. And over the past couple of years, the routes on the flight plans have gone from interesting to downright suspect: mysterious midnight departures originating in Russia or the Emirates, making their way from Belgrade via the 'stans and Cyprus to Iraq and Libya. They've coincided with a spike in trafficking activity through the Balkans in drugs, guns, and hard currency to sustain the regime's proxy militia armies down in Kosovo.

"Probably we know before anyone when war is on the way," Mickey will remember years later, casual as an after-hours minicab driver running down the nightly routine. "Jobs change. A lot of jobs at one spot. Or maybe a different kind of job becomes popular very quickly. It always means something. And it means money."

The Serb businessman and I finished our wine, paid the waiter in new U.S. dollars, and headed away from the hotel to our respective jobs, the next meeting.

BUT I DIDN'T forget what he'd told me, or what I'd seen. From that point, every time I traveled as a journalist, the airfields and terminals glowed with occult significance. I'd find reasons to separate myself, accidentally on purpose, from the press packs in places like Indonesia, Central America, the former Soviet states, the Balkans, Africa. I sat and watched the comings and goings of these giant cargo planes and the men who flew them. Mostly, I'd sit there for hours and nothing would happen; often, I'd attract the attention of the local security or military police. Either way, most of it was spent either explaining or wondering to myself what I was doing there.

But sometimes I'd catch a glimpse of some interesting planes, some interesting people. You got to recognize the crews: the worry lines, the likely hangouts, the incongruous overalls, Hawaiian shirts, and sports clothing. Even the way they'd walk across the asphalt, drink, and wait for their connection together, all watchful-casual just like military units. Watch them through the foyer window for long enough and you could almost feel their civilian clothes making them itch.

I'd spend the next decade and a half tracing these men and their movements and trying to get to the bottom of exactly what they were carrying, where, and for whom. And when I got my chance to hitch a ride with a crew of "delivery men" into Afghanistan in the wake of the U.S.–led coalition's invasion, I made sure I took it.

As it turned out, the pilot and his crew of Soviet veterans would lead me into the shadowy side of the new global economy, from South American guns-for-cocaine drops to the Afghan heroin trade, from the warlord-controlled jungles of the Congo to parachuted suitcases full of cash for Somali pirates. But that was all in the future.

To understand Mickey and his business, I'd first have to hear his story. And to understand the cosmic rupture that threw him, his plane, and a tidal wave of deadly cargo unequaled in history out into the world, we have to go back to the USSR.

PART II

Everything You Know Is Wrong: The USSR

CHAPTER THREE

The Lost Boys

Soviet Union, 1992

By DECEMBER 1992, for Mickey and his crew, not only was the disastrous, drawn-out Soviet-Afghan war over: The Soviet Union had given up the ghost completely, bankrupted by its own arms-race supremacy and torn asunder by the tensions between reformers like President Mikhail Gorbachev and the old guard, between satellite states from Lithuania to Georgia making their bid for secession, and by the instinct for stamping out dissent. From the Berlin Wall to the McDonald's in Red Square, from universal comradeship to the "new Russians" sweeping around Moscow in armed cavalcades of BMWs, the times were changing indeed. When he'd left for Afghanistan in the early 1980s, Mickey had left a home he knew. By the time he'd returned, that home was no longer there.

Drafted in small numbers initially to shore up a "tame" Afghan communist government, like America's Vietnam, the game quickly changed for the Russian military. Now huge numbers of men with the world's best weaponry, tanks, aircraft, and intelligence found themselves struggling to survive the stealth-and-sabotage tactics of Afghans fighting for their own land and familiar with the endless mountain passes. Increasingly motivated by fear, desperation, and the thirst for revenge, both sides quickly developed a reputation for playing dirty. Reports of torture, looting, the massacring of civilians, booby traps and poisoned supplies and indiscriminate dropping of explosives began to emerge. And as the Afghan tribal leaders and mujahideen began receiving covert backing from Pakistan, the Gulf, and the CIA alike, flights of the "Gruz-200s" (Soviet military code for the Il-76 and giant Antonov cargo planes that carried Soviet soldiers' bodies home) stepped up their frequency. Soviet withdrawal went from unthinkable to inevitable, and having delivered and supplied the Soviet armed forces in Afghanistan, Mickey and his comrades became the ferrymen who would spirit them back out, alive or dead.

Returning home, Mickey and his fellow veterans saw everything they'd thought was eternal, secure, and structured turning to ashes in a matter of months. The campaign was lost, their wages (when the government could afford to pay them at all) rendered worthless by a collapsing ruble; the air force itself was a busted flush, the economy going down the pan, and their hopes for any kind of future, in the armed forces or out, were looking bleak.

In a parallel universe, a Russian-set version of *The Full Monty* would portray the sense of listlessness, despair, and betrayal felt by these erstwhile Soviet poster boys of heroism and virtue, suddenly told they're no longer needed, won't be paid, and that everything they fought for was wrong anyway. The Soviet army was on the scrap heap, and whole garrison towns had become dilapidated and abandoned, almost postapocalyptic husks. One of them was Mickey's.

TORRENTIAL RAIN DOES few cities any favors, but it's hard to believe Vitebsk could ever really be beautiful. Perhaps I'm being unfair. Like anywhere, the fourth-largest city of the Socialist Republic of Belarus has its old town, though it's now reduced to a couple of whitewashed promenades, and the center—all potted auto routes, soot-spouting Volgas, and dirty yellow buses full of elderly ladies in headscarves—is no worse than many of the former Eastern bloc's industrial centers. But there's something about the way the slate sky pushes down on acre after acre of horizontal concrete blocks (offices, houses, hospitals, and municipal car parks all seem to have been designed by the same firm of architects who may or may not have been heavily influenced by Tetris) that can make a man itch to get into his car, or anyone's car, and drive very far away, very quickly.

Like so many former Soviet towns, it had its pet industries beyond the

air base and military-transport regiment, and like all of them, the clues
are in the football teams. The two big local names are Lokomotiv Vitebsk
(in the Soviet workers' paradise, the Lokomotivs were originally teams of
engineers and railwaymen, just as the Dynamos were power-plant workers), also known simply as Vitebsk FC, and Kimovets Vitebsk (workers at
the town's KIM tights and hosiery factory). After a disastrous 1995 season, they went under.

Eight miles out of town as you go northeast toward the lorry-choked
E95 motorway and the Russian border, there's a rather bleak military field
with a conning tower, planes, gates, and a few scattered concrete buildings: the ghost of a once-mighty air base that, give or take tours of duty in
Afghanistan and across the Union, was home to Mickey and his crew and
the hundreds of men and planes of the Third Guards Military Transport
Aviation Division. It had all seemed so permanent: The men, the base, the
planes—some thirty giant Il-76s and more An-22s—were part of the
greatest standing armed force the world had ever known. And then one day
that force simply evaporated.

Looking at it from this historical distance, in the rain on the deserted
perimeter, it's hard to see how the empire's sudden collapse and so many
former Soviet states' crazed "transition" to freewheeling capitalism could
have ended up producing anything but a pan-global underground network
of airborne traffickers. Or how the world could have expected anything
but a proliferation of organized crime, profiteering, black markets, terror,
and instability in its wake.

For ordinary Russians, Ukrainians, and Byelorussians, the sudden,
galloping disintegration of the Soviet Union and its subsequent carve-up
by privatizing entrepreneurs was nothing short of a disaster. A universal
share-voucher issue by the Russian state went disastrously wrong when
starving and impoverished ordinary Russians, with little or no idea what
it meant to be a stakeholder in anything, swapped their shares almost immediately for food or vodka. As a result, almost 100 percent of the shares
in newly privatized state operations and utilities worked their way back to
the few men already wealthy enough to buy them up, share by share, with
booze and bread.

Meanwhile, many among the first generation of Western firms to do
business in former Soviet lands more than lived up to the Soviets' image
of the robber-capitalist adventurer, turning up with much-needed liquid

capital and tying Russian companies into swingeing and impenetrable contracts. Some Russian businessmen—soon dubbed "new Russians," or *biznesmeny*—caught on quickly: Coca-Cola's head office in Ukraine reportedly hired its own militia after being raided by gunmen who forced their way past reception demanding the directors sign a "partnership agreement." A Russian friend in credit control succeeded in tracking down a debtor with an invoice inquiry, only to be told by a voice on the telephone that he recognized her accent and her family wouldn't be too hard to trace should they not be able to "write off the debt amicably."

As the economy seized up, ordinary people across the former Soviet Union became increasingly desperate. The World Bank's chief economist Joseph Stiglitz noted in disgust, "Not only was the [former Soviet states'] national economic pie shrinking; it was being divided up more and more inequitably so the average Russian was getting a smaller and smaller slice." The effects were clear: From being a society in which only 2 percent lived below the poverty line—then defined as living on the equivalent of two dollars a day or less—by 1998 Russia's poverty trap had claimed one in four, with over 40 percent living on less than four dollars a day.

But if it was a disaster for ordinary people, for anyone employed by the military—and even by 1985, that figure was reckoned by the Central Committee to be a massive 20 percent of the entire working population of 135 million—it was nothing short of an apocalypse.

As the lands of the Union split away to try their luck as independent states, army units, air bases, nuclear submarines, men, machinery, and warheads suddenly found themselves claimed as sovereign property, as residents or unwilling occupiers of newly independent states far from home. Even at home, funding for the armed forces simply evaporated. Wages went unpaid. Rations of food, fuel, and clothing just failed to arrive. Equipment went unrepaired. Ghostly, hunger-ravaged soldiers lost confidence in the chain of command and simply wandered off. Nuclear warheads lay unguarded in padlocked sheds and on abandoned rolling stock, their guards forced to forage in the woods. Elite weapons scientists on the verge of starvation appealed frantically to an impoverished state for help in keeping their crumbling research facilities going and their families provided with food, shelter, and medicine. High-ranking officers took payment in whatever form they could get, from vacuum cleaners to breakfast cereals, and spent their days AWOL, trying to sell them for their supper on the black market. Army platoons hired themselves and their equipment out for cash, laying roads with their tanks and enforcing security for whoever had the money to feed them, while airmen diverted avgas, planted potatoes in air base soil, did whatever it took to feed their families, their men, themselves.

Pilots and other air force personnel were laid off en masse; those who remained often went unpaid for months, even years. As late as 1996, four MiG-31 pilots at the Yelizovo air base in Russia's far east resorted to a hunger strike in an attempt to claw back several months' back wages. The rate of "extracurricular" deaths among conscripts—from suicides, murders, and unfortunate accidents—jumped from next to nothing to three thousand a year. It had all happened so quickly that the sheer numbers of servicemen returning from erstwhile Soviet posts in East Germany, Poland, Czechoslovakia, Hungary, the Baltic states, Central Asia, and beyond found there simply weren't enough houses for them; camps were set up in which soldiers and airmen and their families were forced to live in tents.

The authorities were rattled by the speed and scale of the breakdown. In a panicked 1992 report, first deputy defense minister Pavel Grachev protested that "of the Soviet Air Force's three military transport aviation divisions, suddenly only two regiments remain remotely operational." To make matters worse, the massive base in Vitebsk, as well as bases like Ukraine's Dzhankoy, Zaporozhye, and Krivoy Rog, suddenly belonged to newly independent countries—which meant that they were not merely outside Russia's control but even more desperate for cash, and potentially even less stable.

Among the hundreds of newly created ex-servicemen at the Vitebsk base, all of whom suddenly found themselves on the scrap heap with no other prospects and often without a final wage packet, were Mickey and his crew.

"What do you do?" says Mickey. "It was a very bad time. There was no money coming in, no housing, no food, the army couldn't even feed us. We all had to find another way to survive—and I mean, really, to *survive*."

But as it happened, they weren't looking for long before the solution found them. Because in a curious twist of fate, the very forces of free-market capitalism that had rushed in to pick over the bones of the USSR and that were now impoverishing its former pilots suddenly came to rest, for the briefest of moments, in the hands of one of the most powerful men in the erstwhile Soviet Union. And that man was about to take a very close interest indeed in the fate of men like Mickey and his crew.

EVGENY IVANOVICH SHAPOSHNIKOV was born on his family's farm in the southwestern Rostov region of Russia on February 3, 1942, into the tense, impoverished calm that descended between two murderous occupations by the SS. Rostov-on-Don had already been reduced to rubble by the Germans. Regarded by Hitler as having strategic importance for its river port, railways, and land rich in oil and minerals, the area had first been bombed, then briefly occupied the previous November. The Germans would be back to retake it in July 1942, when little Evgeny was just five months old.

Growing up amid the rubble, land mines, and poverty of postwar Rostov, and in a society now severely lacking in adult males, the boxy, well-built boy looked to the skies and Soviet film reels for his role models. From an early age, Evgeny worshipped the brave Soviet fighter pilots. "It was my dream to be a pilot from childhood," he says today. "After World War Two, all military, including airmen, were highly respected persons. My house was close to the airport, and I used to watch the planes high in the sky. All my friends wanted to be like [legendary 1930s and World War II Russian fighter aces] Chkalov, Kozhedub, and Gromov. So the choice was obvious."

Shaposhnikov and his schoolmates weren't alone. As with the race for outer space, aviation was very much the sleek, silver shape of things to come in the Soviet Union of the fifties and sixties: Yuri Gagarin himself was a pilot first, cosmonaut second, and the air force was hungry for the best and brightest to man its aircraft—a new, cleaner defense system for the Cold War's new geopolitical borders in the sky.

Graduating from the Kharkov Higher Military Aviation School in 1963, Shaposhnikov was quickly identified as having the right stuff and passed out of the prestigious Gagarin Air Force Academy in 1969. Square-shouldered and handsome, he was the perfect pilot—talented, well liked by superiors and comrades alike, and loyal. By 1991, when he was appointed the last defense secretary of the USSR, he'd already commanded the Soviet Air Force's Sixteenth Army in East Germany. In 1992, when the USSR broke up, he was appointed commander in chief of the armed forces of the newly created Confederation of Independent States—a looser, freer alliance, but one territorially similar to the Soviet Union. Shaposhnikov was a powerful man. And his sympathies, as you might expect, lay very much with air force personnel at this difficult and uncertain time.

That, at least, is as close to an explanation anyone today is prepared to risk as to what Evgeny Ivanovich reportedly did next.

According to documents uncovered by Russian investigative journal *Sovershenno Sekretno* ("Top Secret") and reported by the International Relations and Security Network, in the winter of 1992 Shaposhnikov issued a command granting the right to anyone of battalion-commander rank or higher to dispose of "surplus property" belonging to the air force. They could dispose of it in exchange for payment—though no indication survives that guide prices were given—and to suitable buyers, though it's unclear precisely who, in this impoverished land, might both have cash and want weapons. Nor was it clear to many men further down the line exactly what was meant by "surplus property," as distinct from, say, the entire contents of stores, aircraft, ammo, uniforms, and anything else that wasn't nailed down.

In the split second between the command and the commencement of an orgy of privateering and black-market arms sales the likes of which had never before been seen in peacetime, the world (Shaposhnikov's closest cabinet colleagues included) all asked themselves the same question: *What on earth was the commander in chief thinking?*

"Certain steps had to be taken officially in this direction," explains Shaposhnikov today from his office at the Flight Safety Foundation International in Moscow. "Firing and training grounds were leased to local collective farms; military trucks were used for fetching nonmilitary goods, men were sent to help collective farmers with crops." Then he adds: "And surplus military property was given to local businessmen."

Whether he foresaw it or not, it was a looters' charter. As if a whistle had sounded, the quartermasters' stores from Vladivostok to Vitebsk, and all the air and weapons bases across Russia, Belarus, and Ukraine, became a January sale. Selling at low, low cash prices to the right people—and that meant more or less anyone with the wherewithal to come knocking— lined the pockets of the sellers (with the battalion commander inevitably taking an 80 percent cut for turning a blind eye and signing the docket) and gave the buyers access to weapons-grade material for a fraction (usually less than 10 percent) of the guideline market value. Every serviceman with access to equipment, from high explosives, guns, and ammo down to night-vision gear and regulation thermal vests, liberated what he could. According to senior Moscow military analyst Colonel Oleg Belosludtsev, "Freelance arms merchants took over in cahoots with army officers, plundering the vast surplus stocks and selling wherever buyers could be found."

"It might not have been a written memo," says historian Dr. Mark Galeotti, academic chair of the Center for Global Affairs at New York University, a historian who's spent his career tracking organized crime in the former Soviet Union. "But it's clear that there was an understanding. We can't pay you, so sell what you need to in order to get by. At this point, you've got Russian fields being plowed by 'tractors' that are basically Red Army tanks with the turrets yanked off and a piece of metal soldered over the hole. So in that context, you want an Il-76? Sure!"

At the same moment, the masses of ordnance, ammunition, planes, vehicles, and supplies returning from former Soviet bases abroad had become problematic. If there was a shortage of homes for the airmen, there were certainly no facilities to house the gear being repatriated in a procession of trucks, Il-76s, Antonovs, and ships from erstwhile Soviet garrisons in East Germany, Poland, Central Asia, the Baltic states, the Caucasus, the Czech Republic, Slovakia, Hungary, and further afield. Between the announcement of withdrawal and the last arms-laden Candid leaving East Berlin's Schönefeld airport in 1994, it was widely understood that anyone who could make a buck for himself by disposing of some of the "load" would be doing everyone a favor.

The sheer scale of this pilfering from the world's greatest arms stockpile is staggering. "Ukraine, where [notorious illicit cargo baron and gunrunner to Liberia, Leonid] Minin came from, is a great example, like all the former satellite republics," wrote PBS's *Frontline World* journalist Matthew Brunwasser. "During the Soviet era the Second Soviet Army was based in Kiev as part of the Soviet Union's defense strategy against a western NATO attack. Ukraine was equipped to maintain a standing army of 800,000—almost three times the size of Ukraine's military today. After the Soviet Union collapsed in 1991, Ukraine inherited these Soviet stockpiles of military goods intended for a military far larger than Ukraine's."

In practice, that means that in Ukraine alone military equipment, weapons, and transport sufficient for 630,000 troops was now officially "surplus"—and fair game for anyone with enough cash and chutzpah. Colonel Oleg Belosludtsev estimates that a staggering 80 percent of all arms exports made after 1991 were through these "shadowy," mafialike dealing networks that grew up around the old military bases.

Kremlin mandarin General Alexander Lebed went so far as to claim the entire Russian invasion of Chechnya in 1994 was simply a cover for the massive corruption in military high command. "These so-called generals needed a big war to break out somewhere," he admitted, "so that a large number of armored vehicles could be 'written off.'" Armored columns would leave for Grozny; an unusually high number of tanks, rocket-propelled grenade-launchers (RPGs), ammo, whatever, would be "damaged" on the journey, written off, and replacements sent for. Those "damaged" goods, in pristine condition, would then be sold to whichever broker could meet them on a lonely Chechen road and take delivery.

It was the fire sale of the century. Many of those who had access to the stockpiles simply sold their booty on, becoming dealers either in the "legitimate" marketplace, to Western companies looking to buy up cheap APCs, guns, armor, and aircraft, or to contacts in the rapidly growing local mafia organizations—men like Minin, giving mobsters prime access to former Soviet army stockpiles reclassified as "surplus" small arms. Within a couple of years, defense trade magazines such as the one I was working on were suddenly full of hurriedly written, blurry display ads for MiG fighters and other nearly new defense hardware placed by men like my friend "the Contact."

With uncanny speed, the mafia infiltrated the higher ranks of the military, developing a broad network of suppliers, collaborators, and commanding officers with enough clout to sign off military equipment by the truckload. Writing perfectly good equipment off as "damaged in transit" was a favored method, as it kept not only the buyers happy but the government's suppliers too: the perfect win-win situation and, if they could only forget about the end use for the weapons, a seemingly victimless crime. Enlisted men further down the ladder like Mickey's loose band of associates set up in business—as private security guards, as mercenaries, as drivers . . . and as freelance transport outfits.

So if these reports are correct, then what on earth was an honest soldier like Shaposhnikov—a hero to many, whose good standing, integrity, and trustworthiness were such that President Boris Yeltsin entrusted Russia's "nuclear red button" codes to him for safekeeping—thinking?

"These activities were intended to provide men and officers with free food and goods from local farmers and businessmen," he confirms today. And despite his protestations that "the first post-Soviet winter was difficult for everyone, including our military and air force, but I was impressed that our personnel and operational readiness was up to the mark . . . discipline and loyalty mean a lot to our men," Shaposhnikov himself must have felt that aside from being a discreet way of helping the boys, this colossal military fire sale was arguably the only means left of averting something even more explosive than an arms free-for-all: an all-out armed-forces mutiny.

Russia had endured one attempted coup, the previous year when, in August 1991, government members opposed to President Mikhail Gorbachev's reforms had imprisoned him and used troops to surround the Soviet White House in Moscow. Supreme Soviet Chairman Boris Yeltsin led popular protests against the coup, climbing a tank to deliver a speech denouncing the plotters. It is widely believed that it was only the entreaties of Shaposhnikov (who says he "enjoyed very good working and personal relations with Yeltsin") that turned the tide, forcing the soldiers' climb down. But now the men, unpaid, unfed, cold, and increasingly disaffected, were restive. The specter of hundreds of thousands of highly trained, desperate, and starving servicemen and ex-servicemen turning on their masters was, for a short time, a very real one; and a mutinous air force capable of carrying nuclear warheads and troops anywhere, anytime, would have been a prospect too dark to contemplate in a state all too conscious of the possibilities of armed revolution.

The writing was on the wall. Arms, planes, equipment, and men were going AWOL anyway, and given the choice between allowing the men at least a piece of the action or forcing mutiny and civil war, one can only speculate that Shaposhnikov effectively had no choice. His colleague, Minister for Privatization Anatoly Chubais, said, "We did not have a choice between an ideal transition to a market economy and a criminalized transition. Our choice was between a criminalized transition and civil war."

As for Mickey's team of airmen, they were still in their twenties and thirties but already carried the skills, scars, habits, hardship-forged contacts, and thousand-yard stares they'd brought back from the war in

Afghanistan—today, Shaposhnikov calls it "the Russian version of Vietnam syndrome." For them, the sudden collapse in prospects for the army and air force combined with feverish talk of rich rewards to be made in the burgeoning private sector. Their families were hungry; they themselves had frequently been forced to survive on their wits by foraging and bartering what petty goods they could steal. Now, finally, with the fire sale they had a shot at something bigger.

With the service descending into chaos, the country on its knees, and rich incentives on offer to join the global movement of goods and capital into, between, and from the lands of the erstwhile Soviet Union, the question for these boys wasn't *if* they'd use their skills to go into business, but *how*.

CHAPTER FOUR

The Machine

Post-Soviet Russia, Early 1990s

THE GUNS, AMMUNITION, PLANES, EVEN NUCLEAR WARHEADS flowed out of the military stores, the bases and the silos, even straight off the factory lines and into the hands of anyone with a good contact, a bill to pay, or a score to settle. But for Mickey and his comrades, turning the free-for-all into a worthwhile business would take all the wiles, expertise, and perseverance they'd learned flying their endless sorties over Afghanistan. It would also take the right plane.

After years of neglecting the wider economy in favor of military might, the former Soviet Union now faced a downhill race, just as Mikhail Gorbachev had predicted, to liquidate as many of these assets as possible, as quickly as possible. Warheads, tanks, bullets, guns, jet fighters, ships, grenade launchers, transport planes, the lot.

Arms manufacturers, sensing the approach of a drastic liberalization of the economy, began to adapt to market conditions. But their production lines, used to working toward targets outlined in five-year plans, couldn't react fast enough. Commissioned by a suddenly bankrupt army, dozens of Soviet monster aircraft—Ilyushins, Tupolevs, and Antonovs—often made it no further than the post-assembly depots, left to rust in their dozens outside factories and on silent, abandoned airfields across Uzbekistan,

Tajikistan, Kazakhstan, and Ukraine. Faced with the option—sell them and claw back some cash for yourself, or let them rust—their guardians were only too pleased to let them go to whomever came knocking. But if a new model was still too much—well, there were also plenty of combat-worn planes in various states of airworthiness to be bought, leased, or borrowed on very favorable terms, solo or crew included, from the armed forces themselves.

For a team like Mickey's, trained to a high level but with only one skill to speak of, taking to the skies again in a repainted Il-76 felt, he says, "like getting back to business as usual after all the worry." They had the plane, the crew, and, in the burgeoning black markets of former Soviet states, no end of demand for discreet, speedy transportation to satisfy.

Suddenly, and to this day exactly how remains a mystery, these men with no money of their own and a few solid army connections were in business. They flew whatever came their way, from that first "liberated" Candid in Kazakhstan to whatever hastily assembled patchworks of leased engines and borrowed airframes someone had losing money on a parking berth and wanted crewed. They flew for others and flew whatever unlisted cargo they could for themselves: pilot fish for the new breed of sharks that were suddenly circling international waters. And they soon found they had three "invisible" competitive advantages that would prove crucial as their business activities grew.

The first was a vast, loyal contact network. With ex-Soviet military and crew stationed everywhere from the coast of Afghanistan to Angola, they enjoyed the benefits of the world's biggest old-boy club. For discreet missions at short notice, reliable recommendations—preferably not just for capable crew, but the right sort of people—were often the only way to staff up extra charters. And reliable connections on the ground at destination were often the only way to ensure customs could either be successfully negotiated—or negotiated with.

The second subtle advantage enjoyed by ex-Soviet airmen taking to the privatized skies was a deep knowledge of mission terrain that went way beyond most other pilots'. Between 1979 and 1991, Soviet Il-76 pilots made more than 14,700 flights into Afghanistan, transporting 786,200 service personnel and 315,800 tons of freight. Soviet support for proxy regimes in Africa, Asia, and Latin America like Angola, Cuba, Afghanistan, Korea, Vietnam, and Chile throughout the Cold War meant a large number of the pilots knew more about the airstrips, weather, terrain, and even local infrastructure, customs, and connections than anyone quite realized.

The killer difference, though, was in these DIY import-export barons' relationship with their aircraft. After all, having trained, graduated, captained, and seen active service in Il-76s throughout their careers, often fixing engines by hand and stripping down the interiors to accommodate more men or equipment under duress and in sometimes extreme conditions, they knew their plane like it was part of them. And that meant they knew its hidden secrets.

Today, British aviation consultant Brian Johnson-Thomas sits on the UN's panels of experts on the traffic in destabilizing commodities throughout the world. But as an investigative journalist and former flight manager, he's witnessed these crews' sheer grit, talent, and ingenuity up close. He's also come to admire them, cautioning me when we meet that they are among the finest aviators he's ever seen, and "certainly no worse than anyone else when it comes to moral choices." A strapping, white-bearded fiftysomething with a soft Celtic burr and a tweed jacket, he cuts an incongruous figure among the bony, glazed faces of the former Soviet crews and deathtrap planes with whom he flew for years for NGOs and monitoring groups. This experience has given him a rare insider's view of their operations . . . and their hardware.

"People who don't actually fly them don't realize that Il-76s especially have all these hidden advantages to them," he says. "For example, they can load and unload, land and take off without any ground assistance, so whatever you do, you don't need anyone else's help. But the real surprise for me was the hidden spaces. Nobody ever looked beyond the cargo hold—not once—but it's an open secret among the crews that there are all these spaces down in the belly of the plane. You're flying these things all over the world, and nobody but you knows that there's a good fifteen tons of stowage beyond what it says on the operator's manual.

"Even customs officials, who check cargo off every day, don't ever fly in these things. They have the contents on the cargo manifest, and they tally with the maximum load on the spec. Then, if they stop for a moment, they'll do the maths and sure enough, the manifest takes the plane up to Maximum Take Off Weight. They expect a single hold space, and that's what they're shown, and they tick off what's in it, and that's their job. Beyond that, they don't have the time or the resources. A customs official in the third world might get paid five U.S. dollars a day, on a good day. They aren't likely to stop and arrest and generally make life difficult for the people who fly in and give them a bottle of vodka or case of cigarettes that will fetch five times that on the black market."

It was perfect. It quickly dawned that "the people who'd check the cargo against what we'd say we were carrying had never flown the plane—they hadn't a fucking clue, quite honestly," tuts Sergei.

"They'd look at the manual, see that 192 tons was the maximum take-off weight, and sixty tons of that was cargo. When that sixty tons had been loaded up and accounted for, they'd sign it off! But the thing is, we can carry fifteen tons more under the floor. Maybe sixteen, if we're feeling lucky. You have to start a little way back on the runway because it'll take you that much more power to get airborne, but you can do it. Well, *we* can."

So long as they didn't want to carry all the standard escape equipment that would normally fill those chambers, they had the perfect smuggler's vessel. Not only did the plane itself have what amounted to a fake bottom to it; because of Soviet secrecy around its military, the only people who knew it was even there were the engineers, and the airmen who flew it. And they were hardly likely to ruin a good thing by telling.

So now Mickey, like everybody else with a plane to fly and a living to make in that first desperate burst of free enterprise, just had to figure out a) what openly declared cargo jobs they would take on, and b) what illicit cargo a man of his skill could get away with carrying, for the right price.

For Mickey himself, of course, there was a third question. What hidden extra cargo, in the spaces of the Candid that not even his bosses knew about, would make him the most illicit cash in hand on each journey?

He needed to figure it out quickly. The crews were in high demand. The year was 1992 and things were changing. The Cold War was over, and the free market had trumped ideology. Meanwhile (and thanks largely to the glut of small arms suddenly flooding the market), small, bloody, internecine conflicts were spreading across Southern Europe and Africa.

By 1992, the former Yugoslavia had began its ugly descent into all-out sectarian war: Croatia and Slovenia, having declared independence, were recognized by some Western governments and began looking at what they could take with them, while Serbia geared up to prevent more secession, by force if necessary. On the edges of the old Soviet Union, Georgia, Armenia, Azerbaijan, and Tajikistan were plunged into civil war. Libyan-armed Tuareg rebels were opposing government forces in Mali. The Democratic Republic of Afghanistan had collapsed to the same mujahideen resistance fighters who had seen off the Soviets. Rebel militias were running riot in Rwanda, Liberia, Sierra Leone, Angola, the Sudan, Somalia, Guatemala, Peru, Colombia, Algeria, and Uganda. And in the Caucasian borderlands of Russia itself, another ex-Soviet air force Afghan-war veteran and Chechen separatist named Dzhokhar Dudayev was about to declare independence from the motherland and sign a law giving all Chechens the right to bear arms against their oppressors.

And for Mickey's crew, finding the answers to those questions would lead them into close contact with some of the worst people, and most hair-raising places, on earth.

Suddenly there was a new mission on the board.

IF THE SOVIET Union was broken—and veterans still refer to the snow-balling chaos of 1992 as "the Cataclysm"—its former pilots were unstoppable.

The perfect storm of the imploding USSR that had ripped apart the lives of men like Mickey was soon putting it back together again in some rather improbable, highly exotic, and infinitely more profitable ways. Far from being on the scrap heap, these aircrews found, to their considerable surprise, that they and their planes were exactly what this brave new world was looking for. Suddenly there was a wave of well-paid work for pilots and cargo planes from some unexpected quarters.

Those who'd flown in Afghanistan, like Mickey, were in particular demand. Not only did they know the capacity, and the abilities, of their giant cargo planes like no one on earth; they were also, it turned out, old hands at the "gray cargo" game.

There's a joke Mickey likes to make.

"Was the Soviet-Afghan war good cover for smuggling operations?"

"No, terrible!"

"Why?"

"Because the Soviet-Afghan war *was* a smuggling operation."

The stories are many. Like so many, there was Mickey's first visit to

one of the local Afghan markets near his billet, where he, like so many
other enlisted men, saw not only exotic fruits and foods he'd never laid
eyes on before but tape-to-tape cassette players and microwaves, and he
and his crew, like so many others, pretty much bought or bartered everything they could and hoarded it until they could get it out. It went down
so well that they started "losing" or writing off as destroyed or damaged
items on inbound runs—boots, fuel, even arms and ammo—and swapped
them at the same market for more microwaves and electric shavers to
haul back to the motherland.

Even then, the same discreet two-way silence ensured shadier pieces of
official business, and these crews' cash jobs could be carried out with mutual blind-eye indulgence. Among many similar tales in his chronicle of
the war, historian Gregory Feifer recounts one occasion on which KGB
spooks smuggled loyal former Afghan ministers out of Kabul under the
noses of the authorities, packed tightly inside green boxes pierced to allow
the "cargo" to breathe. On another, Spetsnaz men—the Soviet Union's
own Special Forces—captured the Taj-Bek Palace, and the looting lasted
two days. Trophies were taken: hats, guns, carpets, anything that wasn't
fixed to the walls and a whole lot that was, but the prize booty was the
trove of Panasonic TV sets and Sharp boomboxes. What didn't get found
by the Spetsnaz and sent back was coveted; unobtainable in the Soviet
Union, just one of these unlikely finds alone would make a grunt's crafty
extra baggage stowed away on board the Ilyushin more than worthwhile
on his next pickup back home.

Suddenly, the humble cargo crews with their Il-76s, Antonovs,
Tupolevs, and helicopters were the go-to men for anything their fellow
servicemen, secret agents, diplomats, or their families back home wanted
ferrying in or out on the sly. It ended up so well known that Mickey, Sergei, and the rest were put under special observation by some of the
straighter KGB men, anxious to put a stop to their secret supply-line
favors. Today, one senior Russian diplomat recalls his tour as a young Red
Army conscript in Kabul back in 1984, and the rumors of aircrews who
were said to transport illicit goods. "They had to be careful," he says. "The
pilots and aircrews weren't stationed with the soldiers, and if anyone was
seen speaking to them too much, it would get noticed. The other soldiers
and airmen weren't the problem, but the KGB people stationed over there.
If they thought there was something going on, there would be trouble."

But Mickey was nothing if not resourceful, and he was already per-
fecting ways of staying one step ahead of his watchers. A favored method
of hooking up was in the discreet "Russian-friendly" restaurants in town,
where "accidentally on purpose" encounters between services and ranks
could be engineered and pulled off, albeit with some care. And among
these circles, slowly, these pilots of the giant Soviet cargo planes laid the
foundations of a career that endures today.

Even among 1920s barnstormers and World War II flying aces, few had
the intimate knowledge of their planes that Mickey does. Theirs is a mar-
riage, an equal partnership in business and in life: one born of eating,
sleeping, fighting, and working in the Il-76 for a quarter of a century.
Even watching him prepare for takeoff on a standard run in Africa is like
spying on a bachelor alone in his flat. As I fidget and pace in the plane, he's
outside on the runway, having a last smoke with two Latvians and some
local gofers. They're shuffling about among the cans, weeds, and crows in
the last rays of sunlight, talking, joking, and smoking. No one looks toward the plane.

Then the boots clatter and Mickey appears inside. He takes off his
threadbare captain's uniform and hangs it on a twisted coat-hanger peg at
the cockpit threshold, pulling on a polo shirt and jeans and settling in for
a day's shift work—stepping into the cockpit proper and pushing a newspaper, charts, invoices, clutter from his seat onto the floor, gathering the
paper puddle and stuffing it into a plastic carrier bag on a pile behind
him. Down below, from the glass pit of the nose, Dmitry the navigator, a
strapping, sulky-faced man with sandy hair and slanted Tatar eyes, looks
up and round, catching my eye, then away. Lev, the spooky-eyed, un-
blinking blond flight engineer, pops another chewing gum and makes
one last check that everything's as it should be.

There's a high, sick whine, then the hot roar of the engines as we begin
our taxi. Some of us cover our ears against the earsplitting pitch of the
engines, some of us don't, and I crane my neck to check out the in-flight
movie—the view through the huge, panoramic nose cone, a glass screen
providing such spectacular floor-to-ceiling action it earned the plane an
affectionate nickname, "the Cinema."

There weren't any passenger seats in an Il-76 (there still aren't in most),
so chairs were brought onboard and lined up in hotchpotch fashion: chairs
from offices, schools, terminal buildings where they had terminal build-

ings, sentry boxes where they didn't, but really, just wherever they could find them. These chairs naturally weren't fixed down, so they'd slide about a lot during takeoff, landing, and any evasive maneuvers the pilot had to make, which were many and varied, and of course the passengers would have to link arms while those closest to the fuselage walls just held on to whatever protruding metal lugs, instruments, or bits of loose webbing they could.

For the former NBC newsman and Soviet-Afghan war reporter Arthur Kent, trips with Mickey or his fellow pilots in the Cinema "became a regular treat, every time I skipped over to Moscow with a Soviet troop-transport flight, or into Pakistan and back for more chaos."

In fact, the basic, cavelike interior of an operational Candid is an attractive proposition to many airmen and flight managers, who speak affectionately of its spartan comforts—no comfy seats, just eggs frying on a gas burner, a liberal smoking policy that extends way beyond tobacco, and all the half-inched vodka and warm beer you can drink. Even today, asking a veteran passenger of those Il-76 flights if he fancies taking a trip to Moscow in the Cinema is enough to make him turn white and remember that urgent appointment he's already late for somewhere else in town. One veteran flight manager once described the Candid to me as "two hundred thousand rivets that just happen to be flying together in close formation." But it's only when you cadge a lift with an old warhorse like Mickey's that you really understand what they mean.

Just like the chairs in the Cinema, lots of the fittings aren't nailed, soldered, glued, or fixed down. It makes for an exciting takeoff, and generally adds to the fun when the pilot takes any kind of sudden evasive action, or even decides to swoop down and land somewhere for a pickup. It's quite an odd feeling watching furniture, baggage, and boots moving up and down the plane under their own steam. There are two stoves: One's a standard burner, one's a two-hob hotplate on a cable. (On some old Antonovs there's even a chimney for the smoke.) Lights are strung along a runner. Pots and pans jammed in a box by the side, more ripped-open packages, a couple of thirty-two-packs, some big batteries wrapped in cellophane, a well-cared-for metal coffeepot. Lots of people, most of them Westerners, don't understand the beauty of the setup and make wisecracks about these gas canisters for the stove being our emergency fuel tanks, or they joke that the Il-76 burns vodka, shouting, "5, 4, 3, 2, 1 . . . cleared for Smirnoff!"

whenever they see an overloaded old Candid take off. I actually remember laughing about it to myself once, but that attitude faded as soon as the smell of frying bacon and beans wafted through the pressurized cabin as we flew into the dawn.

The cabin's got that panoramic view, glass all over the nose, light flooding in. Except right now, the crew's clothes are slung on hangers from hooks and rails across the front: a couple of those cloth hanging bags for pressed suits you get from hotel laundries and alterations services form a blanket obscuring the duck-egg green cockpit. Push it aside and you'll see the instruments almost all have needles and dials—a few calculator-style digital displays and autopilot, of course, but otherwise everything's mechanical—and therefore fixable with a screwdriver if you take the console up. Whatever else crashes, you suspect it won't be the onboard computer.

Boxes, crates, ropes; tattered brown padded lagging all over the fuselage and hold; metal-plate signs in Russian Cyrillic saying things like выход ("exit")—"Don't touch that one," deadpans Sergei); masking tape, lockers in the gun-metal gray, a couple metal pallets and a fold-down iron-springed bed about half the length of a human body to lie on; and small, high-up, porthole-style windows just to boost the whole Kursk submarine vibe. Outside, along the side of the bird, what looks smooth and bullet-skinned from a distance is really a network of holes and patches. This one's starting to look like a quilt. If you see riveted patches like these, you know you've got an ex-Soviet air force model, and the odds are it saw action in the Soviet-Afghan war, where the curtain of mujahideen RPG fire around every airstrip meant pilots either had to turn the giant plane into an impromptu and entirely inappropriate dive-bomber, or attempt to land using the Khe Sanh method.

It sounds like a complicated sexual practice, but the method is a good deal more difficult and hazardous. It's a famous under-fire landing procedure perfected by the Americans during the North Vietnamese siege of Khe Sanh air base in 1968. For pilots in war zones who want to hit the runway at just the right angle without coming in low enough to be shot down by light bazookas—and that's all of them—it means flying very high until they're directly over the runway itself, then corkscrewing down in a near-impossibly tight descent. But there's a problem. Because what the ground-to-air missile fire couldn't achieve, the Khe Sanh method often did: After the Soviets introduced it during their Afghan occupation, these

giant cargo planes' fuselages regularly cracked under the stress of spinning round and round in circles tighter than the plane was ever designed
to attempt, and in almost all surviving aircraft, fatigue cracks, fissures,
and holes began to open up on engine skins.

Potentially fatal leaks appeared. Rivets groaned, then popped. Parts
began to fall off. And aviators began falling from the sky. On November
26, 1984, the same guerrillas we'd evaded with Mickey's astonishing piece
of dive-bombing were camped in Kabul's Missile Alley. Only on that particular day, the pilot wasn't quick enough, didn't climb high enough, didn't
corkscrew tightly enough. A rocket-propelled grenade smashed into the
starboard wing of a Candid laden with cigarettes, notepaper, and ballpoint
pens for the troops garrisoned there. Any other time, the plane would *still*
have been able to land without too much of a problem. But this Candid
had flown in one too many tight circles and dives. The fuselage was criss-
crossed with invisible stress cracks like the rips in the inner seams of your
jeans. So that day, as the plane rolled sideways, it simply imploded, disintegrating into metallic powder in midair. Not only did the crew not have
time to send a distress signal; they didn't even have time to cry out. For
weeks afterward, farmers, kids, and soldiers were finding Russian-made
ballpoint pens, cheap writing pads, and packets of army-issue cigarettes
strewn across the countryside.

Always resourceful, the Soviet air force's technicians and ground crew
developed a method of riveting on metal patches—never enough to solve
the problem, never pretty, never meant to be permanent, but just enough
to keep the plane from splitting at the seams from all the diving and
twisting.

But these planes are also remarkable in a lot of other ways. Not least in
the way they owe their current capabilities—even a lot of their features—as
much to the crews who fly them, customize them, cannibalize and adapt
them as to the designers and workers of the Ilyushin and Antonov companies.

Mickey remembers more ad hoc, and certainly less official, ways of
souping up his plane's capabilities with the nostalgic affection of the man
remembering decorating his first home. The wells for escape equipment,
radar, even parachutes and the air-to-ground flares fired during takeoff
and landing to fool heat-seeking missiles, were often hollowed out and
stripped bare, their contents sold off separately either unofficially or with

the connivance of superiors out in the field. On the one hand, says Mickey, that meant no escape equipment, which was bad—but then, you never knew if that stuff was any good anyway, because there had been a lot of problems reported with it, so "We'd been warned not to bet our lives on it." Yet the upside was good enough to make even the prospect of taking on missiles and mountain ranges look like a reasonable risk to take.

The point of these modifications, along with knock-throughs and strip-downs applied to almost every other nook, cranny, and belly space, was to turn the Candid into the perfect deep-cover mule for whatever you wanted to take from A to B at the army's expense. The ploy exceeded the cargo teams' highest hopes: It was so effective, even among army checks, precisely because a lot of these spaces weren't even there on the initial design blueprints or paperwork. By the time your commanding officer discovered you'd ripped out the escape chutes to make space for a few extra tons of rugs, jewels, Stolichnaya, and bullets, went the saying, you'd probably be too dead to court-martial anyway. In truth, shrugs Mickey, his commanding officer was almost always part of the whole deal—the safest way to make sure you weren't thwarted by any of the other officers.

The most profitable journeys, he says, came when you were carrying bulky but light items in the hold. "Tents or uniforms or piping or whatever was good, because all the visible space could be full, but you still had lots of weight left to play with under the floorboards." (More than two decades on, it's a phrase I'll hear echoed by Oliver Sprague, a trafficking monitor at Amnesty International, who's watched these crews perform their cash-job dodges while piggybacking humanitarian aid runs.) But even if you had relatively little load space going spare, you'd always be able to shift something, since Mickey could fly it way beyond its stated maximum takeoff weight anyway.

So that's exactly what Mickey did. And so did plenty of his cohorts. From all over the USSR, they descended on Central Asia in the hundreds for a crash course in survival, physical and economic. Theirs was an operation within an operation, a job both patriotically legit and on the side; biggest of all the Red Army's regiments, battalions, and corps, it turned out, was the Self-Preservation Society.

Mickey shrugs. Conditions at the Afghan war air bases were appalling.

And anyone who could stomach that had more than back pay coming to him. And while the pilots themselves were lodged in hotels wherever possible (partly out of seniority, partly so they could sleep at least enough to fly without smacking into mountaintops), for loadmasters and the rest, something had to give. They kept warm and amused themselves on base by knocking back the pure-alcohol aviation spirit used for cleaning electrical circuits, nurturing a habit that sustains many of them and kills plenty still today. This was "white fever," the scourge of Soviet cargo crews. Andrey, a former Il-76 pilot and Afghan comrade of Mickey's who now runs his own cargo op down in Central Asia, recounts the tale of a young conscript diligently cleaning his engine with pure methanol, only for a wild-eyed airman to stride over cursing him for his wastefulness, grab the bottle, take a long lusty swig, and, with the words, "Idiot! You only need a thin layer," finish cleaning the engine by *breathing* methanol fumes onto the metal and rubbing merrily.

Alcohol was the beginning. Many wiled away downtime, and often uptime, with the local crops, opium and hashish, in which even the air bases were swimming, with some being "donated"—thrown into tanks and over compound walls grenade-style by Afghan "well-wishers" keen to see the pilots and soldiers become addicted—though much of it just went onto the planes and off again at the other end.

These were the experiences, hastily acquired skills, and low expectations that shaped the men suddenly available for freelance flying work. And as it turned out, Mickey's exit from military life was perfectly timed. Not only did he narrowly escape being dragged into the first Chechen war; he was also, he says, surprised to find that the world outside was ready and waiting for his services. For the business owners, all those who'd got themselves a piece of the arms action, and the airmen themselves, these were, he says, good times—the years of expense accounts, room service, tropical destinations, luxury hotels, parties with friendly capitalists, and encounters with exotic women who weren't actively trying to kill him.

Not that it was easy from the start. Just three years on from evacuating Kabul under enemy fire and having being laid off by the military with a single, one-off payment of 150 rubles in lieu of all back pay, the abrupt arrival in this wild new existence of sun, sex, and self-interest came, he admits, as a bit of a headfuck—not just to him but to everyone.

The airmen found ways of coping. Many drank, heroically and often, then less heroically and more often. Some, like Mickey's pal Artem, succumbed full-time to the heroin they'd first tried in Afghanistan, becoming thoroughly unreliable "ghosts." These ghost airmen were a common sight in those days, he says. They OD'd on tower-block staircases, turned up dead in the thawing snow plowed from the railway sidings or under lake ice in spring. The more resilient often washed back down to the 'stans, where they took to opium full-time and worked as fixers.

There were other roads. Some clued-in vets from his regiment fell in with the new *mafiya* gangs springing up across the erstwhile Union, acting as hired muscle, security, drivers, whatever it took. Some got religion, got jailed, or got the fuck out of the country. Aeroflot, suddenly flush with private suitors and cash, soaked up quite a few ex-servicemen—including the erstwhile commander in chief Evgeny Shaposhnikov himself, who would become the firm's director in 1995. Others got entrepreneurial, got settled, and went into business, stayed on the straight and narrow and gritted their teeth. Or they used other skills to start new lives as plumbers, shoe salesmen, and truck drivers.

And some, like Mickey, just kept flying. Hitting forty and still handsome in a lanky, sloping-shouldered way, he simply enjoyed seeing the world, revisiting some of the places he'd last seen in service, and living a little. So long as they were a few bucks ahead of the game and doing the thing they knew best, it was a good life. As Mickey tells it, with a matter-of-fact wave of his cigarette and that eyes-to-the-floor shrug, "There is no plan. Just me, the plane, the next job. I just do it." Then he laughs. "Take the aerial view, or you can go crazy."

It's a truism that the turbulent breakup of the Soviet Union created a power vacuum in which crews like Mickey's could thrive. But a stockpile is just a stockpile making small change on Arbat Street, an Il-76 cargo plane just a chunk of metal, and even a Vitebsk *mafiya* boss lording it over his local neighborhood with all the guns he can sell is just a hostage to fortune—until you match supply to demand. And in the freewheeling 1990s, so full of newly independent countries and post–Cold War movements struggling to be born, the demand was out there, all right.

It was time to go international.

CHAPTER FIVE

The Birth of the Global Network

Russia, 1993

LIKE SOME LOST TRIBE in search of a promised land, these privatized Soviet crews and their networks of partners, agents, bosses, and fixers scattered across the globe. The vast majority were simply earning a buck any way they knew, doing it honestly and transparently, and founding a wave of aviation outfits, legitimate blue-chip names like Volga-Dneiper and Heavy Lift, that span the world today, making sure Pentagon ordnance, rock bands' stage sets, humanitarian relief, and giant wind turbines get to wherever they're needed. And with them, across the world, a whole ecosystem of shadowy contacts and fixers sprang up with what— had anybody been looking at the time—would have seemed uncanny, almost unnerving speed.

Their choice of start-up HQ locations in Africa and the Middle East was about more than the need for Mickey and his like to enjoy a nice spot of distinctly un-Siberian sun and a change of scene. And it will come as no surprise if I tell you there are very few marble corporate offices with brass plaques on the door.

"There's no doubt the real reason was strategic," says international monitor Hugh Griffiths. At just thirty-seven, the young Englishman is a researcher at the Stockholm International Peace Research Institute, whose work in monitoring these mushrooming private airlines has seen him cause more ripples at the UN than many heads of state manage in a lifetime. He's become the scourge of the destabilizing commodities trade.

Lucrative aid and reconstruction contracts, he explains, as well as security and peacekeeping supply jobs will always go to places hit by the double-whammy tragedy that famine, terror, earthquake, or humanitarian disasters bring. Because for every shock, in which food, clean water, shelter, or medicines become scarce, there's an aftershock. This is the critical phase in which institutions break down: Corruption, violence, profiteering, and the law of the gun hold sway.

"The UAE, for example, is a main way-station and hub for the Afghan air bridge, and for aid to the Middle East and South Asia. Places like Uganda and Kenya are the only game in town for flights to Angola. That places them right where they need to be for aid flights and for anything else they might want to take to or from these countries."

Still, international monitors were for many years baffled at the way small arms and black-market goods find their way into disaster zones so quickly—and local resources, from cash and looted treasures to opium, find their way out.

But just as every complex ecosystem evolves parasites, it will evolve predators, scavengers, and masters of disguise and diversion. And, in among the jobbing airmen seizing their chance at a new life, there were others—legitimate businessmen and rogue operators, too, who cannily registered their planes in known-quantity countries with notoriously lax, obscure, or corrupt record-keeping and monitoring regimes like Georgia and Kazakhstan and set up their businesses in the Arabian Gulf and across sub-Saharan Africa. Once there, they formed a whole new class of altogether more freewheeling business owners. And the story of the most celebrated of them, an old air force comrade of Mickey's no less, is the key to understanding just what Mickey did next.

JUST OVER AN hour's drive east from Mickey's old air base at Vitebsk, the green, mossy earth smells of fresh rain and birch resin. Russian, Polish, and German cars, open-topped trucks and transcontinental container lorries hiss and spray along the cracked wet blacktop of the E141 auto route, bound for the Russian border city of Smolensk.

Slow down, indicate right, and pull over. Get out of the car, step off the hard shoulder, away from the whooshing traffic and into the trees, and the dripping silence quickly closes in. Giant, raggedy crows flap and peck over the soft forest earth. The abandoned shells of German Tiger tanks stand immobile and rusting, though even they are now rotting into these giant, misty birch forests through which they once advanced, clanking and roaring.

In the Forest of Katyn, the ghosts are piled six-deep in some places; in others, pieces of human debris turn on twigs in the wind. Either way, it's not a place you want to be after dark. Between 1942 and 1943, under the leaves and dirt, the bodies of as many as twenty-two thousand Polish army officers, writers, lawyers, engineers, and teachers were found, piled several deep in hastily dug pits twelve miles west of the city. On the orders of Stalin's secret police, they had been massacred in the woods in one single day of almost industrial slaughter in April 1940. And here, amid these same birches, they lay—alongside Ukrainian and Byelorussian comrades executed simultaneously and in their hundreds, in Smolensk's main industrial abattoir, and in the NKVD secret-police headquarters in town. The Katyn massacre still poisons Polish-Russian relations, and the ghosts still bring travelers to their deaths.

On April 10, 2010, the Polish president, dozens of war veterans, and the entire top tier of Poland's government were killed en route to a remembrance ceremony for the victims of the massacre. The Tupolev Tu-154M plane of the Thirty-sixth Air Transport Regiment, lost in the fog and attempting to reroute to Smolensk, hit the birches and disintegrated. Of the eighty-seven passengers and crew, not one survived. Photographs show the smoking wreckage of one of the engines, nestled among the birches on the forest floor, precisely twelve miles west of town. It looked like something that had found its way home.

Like Mickey's old base across the border in Vitebsk, Smolensk is home to a colossal military-transport air regiment—the combat-ready Il-76s of the 103rd Military Transport Air Regiment—and a famous Soviet-era military academy. The Military Air Defense Academy of the Land Forces of the Russian Federation is Russia's crack rocket and antiaircraft artillery training school—the first line of defense against the airborne aggression from the West on which, until 1991, the Soviet Union was betting its bottom ruble. Today its recruits play their part in the deployment of

Russian forces abroad as well as in defense of the homeland. But unknown to most recruits and enlisted men, the academy was also the scene
of one of the most bizarre heists in modern Russian history.

Sometime in the mid-1990s—details are understandably hard to come
by—it was decided by the authorities that a fitting statue should be installed in tribute to the academy's graduates and their work for Russia's
armed forces. Calls were made, permissions granted, and the military, with
thanks to the snappily branded Ilyushin-Tashkent Aviation Production
Association down in Uzbekistan, donated a suitable installation: a giant,
pristine Il-76 aircraft to stand proudly as a piece of mighty, industrial-
age sculpture at the entrance gates. It was a huge, jaw-dropping symbol of
Russia's adventures abroad, a reminder of just what was possible. The
authorities and military top brass trumpeted this coup. But on the day of
the great unveiling, the installation was nowhere to be seen. Because
someone—someone who'd been tracking the progress of the Il-76 statue
very closely indeed—had other ideas. According to investigators Douglas
Farah and Stephen Braun, somewhere en route to the academy, the warplane simply vanished.

Tantalizing details slowly emerged, though even they were sketchy. It
appeared that, having first persuaded an official somewhere along the line
between factory and delivery to redesignate the plane as scrap metal, the
audacious would-be owner then helpfully arranged to take the seventy-
two tons of "scrap" off their hands, diverting it to a third destination—
and then re-registered it in a loosely regulated regime and flew it off on its
first job. Anywhere else, it would be the crime of the century. In the context of free-for-all early-to-mid-1990s Russia, with entire, security-policed
payroll trains disappearing from the rails between stations, tanks firing
on Parliament in an attempt to steal the newborn state itself, and tons of
military ordnance vanishing on reaching Chechnya, it was depressingly
normalno—another day, another screw-over.

"Of course, there was the big sell-off of military equipment—but theft
is the other big way in which planes got 'liberated,'" says Mark Galeotti.
"Never underestimate the sheer amount of malfeasance in the former
Soviet Union at that time. A lot of kit got written off as 'destroyed,' and
just disappeared when units were being transferred back to Russia from
far-flung locations. It's horrific how much. Even before the Soviet Union
collapsed, much of the kit that was being brought back from East Ger-

many seems to have 'got lost' in transit. Estimates of how much vary dramatically, but the main ones were things that had practical civilian use. According to one figure I've been given, half of all the Soviet armed forces' motorbikes disappeared! Because that's something you can literally just wheel down to the local bar and say, 'Anyone like to buy a motorbike?' And admittedly, RPG-7 grenade launchers are a bit trickier."

Clearly, he says, given the difficulty in selling an Il-76 in a bar, whoever got the installation written off as "destroyed" then flew it away, having had what Galeotti calls a "practical civilian use" in mind for it.

It's a mystery that's likely to remain unsolved. Dmitry Kholodov was the last Moscow investigative journalist to launch an inquiry into the fake "scrapping" of large items of military equipment for black-market purposes, having written a series of articles about the possible involvement of none other than Defense Minister Pavel Grachev. He was passed a briefcase purportedly containing documentary evidence but the moment he clicked open the lock, he triggered a booby-trap bomb that blew him to smithereens and turned his office at the *Moskovsky Komsomolets* newspaper a bloody shade of burnt. So nowadays, those who may know are understandably circumspect about naming names when it comes to "scrappage" stunts like the life-size Il-76 sculpture that simply flew away.

But some names do keep rising through the murk. And whoever you ask—airmen or businessmen, cops or robbers, inside or outside the industry—you don't ask for long without hearing the name of a one-time comrade of Mickey's at the Vitebsk base whose career mirrors Mickey's own in some ways, while showing the difference a white-collar background, impeccable connections, and boundless ambition can make: an officer and army translator named Viktor Bout.

There are as many different biographies of this most controversial figure as there are people who'll claim to have had a brush with him. But for such a cause célèbre, so frequently photographed, he's still curiously difficult to pin down.

As far as anyone knows for sure, he is, or may be, any one of the following: Vitebsk airbase veteran; model businessman; ex-colonel; fairly low-ranking military translator; maverick aviator; illicit arms trafficker; friend to dictators and warlords; philanthropist; conduit for Colombia's FARC militia; black marketeer; Merchant of Death; innocent victim of a smear campaign on the part of embittered former business contacts, including ambitious arms-trafficking monitors, CIA-run rival cargo businesses, and the U.S. government; rogue FBI double agent; pawn in the Bush-Cheney administration's war games; valued partner to the U.S. reconstruction effort in Iraq; embargo breaker; puppet; delivery man; elusive phantom. Some say it's likely that at different times he's been all of the above. And as one *Guardian* reporter wrote on his 2008 arrest, "If Viktor Bout did not exist, a thriller writer would have invented him."

It would be tempting to say that the only thing anybody really knows about Viktor A. Bout is that his name is Viktor A. Bout, but even that's not always been true. He's carried at least five different passports and could at any moment have been Viktor (or often Victor) Buyte, Butte, Butt, Budd, Bulakin, Boutov, Bont, or Byte. Or Vitali Sergitov, or Vadim Markovich Amonov. Or simply "Boris."

Though his Web site, one of his passports, and a home video he recently put online all locate his birthplace as Dushanbe, in the former Soviet state of Tajikistan deep in the Central Asian crossroads between Russia and Afghanistan, he's claimed in a radio interview that he was born in Ashgabat, Turkmenistan, on the shores of the Caspian Sea. Then again, no less a source than Interpol had information (used in his arrest warrant) that he came from Smolensk itself. Another Interpol warrant put him down as a Ukrainian. Ukraine's Director of Military Programmes Leonid Polyakov, meanwhile, calls him a Russian born in Kazakhstan. Even the Russian government, having identified him as a Russian citizen and cooperated with attempts to extradite him for years, turned around in 2006 and tartly announced he wouldn't be extradited, as he'd never actually been a Russian citizen at all—then fought his extradition from Thailand to the U.S. and, after his extradition was finally ordered in 2010, announced it would do everything it could to "bring him home to his Motherland."

Ironically, the only thing one can really be sure of is that at the time of this writing, Bout had never been convicted of a single crime; even his harshest critics admit that, while they'd rather he didn't do what he does, none of it has been illegal. Whether that will still be the case when his trial is concluded is for others to decide. But only a fool would bet with the odds on a man like Viktor.

Bout is prominent enough to have enjoyed Armani-clad lifestyle-shoot treatment in the *New York Times Magazine* as well as having the world's most august intelligence agencies on his heels for over a decade. Which makes the degree of uncertainty about him incredible. Either Interpol, the CIA, the UN, and the U.S. and Russian governments are all comically inept (which is by no means out of the question), or someone's been constructing a pretty big smokescreen.

In fact, Bout's story is a white-collar version of Mickey's own: an operation founded with the purchase of ex-Soviet military Antonov An-8 planes in the same Big Bang that spun and spat Mickey, Sergei, and the rest across the globe. "Upon the collapse of the Soviet Union," says his Web site, "Victor decided to leave the military service and start his own aviation business, the field he was always fascinated by. And with some help from his family and his wife, Victor was able to purchase four Antonov-8 cargo aircraft that became the core and starting point of his fleet and his business."

That sudden acquisition of a fleet of cargo planes in those straitened times has raised many questions over the years, and recalls Mickey's words about simply "liberating" a plane down to Kazakhstan. Sure, there was a fire sale, but even then, with the reported price for these aircraft a bargain $300,000, that must have been an awful lot of money for an army translator from Tajikistan and his "friends and family" to scrape together. Then again, it depends on the friends—and unanswered questions about the nature and identity of these people will cast an ever-present shadow over my time with Mickey.

Bout's network of planes—a patchwork of Antonovs and Il-76s, purchased, begged, "liberated," and borrowed from different sources, which some claim include a plinth in front of a certain Missile Academy—grew throughout the maelstrom of the early 1990s, as did his influence. Soon he would be running those giant military-spec cargo birds throughout Africa, Central Asia, and the Arab world from his base in Sharjah, supplying arms to the likes of the Taliban, African warlords, and the Pentagon alike.

There are odd echoes of that first casual chat with Mickey on a dusty runway in Bout's self-description as "the typical and ideal picture of the new generation of Russian businessmen." Only where the blue-collar pilot seemed sheepish with the terminology of the New Russians and *biznesmeny*, to the polyglot, designer-double-breasted, coiffed, almost yuppie-like Bout, aspiration and achievement are nothing to be ashamed of. He is, if he says so himself on his personal Web site, "dynamic, charismatic, spontaneous, well-dressed, well-spoken, highly energetic [and able to] communicate in several languages including Russian, Portuguese, English, French, Arabic, among several others . . . a born salesman with undying love for aviation, and eternal drive to succeed." That is where he and Mickey differ. Because where the cataclysmic end of the Union meant working men like Mickey had to find some way to survive, for Bout it was all about seizing a great business opportunity.

But there are more similarities than differences. Like Mickey, Bout contends he's just a simple cargo guy: a postman, not an arms trafficker, and that whatever customers might be sending through his postal service is for them to sort out. Indeed, in an unexpected, and indignant, 2002 phone call to the *Los Angeles Times* by a man claiming (though the paper never managed to verify it) to be Bout's brother and business partner, Sergei, Bout was likened by the caller to a cabbie. "Imagine a taxi driver who is supposed to give a lift to a customer who asks him to take him to a certain location. But suddenly the taxi driver asks what is in your suitcase. It's not my bloody business what my customer has in his trunk. I am a carrier."

Over the years, Viktor Bout has become a cause célèbre, a thorn in the side of an ever-larger band of arms-trade monitors, plane watchers, UN investigators, and governments who can't quite believe it should be so hard to stop the deadly cargo of missiles, planes, guns, and ammunition to an unstable developing world full of cash-rich customers. His aviation companies have shape-shifted so often that nobody, not even Interpol, the CIA, or MI5, seem to this day to be exactly sure what, or where, they are.

But for now, all that—the fame, the photo shoots in glossy magazines, the arrest warrants—was still in the future. He was the undisputed cargo kingpin of this new age, and business was good. And Bout was nothing if not a big thinker. In the months ahead, as he rose to prominence as the operator of several ex-Soviet planes, he would move to South Africa, locate bases in the Middle East, become Boss Hogg of a remote airport near Mafikeng, and in time draw allegations of being a platinum-service gunrunner simultaneously to both the Afghan Taliban *and* the U.S.-backed Northern Alliance, arms trafficker to Angola, smuggler of blood diamonds and more. He was, if not first to market, then certainly the best.

But he wasn't alone.

CHAPTER SIX

The Warlord Is Always Right

The Caucasus, 1994

THE DEAFENING WHINE CHANGES TO A HOLLOW, throaty roar as the engines surge. There's shouting and pointing in the cockpit, the copilot's tapping on the glass at something below; everyone's looking down. We're too high for mountains and the sky's been as smooth as a monorail. Then a nod from Mickey and it's over, the roaring silence and the blackness closing around us again.

Steely glances and forget-about-it shrugs ricochet around the fuselage as shadows melt from the bathroom-lit cabin and into the half light of the fuselage. We've been curled, slumped, and slouched, entering a kind of willing suspended animation like men trapped in a bank vault or down mines in disaster movies. Now the spell snaps. Alarmed by the shouting, it's a while before I can find out what's going on.

"Chechnya," tuts Dmitry, turning out of his pod to grab a bite. "The idiots are shooting at us." He rolls his eyes. "Again."

"What's the point? We're too high. Much too high," sighs the flight engineer. Everybody shrugs. Someone opens a can of Sprite, but it's been shaken and explodes out, to much cursing.

Apart from the word *Chechens* passing back down the cabin, nobody says anything after that. I look round at the faces. They are blank, intense but vacant, and it's hard to tell if they're just doing their jobs, lost in the automatism of aircrew life, or thinking about being shot at, beyond range or not.

Despite the crew's obvious disdain for the possibility that someone's shooting, it often can and does end badly, even here. On a clear and starry night like this in August 2002, a giant Russian transport helicopter was shot down by a trigger-happy Chechen warrior on this same spot. The giant helicopter crashed in the midst of a minefield, one of the inky-black, unlit areas now visible through the navigator's glass. In the biggest single loss of Russian life of the whole Chechen war, 119 aircrew and Russian soldiers died, and a used rocket launcher was recovered close to the crash site.

There's been antiaircraft activity around Chechnya for years. Mostly they're wreckers just like the nineteenth-century lantern carriers who'd steer ships onto rocks in the hope of plundering some of the valuable cargo that survived the wreck. But animus against Russian planes specifically plays a part too—for the scorched-earth bombing tactics deployed against civilians in Grozny during the war. On September 9, 2010, a female Chechen suicide bomber dressed as a medic blew up a busful of Russian air force personnel on its way to Mozdok air base in North Ossetia.

"A really experienced pilot can fly his Il-76 anywhere," grins one Ukrainian I talk to later. "Snow, heat, fucking anywhere. But Chechnya still makes everyone nervous."

"Not really true, I think," frowns Mickey when we next speak. "No problem at high altitude. And even if you take a hit, maybe it doesn't damage you too badly. I could crash-land it, probably." He coughs up a wheezy little laugh. "Maybe even in a minefield."

The savage irony nobody mentions is that these rebels are firing weapons from the very same stockpiles as the ones Mickey's team is carrying. Because one unintended consequence of the global move toward self-determination that the collapsing USSR kicked off is that you get a whole lot more of these freelance psychos with rolling eyes, itchy fingers, and a bellyful of plum brandy or religion taking wild potshots at your Candid from the rooftops, hillsides, and treetops of places like Grozny. And when the market rules, these whooping vigilantes will always have more than enough rockets. The dawn of the era of the customer was also the beginning of a new kind of terrorist.

Back in 1992, it took a special kind of sixth sense to see just how snugly the two new doctrines in town—political self-determination and personal consumer choice—would fit together; to see that large groups of people, from the former Yugoslavia to Chechnya, Armenia, Azerbaijan, and Macedonia, were determined to have it *their* way. And that like all consumers, they were prepared to enter the open market to get whatever it took.

Not that armed militias were anything new: In the superpowered past, rebel groups had always been supported by one bloc or the other. The long-running Angolan wars (1961–1975, 1975–2002) had long been proxy Cold War confrontations, with the UNITA rebels receiving military assistance from the U.S. and South Africa, and their enemies the MPLA backed by the Soviet Union. It was all part of a larger game, there was no doubt as to who was in charge—the phrase "puppet regime" said it all—and, of course, there was always a political and military quid pro quo. But suddenly things were different. Now access to the finest, most powerful military hardware—along with anything else—wasn't a favor they needed to beg of anyone with a broader range of interests at heart; not the Kremlin or the White House or China, not the CIA or the KGB, or anyone else for that matter. The hardware, the bullets, the mercenaries, the mayhem was their right as consumers, and their money (or homegrown cash crops, natural resources, whatever they could trade) was calling the shots now.

In Angola, Liberia, Rwanda, and Sierra Leone, diamonds bought those old Soviet stockpiles; in the DRC, timber, gold, diamonds, furs, and coltan called the tune, with operators like Bout and Leonid Minin (a heftily built Israeli-Ukrainian, boss of the Odessa mafia turned trafficker and all-around wheeler-dealer who'd recently set up a business called Exotic Timber Enterprises, flying innocent-looking cargo flights between Europe and Africa on a regular basis) making the deals and men like Mickey flying in and out packed to the rafters with extras on the side.

It looked like chaos. It was a thriving market. The International Relations and Security Network, part of the Zurich Center for Security Studies, nails the spirit of the 1990s globally when it calls Minin's and Bout's trade in stockpiled weapons to whomever was paying "a diffusion or democratization of military power."

Suddenly everyone was a potential arms customer no matter what the international community said. Provided they had the cash, or payment in kind, that is. However underdeveloped and poverty-stricken your country was, you had *something*. And, just as globalization cheerleader Tom Friedman told us to do in *The Lexus and the Olive Tree*, whatever they had, they leveraged it, sold it, traded it, just to get into the game. In Africa, that meant dictators were free to trade blood diamonds for weapons and shipped-in mercenary support. In Serbia, mafia control of the airports created ad hoc free-trade zones, shipping arms to rogue states like Libya in exchange for hard currency, and the blossoming of a drug-and-bootleg route that still marks Europe today. Meanwhile, at the bazaars of Tajikistan it meant heroin for arms, flown down onto dusty, barren scree and disused runways by Mickey or any one of a dozen other outfits taking their new-found customer-is-always-right creed literally.

Everything had changed. Everything, that is, but the forces of law and order—agencies like the UN, the FBI, the CIA, MI5, Interpol, and the rest of the police, intelligence agencies, and regulators who, for the past forty years, had been dealing with the kind of transnational organized crime you could pin a structure on.

IT'S POSSIBLE THAT, at any other time, these night-flying crews in their battered Il-76s and Antonovs would have rung alarm bells; that the men behind their cargoes would have been targeted, investigated, neutralized—if not by their own governments, then by those in the West, and wherever else they operated. But this time, conditions made that impossible.

Amid the global recession that cast a pall over trade and politics from Europe and the Americas to Asia in and around 1992, a new mind-set had taken shape in the West; one focused squarely on "delivering value." The word *outsourcing* entered usage in English in the 1980s, and by the 1990s, with all that cheap labor suddenly available in the former Communist bloc, it was the economic buzzword, rooted in the very concept of good governance. And as state agencies increasingly spoke the language of the boardroom, Western governments (all far less spooked than they had been by the idea of people doing whatever the hell they liked to each other in places like Guatemala, Rwanda, Afghanistan, and the Philippines now that we knew they weren't about to be turned into "Soviet puppet regimes") focused on pleasing their stakeholders, putting more dollars in their pockets by driving down the costs of any nice-to-haves. Which included contributions to remote, fluffy agencies like the UN.

But for the UN itself, the world stayed the same size—in fact, it got bigger. Where there'd been one big old Soviet Union, here were dozens of new places with names like Armenia and Azerbaijan that seemed to have a whole lot of problems suddenly flaring up and no one else to look after them. Membership suddenly shot to 177 member states. Then there were countless smaller countries from Africa to Central America whose Cold War "sponsors" on either side had suddenly melted away. The UN had to police them all. So as the cost of peacekeeping operations skyrocketed, the big payers found themselves being asked for more. In 1991, UN peacekeeping ops cost a fairly typical $490 million, and payment arrears amounted to $358 million. Suddenly, just one bloody year later (a year in which Georgia, Armenia, Azerbaijan, Tajikistan, Mali, Afghanistan, Rwanda, Liberia, Sierra Leone, Angola, Sudan, Somalia, Guatemala, Peru, Colombia, Algeria, and Uganda all plunged into the abyss), the cost of the UN's peacekeeping operations around the world had nearly quadrupled to $1.76 billion. Meanwhile, the arrears in paying for these operations had doubled.

Things quickly spiraled out of control. By 1995, the UK's permanent representative to the UN was complaining of the "crisis of funding caused by the disproportionate sums paid by certain countries . . . the USA (30 percent), the EU (30–35 percent) and Japan (11 percent) contribute 75 percent of the total. This has a particularly negative impact in the U.S. where Congress and influential elements in public opinion argue that America should not have to pay one third of the cost of operations in which . . . there is no direct American interest."

Panic set in, heightened by the fact that the U.S. had become a notoriously late payer of its contributions, when the incoming Clinton administration discovered to their horror in 1993 that the budget deficit they'd inherited from successive, big-on-defense Bush and Reagan governments was almost double what they'd been told. It was a deliberate and cynical overspend known as Stockman's Revenge, after its mastermind, Bush's chief economist, and was intended to sabotage any incoming Democrat administration by leaving the government so broke it would be unable to initiate any welfare or other expenditures. The all-powerful Federal Reserve Chairman Alan Greenspan would consider the new administration's budget plan credible only if they could show immediate savings of some $500 billion. In this context, and with the disastrous "Black Hawk Down"

Battle of Mogadishu making overseas adventure look like a loser's game, funding the UN's overseas adventures plunged down the list of priorities.

At the height of this crisis, the UN itself was so spooked about how to pay for all these new deployments that it prepared a list of ways to boost funding that even included borrowing on the commercial market— effectively, meeting the bank manager and applying for a loan to buy a nice new peacekeeping operation. So as any organization would in its shoes, the UN focused on driving down its own costs by outsourcing "noncore" activities. And that meant aid delivery and cargo transport. And as luck would have it, the biggest pool of pilots and transport planes the world had ever seen had just become available, and the word was that these former Soviet crews would work for peanuts.

And they would, provided there was a way to boost their wages under the counter.

For his part, Sergei says he rarely knows what's in the main shipper's cargo—as another Il-76 pilot says, "It's all just *cargo* to us." Charter agent John MacDonald points out the "need-to-know" nature of most jobs they do, and that one of the standard conditions of his employment, or at least an understanding on many of the jobs, is that the crew won't ask and the shipper won't tell. A rogue Il-76 seized in Thailand in 2009 on an illicit, embargo-busting arms run between North Korea and Iran via the Emirates, Azerbaijan, Sri Lanka, and Ukraine bears this out. The crew were captured, imprisoned in Bangkok, then somewhat unexpectedly released without charge. One reporter, from *Air Cargo News*, managed to talk to their relatives, who spoke of the big paydays their husbands, fathers, brothers, and friends would get from their bosses in return for being prepared to fly the plane no matter what the job, how dangerous the conflict zone, or how poorly maintained the plane. They mentioned missions to Sudan and Somalia. One man, quoted as Mikhail Petuknov, a friend and once fellow pilot of one of the crewmembers, told *Air Cargo News*: "It's not easy . . . their planes are old, so the flights are dangerous. And it also means being ready to break pretty much every aviation law in the book. But it's work, and they pay well."

There was one more important condition: that they would ask no questions about the cargo, and would keep their own mouths shut.

Still, Mickey shrugs, the secrecy cuts both ways. With most of the cash jobs, neither charter bosses nor cargo clients know—or maybe even want to know—what's piggybacking with their stuff, and when they do they're mostly willing to turn a blind eye so long as everyone's happy and their consignment gets through. So that's when the crews begin to make "real money"—by delivering the official payload and either taking private orders for other stuff on the quiet, or just flying it in on spec. And so skilled were these crews at making their margin on the extra tonnage they carried, objects as big as cars and weighing several tons could be made to melt into the very fabric of the fuselage.

Even clients who see what they shouldn't are persuaded to look the other way for the blink of an eye it takes to make the switch. Brian Johnson-Thomas has fond memories of one crew who never missed an opportunity to double their upside, even if it meant contravening a few rules—including, seemingly, the laws of physics.

"They were the guys who managed to make two whole Lada saloon cars simply vanish inside the plane," he laughs. Johnson-Thomas was flight managing for an NGO at the time, taking forty-five tons of blankets by Candid to a humanitarian emergency. "I had to hook up with an Il-76 and its crew who had been doing another job, but were now free and were being diverted with the blankets into the disaster area," he recalls. Johnson-Thomas arrived at the landing-berth rendezvous and waited. The aircraft arrived, the ramp came down, and to his surprise, Johnson-Thomas saw two large Russian-made Lada cars sitting inside, where the aid was supposed to go.

"I said, 'What's all that about?'" he remembers. The loadmaster explained: At that point, Ladas were actually cheaper in the West than they were in Russia, and you couldn't get the spare parts back home—so they were buying secondhand Ladas in the West, taking them back to Ulyanovsk, and cannibalizing them for sale.

Johnson-Thomas was having none of it. They were absolutely full up to maximum capacity and beyond with the official load, he explained. The Ladas would have to stay behind.

"I said, 'Look, I'm afraid the aid cargo's got to go in there, and there's no room for your dodgy Ladas,'" he laughs. "But the navigator just took me aside and said: 'Captain Brian, please: You go next door, you have a beer, and when you come back in one hour, you will not see any Ladas.

And I will give you balance sheet, and I promise you, it will be good enough to pass.'

"Well, what could I say? So that's what I did. And when I came back, the blankets, the aid boxes, they were all in, and the cars had vanished. *Nothing.* Oh, they were there all right, somehow, but they were hidden, and true to their word, they'd made the balance sheet 'good enough to pass.' And that's all it ever has to be."

As a model, it's remarkably simple, the equivalent of the small-town cab driver dealing cannabis from the glove compartment with or without the say-so of Control. Only for a battered Toyota, substitute an even more battered Soviet air force flying machine. So simple, in fact, that anyone remotely capable of standing back and looking at the free-for-all that was developing could have seen what would happen, even before Il-76 crews like Mickey's started being downed by RPG-toting pirates in the Horn of Africa, blown up in Angola, and kidnapped by the Taliban—and before all that contraband spilled from the stockpiles onto the battlefields and urban jungles.

But nobody *was* capable of standing back. For the West, this was the peachy-keen 1990s. The Cold War was over. Now let the markets self-regulate and bring peace and prosperity. Never mind the fact that the living standard in Russia itself had plummeted since free-market reform. Never mind that life expectancy was falling. Never mind the bloody conflicts from Nagorno-Karabakh to Rwanda. Unfettered movement of goods across borders had to be applauded, not hindered. These were birth pangs for a new universal order of peace and prosperity in which the angels of the free market would make this the best of all possible worlds. In America, the Clinton administration was so sold on this vision that even when they were told about the mafia takeover in Russia, they dismissed the evidence: One report was returned from the desk of Vice President Al Gore with "a barnyard epithet"—reportedly the word *Horseshit*—scrawled across the front.

At the same time, across starved, bankrupted early-to-mid-1990s Russia, a phenomenon called "shuttle trading" was taking shape. Using the newfound freedom to travel and the last few rubles they could scrape together, Russians took overnight buses to Turkey, Greece, or Italy to buy cheap, but to many still impossibly exotic, tablecloths, dresses, plates, whatever, and sell them back home at a small profit, having paid off the customs men at the border. It was a return to the Middle Ages; a Silk Road stalked by killers. The casualty toll was enormous: In the yellow light of the night stations and coach terminals, muggers and cutthroats picked off the traders, and bent police and border guards would routinely steal the gear and the money. Rapes, beatings, and killings of shuttle traders were common.

Mickey's team, he cheerily admits, were a bit like shuttle traders. The difference was they had the plane, so they could sidestep the hassles and turn it into a high-volume business. The fact that transport costs were soaked up by the shipper of the stated cargo and they could cover distances their grounded compatriots could only dream of made their business within a business irresistible and devastatingly profitable—especially since new orders could be telephoned through often at a moment's notice, and practically any time before the plane doors shut.

Others were having the same idea. Suddenly, demilitarized crews and their Candids were flying weapons and contraband in and out of Russia, Ukraine, and Belarus for everyone and anyone—including the newly named Taliban, whose fighters had only a couple years ago been shooting Il-76s out of the sky but who now reportedly became valued customers for arms and ammo shipments.

Rumors of official toleration of, even involvement in the booming illicit and sanction-busting arms trade—by government, big business, the foreign intelligence GRU, the KGB, or its successor the FSB—have never completely disappeared. Throughout the 1990s, the authorities in Russia, Ukraine, and Byelorussia appeared to have bigger fish to fry: Simply regaining control of their armies and maintaining civil society took precedent over chasing down smugglers. Besides, weren't they clearing the former Red Army's own stockpiles, and emulating the best capitalist tradition of entrepreneurship in doing so?

CHAPTER SEVEN

Rogue State

Yugoslavia, 1994–1996

RUMORS OF OFFICIAL, even governmental, collusion with the arms pipe-line that had opened up all along the former Soviet lands seemed just that—rumors, the ravings of conspiracy theorists and ousted politicos with axes to grind. But as fate would have it, the world would soon get its smoking gun. The events of the stormy small hours of August 19, 1996—and the dogged, even foolhardy persistence of a small group of local reporters-cum-snoopers determined to uncover the truth—would alert the world to just how influential some of Mickey's paymasters are. And just how far they were prepared to go to avoid detection.

The Il-76 screams through the humid blue night, a black shape slipping over the Belgrade Hyatt and through the low clouds on the edge of town. It's silhouetted against the lightning, clearly visible for a split second to drinkers, late diners, and businessmen at the bar of the Hyatt, before it all goes black once more. The shadow roars over the river and dives into the forest of office blocks on the far side. At the very last second, the wingtip rises clear of the tallest high-rise, and the fuel-laden Candid screams on through the city center, low enough to tear aerials from skyscraper roofs. Eyes wide in the black, the pilot peers into pitch darkness beyond the cockpit glass. They're eyeball-deep in the shit now, and no two-thousand-dollar bonus payment on earth is going to get them out of it.

The pilot is a man named Vladimir Starikov, a jobbing cargo pilot and former Soviet air force comrade of Mickey's, on a run from Ekaterinburg in Russia, south via his last stop, Belgrade. An old hand, he refuses to panic, but he knows he's running low on options as he circles his Il-76 endlessly above the darkened streets, blocks, and bridges of Belgrade, searching for a way down. He's been in tight spots before and he'll get out of this one just the same.

What had started as just another night flight from Ekaterinburg to points unknown, stopping over for a change of cargo in Belgrade and with another planned in Malta, will, by dawn, become one of aviation's great mysteries, up there with Bermuda Triangle flight 19 and the disappearance of Amelia Earhart.

The crossroads of East and West are studded with sketchy refueling and off-loading stop-offs; tiny islands like Malta and Cyprus, where import-export is the only business there is, and nobody's watching. Both were popular with the Yugoslav regime's gofers. Since the 1970s, Northern Cyprus had been a popular ops base for Middle Eastern terrorists and KGB agents directing "black ops" in the Med and Middle East. "In the 1990s," reported *Zavtra*'s Valentin Prussakov, "thousands of 'redundant' secret service agents lost no time in shedding their epaulets and going into private business. Many opened offshore companies based on the island, followed by a heavy flow of Russian capital." But it was not all Russian. By 1996, both islands were much-loved flags of convenience, letterheads, and stopovers for a host of post–Soviet bloc contraband-trafficking boats and planes alike.

For this shadow world of international smuggling, trafficking networks, and secret agents, tonight's repercussions will continue long after the fires have been put out. But right now, for the pilot and crew, the fight of their lives is just beginning.

Starikov orders up wheels: no wheels. Lights: no lights. He curses the chances. On landing in Belgrade after their inbound flight from Ekaterinburg, he'd headed off for some rest while the crew, and some ground guys, carried out the usual inspection. When they'd told him how the onboard power fizzled and faded, he'd insisted there was no way they could go on to

Malta that night as planned. He hates himself now, silently, like they all do, for having been persuaded by the extra two thousand dollars each that the boss had stumped up. But hell, this is 1996. For a bunch of ex-Soviet air force flyboys living job to job, two thousand dollars cash is a whole lot of money for a night's work.

Sure enough, at 12:25 A.M. on Monday, August 19, 1996, just fifteen minutes after takeoff from Belgrade's Surcin airport en route for Malta, the onboard electrics on flight PAR-3601 blink, surge, then fail completely, plunging them into darkness. The instruments go dead. The radio fails. At the same instant, the plane's external and landing lights fail. All instruments are now dead. Desperate calls by controllers on all frequencies are in vain. Just radio silence, and the eerie rushing of the breeze around the control tower. To the ground, the Ilyushin is now a silent blip on their screens.

If the cargo is what pilot and crew had begun to suspect, they must be trying hard not to think about it. Inside what is now a blind-flying 176-ton petrol bomb, they frantically try to bring the electrics back online.

Starikov and his copilot Vladimir Barsenov have forty-four years of flying experience between them. They are coolheaded men, and they and the crew—including a veteran flight engineer, a radio operator, and a navigator—aren't going down without a fight. Unable to raise ground control on their radio and in the sudden blackness of a powerless cockpit, Starikov knows they have only one choice: to abort the flight and try to bring the 176-ton plane down—packed as it is with 109 tons of jet fuel and a hold that's way too full of black cargo.

The pilot turns 180 degrees, or as close as he can judge it, and heads back toward Belgrade. If they can find their way back to the city without navigation, ground contact, or lights, he's hopeful, even in the midnight darkness, of spotting the airport and runway through his cockpit window amid the grid of streets and fields below. Then maybe, just maybe, he can bring this thing down gently.

For three hours, the stricken Il-76 roars desperately in circles above Belgrade, silhouetted against the flashes of the stormy night sky, its instruments still dead and its radio silent, all navigation gone. Even the bulbs by which the crew would normally be able to see and move about the plane are gone, as are the plane's external lights—including its headlamps. The darkness up there in the cloud is absolute, and Starikov's only choice is to try to remain low enough to see beneath the storm clouds but high enough to clear the city's bridges and buildings.

The overloaded Il-76 is now heading back over the crowded capital of Milošević's mafia kingdom, hidden by clouds and invisible to other aircraft. Inside the iron giant, the crew works in total darkness, or by the meager light of a torch or a cigarette, to bring the systems back online. Using their watches and a magnetic compass, they calculate their entry into Belgrade airspace and descend through the soaking black cloud with a roaring noise that shakes buildings as they pass, way too low. There it is below—Belgrade city center. Descending to 150 meters, they search frantically for their bearings—witnesses see them narrowly miss the top of another building, the twenty-four-story Beogradjanka skyscraper, at around 1:30 A.M. Some lean from windows, try to take pictures, ending up, said one, with nothing more than a dark passing shadow, a blurry Loch Ness photo." Then the monster disappears off into the suburbs, before screaming in, just as low, for another pass.

Some eyewitnesses claim Starikov's panicking now, disoriented and scanning the ground, lower and lower, for the airport, while others at Surcin reckon he knows exactly what he's doing as he keeps passing low over the airport, gauging the ground for landing three or four times, in a clear attempt to raise the alarm. And still the stricken Ilyushin-76 circles, tighter and tighter, lower and lower, not wanting to lose its bearings— over the airport, the city center, and the thronging, partying Hyatt and InterContinental over in New Belgrade—roaring back and forth in what the waiting crash teams now know is Vladimir Starikov's attempt to burn as much fuel as possible before he takes his final gamble.

At 3:00 A.M., residents see the plane narrowly clear Block 44 in New Belgrade and head low over Bezanijska Kosa, its landing gear lowered. Without electricity the crew have labored desperately in pitch darkness to lower the wheels of the giant plane by hand. At the airport, the fire crews are scrambled. Helpless, they can only watch and wait. Finally, the plane turns 180 degrees over Surcin airport and aims for the runway from the northwest, coming in fast, an earsplitting black shadow.

In a split second, it's over. When the Il-76 explodes, its wingtip touching the ground and slamming the plane into the fields at the runway's end, the fireball is so intense that it slams shrapnel and aircraft parts into the control-tower walls, smashing the concrete. Starikov, Barsenov, and anyone and anything else onboard are vaporized, blasted over hundreds of meters of airport land.

And that's where Vladimir Starikov's last flight gets really strange. Because instead of investigators, rescue teams, and fire crews, the first forces to the crash area were the secret police. Faces shaded, backed by soldiers, they began to fan out across the area.

The Men in Black worked fast through the dawn, methodically erasing evidence of the plane's cargo. Witnesses were spirited away, cameras confiscated, recording equipment smashed, residents advised at gunpoint to forget anything that may, or may not, have happened that evening. The agents fanned out along the adjacent motorway, blocking exits and preventing traffic from slowing down as it came within eyeshot of the burning wreckage. The suburb was shut down. The men guarding the perimeter had clear orders: "Not one living thing comes in or goes out."

By sunrise, they'd turned the runway into an Area 51–like compound: total blackout. But even as the secret police and airport security chased off journalists, a couple of reporters considered tame to the regime were not only allowed through, but invited for an official briefing on the cause of the crash—though the wreckage continued to burn too fiercely for anybody to approach the plane. Something about the wreck of flight 3601 was so sensitive that even Russian diplomats, responding to the news that a Russian plane carrying Russian nationals had crashed, were barred from the site by black-clad men with automatic weapons.

Belgrade-based photographer Igor Salinger, who rushed to the site, had heard the plane on several occasions, enough to become used to its distinctive roar. "I'm used to plane sounds," he recalls today. "As well as being professionally connected to aviation, I live on the path to Runway 30, around the outer marker."

This time, he figured something was very wrong from the overhead roaring, even through the fog of sleep. The crash, he says, sounded from his bed "just like a series of distant explosions like . . . well, kind of like firecrackers." Salinger fell back into a fitful sleep, waking again as day broke. Pulling on his jeans and jacket and grabbing his cameras, the photographer made his way to the crash site. Something large was burning out past the perimeter, but Salinger found himself barred by a cordon of men in blue uniforms. They were everywhere; alongside the motorway, the pavements, the roads, even the fields where the black twisted mass burned and smoldered. "It was August, so the corn was high—easily man-height —and it helped hide what needed to be hidden," he recalls. "At that point, you could only see the big 'T' of the tail still sticking up." Salinger tried to get into the Yugoslav Aeronautical Museum, whose windows offered a perfect view down onto the site, but already police and staff had cordoned the building off. Still, he bumped into an acquaintance there—one of the men who'd been clearing the site. The man said something that made Salinger's blood run cold. And little by little, the truth began to emerge.

"The guy was, let's say, someone who knew about these things, and he'd seen the wreck," recalls Salinger. "And all he said to me was, 'It looks like Qadaffi's not getting a flypast at his military parade this year.'"

Still, Salinger had his work cut out. "The crash site was sealed off for, if I recall, thirteen days," he says. "Until they had picked up everything that should not be seen." The photographer finally crept through the farmland and thicket on the far perimeter and managed to snap a few shots; first from a distance, through the corn, and then finally, the wreckage, which the police thought they'd combed and "cleaned" properly. They hadn't. When he managed to sneak through, he found that among the wreckage were aircraft tires and avionics parts, way too small to be from an Ilyushin.

More men called in to do the "cleaning" of the site began to gossip. They reported seeing 23mm ammunition among the wreckage in large quantities. The cleanup was not as thorough as the authorities hoped. Then avionics parts for Yugoslav-produced Galeb and Jastreb fighter planes, then 23mm cannon ammunition.

On his last visit, desperation at the thought of all evidence being erased that there had ever been a crash, he snatched a burned piece of wreckage from the Il-76: "A sick souvenir," he admits. It would be something to hold on to when the official denials started.

Opposition newsweekly *Vreme*'s Russian correspondent in Ekaterinburg, Sergei Kuznetsov, called in some favors from military sources there. They discovered that the doomed Il-76 had, somewhat oddly, been insured by the Russian military. But he was told "that does not mean it was carrying arms . . . most of our clients are renowned organizations like the Russian Security Service, the General Staff Military Cooperation Department, or President Yeltsin's transport service."

Meanwhile, the investigators at *Vreme* started digging, led by a determined veteran reporter named Milos Vasic—one of the paper's founders and himself an aviator who'd flown helicopters in Asia in the seventies as a reporter for a news agency. Vasic and his team smelled a rat. So doggedly did he pursue the story—and such were the lengths to which the secret police went to stop him—that today, talking at his home in Belgrade, the sixty-five-year-old with dark "deadline circles" under his eyes laughs himself into a wheezing cough remembering slipping onto a train to Budapest "every time I needed to phone our contact in Russia, so I knew I wasn't being tapped."

"Milos has a lot of experience in people going after his head," grins Salinger. "Because he's the one who really pokes his nose right in it! I'm just an aviation photographer." Sure enough, Vasic was a thorn in the regime's side and was used to its threats, obstructions, and worse. The ruling cadre, he rages as he remembers the danger he and his team endured in their investigation, "was just, 'Fuck you.' Just we don't give a fuck, we can do anything. *Anything.*"

But in the end, they couldn't stop the story from gathering pace. And when the truth finally came out, it revealed a world of *X-Files*-like complexity, secret patronage, state corruption, sanctions busting, and privateering that not even the most paranoid prosecutors had dared to suspect. Only this time there was no conspiracy of Illuminati, no mystical order bent on brainwashing the enemy or enforcing submission to any all-powerful manifesto. Just a dark corner where the worlds of small business and big politics met.

THE NAME TOMISLAV Damnjanovic had never been so much as whispered by the media or investigators before that night. Even now, some investigators call the slim, tanned, and silver-haired Yugoslav Steve Martin lookalike "the invisible man." He was, all agree, your classic shifty, small-to-middleweight operator. For years, according to an International Peace Information Service (IPIS) report on arms shipments flooding out of the former Yugoslavia, Damnjanovic had "formed part of a transnational cigarette-smuggling network that operated in the Balkans during the 1990s [and] which, according to European Commission documentation, also involved arms traffickers." His story was summarized in a United Nations Development Programme–funded report compiled by arms-trafficking investigators Hugh Griffiths of SIPRI and another Englishman, Adrian Wilkinson of the South Eastern and Eastern Europe Clearinghouse for the Control of Small Arms and Light Weapons. According to the report, Damnjanovic made his name

> ... trafficking to rogue states and African dictatorships under UN sanctions while at the same time supplying arms on behalf of some of America's biggest companies, such as General Dynamics and Kellogg, Brown and Root, before transporting arms for US companies and other arms suppliers such as Taos, Inc., and the network in which he worked supplied Saddam Hussein, Charles Taylor, the Burmese military *junta*, the Islamic militias of Mogadishu, and Colonel Muammar Ghaddafi's regime in Liberia. Like the more infamous Viktor Bout, Damnjanovic has chartered planes throughout Africa, the Middle East and Eastern Europe, supplying everything from humanitarian aid to hand grenades.

Damnjanovic has denied this. Indeed, even amid the mafia hits, crony politics, and chaos of war-torn 1990s Yugoslavia, nothing about his business dealings appears to have been illegal. "Damnjanovic isn't an arms smuggler exactly," laughs Salinger. "Just a man in the business who's found a way to do, as we say in slang, Ilyushin business."

His story is typical. As an employee of the state-owned Yugoslav national airline JAT throughout the 1980s, he was often stationed in Dubai, where he developed a taste for international high living far from his increasingly fraught home city of Belgrade. As Yugoslavia broke up and Slobodan Milošević's regime began prosecuting a series of wars in Bosnia and beyond, the UN imposed sanctions that effectively grounded JAT by preventing them from landing outside what was rapidly becoming the former Yugoslavia. By 1992, his JAT office in the Emirates had closed, and Damnjanovic, like Mickey, started scouting for new opportunities. Now used to the luxury of Dubai's air-conditioned expat bubble, he wasn't about to head home to a life of sanctions, shortages, rocketing inflation, and war in Belgrade. Especially not now that he'd seen how easy it was to make money flying in and out of the Emirates carrying whatever paid best, to whoever bid highest.

In those heady days in the UAE, everybody was at it, it seemed. Rumors of Sharjah's next Big Idea—an anything-goes gateway for whatever you've got—were rife. Dubai itself was great for anyone with an old plane and an eye for an illicit buck. A transport hub linking Europe and the Caucasus, the Middle East, the Horn of Africa, and Pakistan/Afghanistan, it was a free-trade free-for-all in which seemingly anything, or anyone, could be bought and sold for the right price. Sheikh Mohammed bin Rashid al-Maktoum, the crown prince, was not only the visionary behind the Emirate's breakneck growth but its major investor, financing luxury hotels, malls, prestige horse races, and airports with equal élan. He was also one of the first to recognize the Taliban's claims of sovereignty during their pitched battle for Kabul. Under him—though there's no suggestion that the sheikh himself either knew or approved—the authorities seemed willing to let whatever cargo come and go through Dubai's once-pirate-infested port and airport, as long as it did so discreetly.

Sharking around Dubai looking for a partner, the slim, smooth-talking silver fox Damnjanovic fell in with a Russian wheeler-dealer and former chief in the KGB who had fetched up in Dubai like many of his former colleagues, keen to make a killing in this haven for hands-off cargo ops, money laundering, and high-class hookers. The two instantly spotted an opportunity in each other: Damnjanovic, to latch on to the Russian's air-cargo operation and get a foothold in an aviation business that was rising fast; and the former FSB man, an inside line on the boom market for shady cargo. Belgrade was experiencing a mafia boom comparable to Russia's, and sanction busting was the way to make big, big money.

Quietly, secret police chief Rade Markovic and customs head Kertes began taking a close hand in airport security, Markovic taking orders that came from the very top while Kertes coordinated shipments in and out. And after dusk, the terminal echoed with familiar thunder as Il-76s and Antonovs swept onto the asphalt and lined up alongside those last JAT flights out of the country. Slowly but surely, crews like Mickey's became the regime's own deniable conduit for anything Milošević and his cronies wanted done. And as it turned out, their timing was perfect.

Desperately in need of stable foreign currency to finance their government's coffers, their lifestyles, and their proxy militia armies in Bosnia and Croatia, the Yugoslav regime was also aware that they were in a position to sell certain highly desirable commodities further afield. Salinger recalls a series of fake emergency landings near the smaller Montenegrin capital of Podgorica throughout the 1990s: The forced landing was a favorite pretext for stopping to drop off and load up with black market cigarettes away from watchful eyes, after which they'd fly on, "minor fault" miraculously fixed. They set about organizing a giant smuggling ring, using secret police and customs at Belgrade airport as the quartermasters and foremen, and cargo planes chartered by men like Damnjanovic to take the goods further afield. This was the boom time of the Eastern European cigarette-smuggling pipeline into the EU: The regime bought them cheap and in huge bulk from in-country outlets and suppliers (and, of course, many of the airmen bought their own to sell on the side either locally or in Russia, tax-free to Afghan vets), and transported them by aircraft from Belgrade out to the international twenty-four-hour money Laundromat that was Cyprus. (Damnjanovic and his partner "Misko" Djordjevic relocated to the island themselves in 1994.) They would then usually go on by boat to Greece or Italy, where the local syndicates would hand over cash and distribute them within the EU. Western European smokers in the mid-to-late 1990s would regularly buy cheap cartons in bars and on the street with warnings in Russian, Turkish, or Bulgarian, flown in by Il-76 from the Balkans, duty-free. Everybody won, except the people in a far-off foreign land being shot at by Serb militiamen.

To do all of this, of course, Damnjanovic needed the right planes, and men with his own special brand of the Right Stuff: fearless, highly skilled men just like Mickey and Sergei whose resourcefulness, professionalism, and lack of curiosity about their missions had been bred into them by tough years of military service. Men who could fly them anywhere, with anything, under any conditions—no questions asked. He began making contacts in Ekaterinburg—a highly secretive former KGB stronghold in Mickey's home region of western Siberia, dotted with former military bases and arms depots.

The city had (indeed, still has) a well-deserved reputation as Russia's "mafia city," where anything could be done, or anything (or anyone) made to disappear for the right price. More important, it was home to the obscure Il-76 cargo outfit called SpAir (whose assets, in an interesting footnote, the IPIS/Amnesty report points out would later be transferred to Air Cess, the company started by Viktor Bout) and scores of job-hungry pilots like Starikov and Barsenov.

The flights grew more profitable and more frequent. But still, with the number and scale of its wars—present and planned—spiraling, the Milošević regime wanted more cash than it was making with cigarettes. For a while, though there's no evidence linking the prodigious narcotics flow to Damnjanovic's own chartered flights, the famed "Balkan pipe" worked well for many others, with heroin coming from the Caucasus, Albania, Turkey, and Afghanistan and going by land, sea, or air into Europe. Coke and Ecstasy went the other way to feed the Russian new rich and Serb high society. The differentials in cost at purchase and return at sale were enough to make them all good business for the regime, the smugglers, and for Mickey.

By 1994, Damnjanovic and business partner Djordjevic had moved back from Dubai, lingered in Belgrade, and promptly set up an office in Cyprus, where JAT flights carrying bankers and plainclothes cops would bring cases of hard currency to be laundered, night after night and day after day. Virgin cash would be deposited with shell companies in Panama, Israel, Greece, and Albania. Their goods and clean, hard cash would come back, via paper-only companies and shell operations, to Belgrade.

Then there were arms. According to a SIPRI report, it was while in Cyprus that Damnjanovic got the nod from the Serb authorities to start trafficking weapons in an effort to boost their coffers once again.

By 1996, they had turned arms smuggling into a huge business. Milošević's regime was regularly supplying Qaddafi's Libya and Saddam Hussein's Iraq, both under tough sanctions, with regular big-money shipments containing everything from antiaircraft systems to artillery and spare parts for Qaddafi's own fleet of Yugoslav-made Galeb fighter planes, courtesy of the then-Yugoslavia's state arms manufacturer, YugoImport SPDR.

According to Hugh Griffiths at SIPRI, Damnjanovic's new outfit Mensus Trade promptly "organized dozens of sanctions-busting flights into and out of Yugoslavia and they became the people to contact when state arms companies or the government needed goods flown in or out, to or from Russia or the Middle East." He was now a state-sanctioned trader of the kind that, in any other time and place, would have been highly risky; but instead of being arrested, his cozy relationship with the regime gave the Yugoslav government deniability and cover, and him as much business and secret police protection, at home and abroad, as he could wish for. It was a sure thing.

Then, in August 1996, Damnjanovic and Djordjevic called SpAir in Ekaterinburg with a job: fly some jet fighters, in parts, to Qaddafi's Libya, a "rogue" state already under UN sanctions but desperate for an air force revamp. Phone calls were made between Damnjanovic in Cyprus and Djordjevic in Belgrade, who agreed to accompany this highly sensitive cargo to its ultimate destination to avoid slipups. Starikov, Barsenov, and their Candid had already been making these trips for months. They knew the route, knew their plane, maybe even knew the cargo. They just didn't know this time would be different.

So it was that Starikov and his Il-76 crew dealt with Damnjanovic and Djordjevic and flew what they were paid to fly—unaware that they were pawns in a game being played by the highest levels of the Milošević regime itself. These gunrunning Il-76 flights to Libya would finance their cadre's grip on power, their friendly militias and mafia clans, and the campaign of ethnic cleansing in Kosovo that would result in the deaths of many thousands, NATO strikes on Belgrade, and the fall of the regime itself.

But oblivious to any of this, and with a good cash bonus in sight, pilots Starikov and Barsenov flew their Ilyushin Il-76 into Surcin from the Urals. And just after midnight, having executed what the state media claimed was only a technical stopover but what other sources testified was a heavy weapons pickup, and with Djordjevic onboard to make sure the secret cargo was delivered at the other end, flight 3601 took off into a stormy black Belgrade sky bound for Malta and ultimately Libya.

Embargoed or not, it would be a chance for a nice, hot stopover, and hell, North Africa was better than what they were leaving behind in Ekaterinburg for a few days.

Besides, just at that moment Africa and the Middle East were heating up in other ways. There was good money to be made out there. Rumor was that one rather unlikely spot in the Arabian Gulf was becoming a particularly profitable base for ex-Soviet crews and their illicit payloads.

PART III

Gold Fever: The Middle East and Africa

CHAPTER EIGHT

The Men with No Names

The Arab Gulf, 1995–1997

ANOTHER FLIGHT, heading for the Caucasus. I wake from excited half sleep in the belly of the Candid. For a few disorienting seconds, my brain is as fuzzy as one of Mickey's cargo manifests. I look at my pager, where the digital display says it's just before 1:00 A.M. By now we've got to be over Ukraine, or maybe the Caucasus Mountains already. I'm freezing, but at least the claustrophobia, like the stink of men at close quarters, has faded. The metal hums so loudly everything went quiet about half an hour after takeoff, and the effect at night is oddly disorienting. The antique gaffer-taped fuselage shakes steadily. Just yards away in the night, four engines roar so loudly they've got the Il-76 banned from most European countries.

Dmitry, the navigator, sits at the cockpit entrance, pulls a pair of fingerless gloves from the lunchbox by his elbow, and slips back down the sloping floor to his hanging, front-gunner-style cubbyhole, where he settles his lofty frame into a comfy posture and watches the night roll by through the glass beneath his feet. Pens laid out on the folding desktop; charts out, notebook open. My fellow stowaway on the flight, a Scots-Canadian photographer named Doug McKinlay on assignment to shoot the dynamited Buddhas in the northern Afghan hills for CNN, cracks off a photo of the

79

glass pod. Dmitry, surly at the best of times, jumps. He isn't too happy about the distraction from the flash and wheels round, eyes blazing, arm flailing at the camera with a curse. Doug backs off, for now.

Silence settles in again. The flight engineer sits on a fold-down metal bench the same battleship gray as his overall top and track bottoms, and closes his eyes. Sergei, draped in an outsized jogging shirt, is drinking from a plastic cup and compulsively rubbing his eyes. The spring bed is taken—I can see a pair of feet from here—so I lie sideways on a small quarter of available fuselage space on a ridged metal bench jammed to the wall just behind the cockpit area with my head on my jacket, as I've seen the guys do. It's horribly uncomfortable, but it's all there is.

In Mickey's flying warehouse, even if your tiny wire bench is taken, you can sit, or stretch out among the mountains of tethered crates of rice, open pallets of clothing and stacks of boxes, opaque twelve-kilo sacks, wooden crates, and blue plastic sheeting. I wonder if these are the so-called green boxes Mickey's hinted they carry on runs like this, used to transport ammunition and small arms. And if they are, whether they're licit or not. So tightly are they packed that there's no hope of getting farther back, or burrowing between the tethers and boxes looking for stenciling.

There's no point asking the crew, not really. The "double-blind" nature of the illicit stuff means that they'd be the last to know, or to ask. As for what happens at the other end, on paper at least it's not their problem. They're just the couriers, and—again, on paper—never need to cross the customs line with anyone's smuggled gear but their own.

And it's not as if that's ever a problem either. It helps that many of the hubs these humanitarian cargoes fly from—like the wreck-studded cargo perimeter at Sharjah in the United Arab Emirates—have been notoriously lax about customs and security, frequently allowing cargo to come in and leave the airport without being inspected, failing to run the requisite checks on its airlines or keep records of airline business at the airport.

Sharjah is a word that keeps cropping up in conversations with Mickey and the team about their past and their plans. It's their safe haven, they say, their R & R, just like home leave in the air force. There, nobody's taking potshots at them; there's air-con in the bars and hotels; they don't get any hassle from anybody. Sergei can't resist giving me too much information. "You know, you can always get a great shower in Sharjah," he laughs, shoulders shaking, "and you take it, because you never know when you'll see another."

You will not be surprised to hear that *Sharjah* is a word that also figures prominently in whispered conversations, classified reports, and official correspondence about rogue aviation outfits in general and about money laundering, the international black market, gunrunning, the Afghan heroin trade, and human trafficking in particular.

Still, if you've never heard of it, that's not an accident either: You and I were never meant to.

When its larger, splashier, less fussy neighbor Dubai opened up to trade and tourism with the goal of becoming the "Singapore of the Sands" and immediately began riding a monster two-decade boom, the tiny emirate of Sharjah saw the immense wealth that could be generated by turning a sparsely populated, feudal, Islamic desert city into a destination in its own right, a freewheeling hub for people, goods, and business. Only rather than open the Pandora's box of tourism and attempt to attract fun-seeking foreign riffraff to its uniform, beige-and-cement city center—where a particularly puritanical form of Sunni Islam similar to Saudi Arabian Wahhabism held sway and all alcohol, short trousers, and popular music was forbidden—advisors to the ruler, Sheikh Sultan Bin Mohammed al-Qasimi, had one or two better ideas.

Their first plan—to turn Sharjah into the global center for Islamic studies, packed with madrassas hosting boys from devout families across the globe—turned out to be a dud: too much investment, not enough quick return. Besides, it meant building a brand name from scratch. In religion, that's no easy task. So by the mid-1990s, his advisors presented the sheikh with plan B. The small, single-runway desert airport that would make Sharjah's foreign-investment fortune would not bring planes laden with unpredictable, high-maintenance tourists, or compete with Jeddah for the Islamic dollar. It would bring quiet, low-profile, easy-to-manage crates of cargo. Any cargo.

Of course, financial incentives and tax breaks were part of a package designed to lure freight and transport businesses to operate from the airport. But equally well understood was that this would be "a place to do business"—somewhere companies could come without fear of interference or overzealous regulators. And while the sheikh may not have seen it happening, bit by bit, for the duration of the 1990s, Sharjah airport gained a reputation among insiders as a gray cargo hub.

As early as 1993, former Soviet-issue Il-76s and Antonov An-12 and An-124 aircraft and their ex–Red Army pilots and aircrews were flocking there. By 1995, it was clear Sharjah had a hit on their hands. Which meant that the sheikh's men, like the mayor of the Maine seaside resort in the movie *Jaws*, came to rely on the money that was flooding in so much that even as the really big sharks started sniffing around, they simply turned up the music and ignored the warnings. The emirate had a sketchy past as a trans-shipment hotspot in the nineteenth century's hashish- and opium-smuggling trade, with drug-laden dhows flocking the waters around the dock, so it's possible the sheikh's court simply misunderstood any warnings they received about some of the custom Sharjah was attracting, or that he wasn't kept as informed by his staff as he might have been. At least until he decided to take a direct hand in matters.

The sheikh hired a delicately spoken, fine-boned Syrian-American named Richard Chichakli as commercial manager of Sharjah Airport International Free Trade Zone. Chichakli is a talented alumnus of Riyadh University in Saudi Arabia, where he and one wealthy young student named Osama bin Laden had been friends. (He's reported to have recalled how the preradical bin Laden "was a lot of fun in those days.") A certified public accountant, real estate guy, and car dealer with an office in Texas, who served in the U.S. military in the early 1990s and prides himself on "a strange hobby that involves creating highly decorative fruit plates," Chichakli seems an unlikely candidate for the title of international aviation player. Yet this likable amateur chef is also, by his own admission, "one of the world's top experts in managing [air]fleets . . . setting up airlines and managing and administering all financial operations." And after leaving the army, Chichakli put all the aviation knowledge he'd gained there to spectacular private use.

The Free Trade Zone boom Chichakli oversaw became Sharjah's gold rush. Soon, newspaper reports in the region were gasping at the speed and success of the enterprise. Indeed, Chichakli would later protest that those who accused him of a full-time role helping Bout have "no idea" of the workload involved in running an airport. The figures certainly make impressive reading. The airport's special zone opened in 1995 with fifty-five aviation outfits based there, and doubled that figure within a year.

By 2003, a staggering 2,300 aviation outfits were based there. One of the aviation specialists who turned up early and became "a brother and a friend" to Chichakli, he says today, was Viktor Bout.

It's quite possible that even Chichakli himself never guessed quite what was brewing out there on the tarmac and in the shade of the hangars as the sleepy emirate began to change. But as more and more former Soviet aircraft circled and landed and left again, the twentieth century's black-market boom took hold.

These were dusty, sun-baked, lawless Sharjah's Wild West days, when anyone who arrived at the frontier with guts and cunning and a fistful of dollars could grab himself fifty acres and a mule—or at least a huge tax break, a landing berth, and a no-questions-asked policy on what went on, and came off, his plane. Strangers blew into town with shady connections and out again with fortunes, and everybody was, effectively, the Man with No Name.

The sands around Sharjah airport still bear mute, grisly witness to the wing-and-a-prayer flying of many former Soviet crews, with plane fuselages sticking up from dunes, and tailplanes visible under the drifting sand. "They just leave them where they crash," says Sharjah veteran John MacDonald. "The end of the runway's littered with them, just stuck there where they came down or blew up in the sand."

By 1996, bookish, bearded, and rather humorless young men in Afghan *salwar kameez* were stalking the hangars at dusk, sauntering from cooling plane to cooling plane and desk to desk asking pretty much anyone still in the area about doing some "don't-ask–don't-tell" cargo runs in and out of Kandahar, as cash jobs of course. One fiery-eyed twentysomething cleric named Farid Ahmed briefly became a local figure of fun, sneaking round the secure areas and introducing himself to anyone he (literally) bumped into as the buyer for a then-still-obscure organization called the Taliban, a nascent Islamic movement with an extreme interpretation of Koranic imperatives borne out of Afghanistan's religious madrassas who saw themselves not just as the rightful successors to the anti-Soviet mujahideen as the saviors of their country, but also as the solution to Afghanistan's problems with corruption, opium, petty crime, and foreign interference. Their agenda—strict observance of a particularly austere view of Islam—we now know. But at that time, they were just another rebel group with pockets full of secretly donated Saudi and Pakistani cash. And it wasn't long before Ahmed found a man with a plane ready to talk money, in the shape of Viktor Bout.

While most operators were on the level—or at least as close as you could stay to level in an environment like Sharjah—they found themselves lined up alongside other ground staff, crews, and owners some of whom routinely changed their planes' registration numbers overnight, under cover of darkness, to avoid being fingered for any particularly cheeky arms-running jobs. Airlines and cargo operations that appeared on the paperwork may or may not be the ones who owned the planes, and the signatories on the registration, tax, customs, and ownership papers may or may not be real names, or pseudonyms for a real person, or made-up names for entirely fictitious owners of fictitious companies running un-logged flights. Taliban gold was now being flown into Sharjah and Dubai alike by Il-76 or Antonov, bound for Pakistan and the Sudan; blood diamonds, guns, ammunition, explosives, caviar, fur, drugs, and currency all made their way in and out, and nobody there, it seemed, knew a thing.

Today, one seasoned cargo aviator still has trouble believing the no-questions-asked regime around the airport at the time—and well into the 2000s. "There wasn't any security at all—not around customs, or the hangars. Nowhere. Practically anyone could just walk into the airport from the street and up to, around, and into the planes. It was really incredible. Even tourists could buy tickets entitling them the freedom of all areas of the airport, going up around the planes, everything. And you could see cargo coming into the airport straight from boats and the road, without being logged in or out or checked or anything, put on planes and flown off to wherever. My airline did it, and though there's no suggestion we were carrying anything improper, we easily could have, so easily. Nobody kept track. Anything was possible."

The murk, whether the result of a calculated obfuscation or naïveté on the part of the local authorities, made any attempt to chase the trail of illicit cargoes quite scattershot, with conscientious operators soon being caught up in the same wide dragnet of suspicion and investigation as the gunrunners. Indeed, so arcane and complex was the web of bought, sold, part-owned, leased, chartered, borrowed, loaned, verbally transferred, and informally operated planes, logos, and businesses in which Bout was involved at the height of his influence that the authorities were reduced to "linking" planes to him in a desperate attempt to keep tabs on him—or even simply to get some idea of where he'd been.

"It's just got ridiculous," says one UK-based charter agent. "We're a highly legitimate company, and our reputation is important, but some people out there make so many spurious connections that all the big leasing agents like us are totally paranoid. We've got to be careful now that we don't even lease a chassis that he once had anything to do with—even one he previously owned, several owners ago—because people start coming after you. A relative of mine was claimed to be somehow 'linked' to his 'network' on some bloke's Viktor Bout–monitoring Web site, though he'd never had anything to do with him or his aircraft. It's *that* confused."

The airport, its hangars and loading bays, rapidly became a sanction-breakers', black marketeers', and traffickers' playground, and a natural honeypot for Mickey's connections and, quickly, Mickey himself. Soon, air-conditioned restaurants with Russian-only menus, discreet vodka bars, and handling-agent types from Odessa and Vitebsk were part of the crew's monthly, if not daily, routine. Bank accounts were opened, apparently without ID or with the same people using different passports every day, in names nobody knew; paper companies were born, registered, and then immediately seemed to disappear. Douglas Farah and Stephen Braun, investigative journalists and the coauthors of *Merchant of Death*, wrote that by the end of the 1990s, when HSBC Sharjah did a housekeeping audit, it found that some 1,186 bank accounts had been opened by hundreds of different Russians in one branch alone. The speed at which the accounts opened, were used to transfer huge sums, then closed again, was, they concluded, proof of "money laundering on a huge scale."

Across Sharjah and neighboring Dubai, the *hawala* system of Islamically correct banking, in which large sums could be given, loaned, invested, and repaid without the need for interest—or, crucially, transfer records or receipts—was an open door for smugglers, launderers, and mafia from all countries looking to "clean" the suspiciously large profits from their illicit ventures. Airline employees taking home less than two thousand dollars a month would receive transfers of millions in and out of their accounts. In one incident, bemused investigators challenged one such aviation worker, whose indignant response was that he'd just been amazingly lucky with a few flutters on the stock exchange. (As scrutiny grew in the wake of the 9/11 attacks, and the world's eyes turned to the Emirates as potential havens for terrorist funds, Dubai at least set up an investigation team—though many view it as lip service. Later that year, a Sharjah national on the Dubai Central Bank's money-laundering investigation team had his house attacked by a group of suspected Russian money launderers. With uncanny timing, another promptly began receiving death threats.)

But through the mid-1990s as free-and-easy Sharjah grew, such scrutiny seemed unthinkable. First more planes and crews, then more menus, prostitutes, and businesses were from the former Soviet Union. There was no doubt who was running things now. Mickey began first visiting, then staying. Seemingly without anybody noticing, the Man with No Name who blew into town with a battered old Il-76 or a couple of fuel-guzzling An-12s to his name had become the Man with a Dozen Different Names and Bank Accounts. The only difference was that in this spaghetti western, when he disappeared off into the sunset nobody even asked who that enigmatic stranger was.

But Sharjah wasn't the only one of these wild frontiers rapidly becoming a honeypot for screaming super planes, local mafia, contraband, and hell-raising former Soviet aviators. There were many others, from Ostend in Belgium to Maribor in Slovenia, which locals call "Mafiabor," though Mickey and Sergei affectionately call it "Marlboro" in honor of the huge mob-run cigarette-smuggling pipeline from Serbia and Montenegro to the EU that its airport served through the 1990s. And yet more from Freetown in Sierra Leone to the former Soviet states in the Caucasus, who were close enough to political fault lines, rogue regimes, and war- and disaster-prone areas to know a good business opportunity when they saw it and jump on the open-market bandwagon.

Like Bavarian beer or Savile Row suits, says Mickey, every airstrip had its own "thing"—its own specialism. For Afghanistan's Kabul, Herat, Jalalabad, and Kandahar, it was humanitarian aid, illicit booze, consumer goods, arms, and cash in; heroin, siphoned-off aid money, raw materials, artifacts, people (both willing clients and unwilling marks) out. Across the Balkans, it was humanitarian assistance, luxury items, black-market cigarettes, guns, heroin, and cash. For Rwanda, Congo, and the rest, humanitarian aid, guns, and helicopters crossed paths with raw materials, foodstuffs, and natural resources—including blood diamonds.

The transportation business model was perfect in its evenhandedness, in the way it spread the money around: the operator, the owner, the crew who fill up whatever extra space they can find with their own cash jobs. But the best part was the way the dynamics of catastrophe meant they got paid by both sides, on their way in and out of each destination. The crews will never fly empty if they can help it, so on the way out they make sure they fill up with whatever it takes. And on runs in and out of "fucked" countries, that could be anything—chickens, fruit, fish, wood, rugs, bricks, sand, coffee, whatever.

In his 2004 film, *Darwin's Nightmare*, about the effect of globalization on Central Africa, Austrian filmmaker Hubert Sauper recorded the sudden coming together of aid, business, and smuggling in the holds of the now-ubiquitous Il-76s flocking to Africa on fat aid contracts and even fatter gunrunning jobs, and the birth of a new kind of chaos wherever Mickey's hordes went. He issued a statement explaining what he called the film's "trigger":

> In the Democratic Republic of Congo in 1997, I witnessed for the first time the bizarre juxtaposition of two gigantic airplanes, both bursting with food. The first cargo jet brought forty-five tons of yellow peas from America to feed the refugees in the nearby UN camps. The second plane took off for the European Union, weighed down with fifty tons of fresh fish. I met the Russian pilots and we became *kamarads*. But soon it turned out that the rescue planes with yellow peas also carried arms to the same destinations, so that the same refugees that were benefiting from the yellow peas could be shot at later during the nights. In the mornings, my trembling camera saw in this stinking jungle destroyed camps and bodies. This booming multinational industry of fish and weapons has created an ungodly globalized alliance on the shores of the world's biggest tropical lake: an army of local fishermen, World Bank agents, homeless children, African ministers, EU-commissioners, Tanzanian prostitutes, and Russian pilots.

The picture Sauper paints is like a scene from a modern-day Hieronymus Bosch. But as with Sharjah, the sense of chaos and confusion may not be quite as accidental as it seems. Indeed, the appearance of disorganization is a positive boon to crews and their charter masters keen to traffic in illicit goods.

"The illicit stuff is how your crew makes its *real* money," says Johnson-Thomas, who's flight-managed former Soviet crews on Il-76s and An-12s all over the world. "Most of these particular pilots are freelance—they don't work for anybody, just whoever needs them. And because they're freelance, they're not in any union, or on any payroll, so they're very, *very* difficult to keep tabs on, and they can carry whatever they like."

He can't help beaming with admiration as he recalls how one Il-76 crew hit on the brilliantly counterintuitive idea of making more money by offering to do all their aid flights for charities for free. "The pilot made his fortune on the fifteen secret tons of belly cargo he'd carry in addition to the official payload. Depending on the destination, he'd fly something for free for you—he'd fly all the official cargo for no charge whatsoever—providing you let him carry what he wanted in the belly cargo space. The aid organizations, bless them in their innocence, all just thought he was being enormously public spirited!"

The thing is, most people didn't know that it was there. But even if they did know, money talks, so it was no problem just the same. The organizations were getting their main cargo to the destination for free, so they kept taking him up on it. On a typical trip, remembers the veteran flight manager, he'd take his official cargo of aid or pineapples between Mogadishu and Ostend, but in the belly cargo he'd have fifteen tons of whatever else. It might be ammo in or coffee sacks out.

"That's what eventually got him his lovely house," says Johnson-Thomas, "and his-and-hers sports cars. And not one penny of that money showed up on any cargo manifests, let alone the tax returns! It wasn't on any declarations, and as far as the world was concerned, the plane was full to capacity with the official cargo."

Like that anonymous master of commerce, Mickey and Sergei make it their personal business to know the perennial hot tickets in most cities, too—devouring local news, sweeping for rumors everywhere they go, and even checking in with distant contacts by telephone constantly. "Sometimes you hear things when you're out or talking even to airport and customs officials," shrugs Sergei. "Someone will maybe say, we really have trouble getting toothpaste, or we can always use more mineral water, or whiskey. Maybe you will know if a new business is coming to your city, and you tell us. And then we know what to do next time we are in town. It is quite easy."

"These crews are the epitome of globalization," says Moisés Naím, former executive director of the World Bank, Venezuelan minister for trade, and author of *Illicit*, an award-winning report on "how smugglers, copycats and traffickers are hijacking the global economy." "The common theory is that this was chaos. But there's nothing chaotic about it at all! What we've been witnessing here is not *dis*organization—it's markets at work.

"There were superpowers, and now they've gone. But that doesn't make it chaos—anything but. This is like saying that before, you had an organized oil and energy market because you had the Seven Sisters—the seven big oil companies—and that was an organized market, and that now you have a disorganized market because you have thousands of independent oil companies. Wrong: What happened is that the barriers to entry in that market have lowered. So now you have new people—you're right, they are not foot soldiers, they are SME businesses—operating in this market. Before, they were dominated by big organizations that had first-mover advantages and were able to capture a large chunk of the market. Then as a result of competition, government intervention, disruptive technologies, changes in consumer behavior, changes in supply, demand, financing, logistics, and everything else, that same market is no longer dominated by the equivalent of the Seven Sisters—the Mr. Big types, the Viktor Bouts and Pablo Escobars—but it's an open market where you have hundreds or thousands of independent players. Some are very big, some are very small, some are medium, and it's all just a market."

Like any SME, the key advantages they had from the start were things like agility, their flexibility, their low overheads, and their speed. But there's an added dimension, too: They're importing tax-free and pay not a penny in transport costs.

Whoever Mickey, Sergei, Lev, and Dmitry are flying for, they are a business within a business: The client gets what they get, they overload with whatever will make them quick cash, and everybody wins. Once they know their next stop, says Sergei, they can make swift decisions about what to buy in Belgrade, Bangkok, Minsk, Frankfurt, Istanbul, or Shanghai; essentially, what will be most profitable and easiest and safest to sell, leverage, or drop off at their destination. Dealing with customs isn't their problem for the main loads—they just drop the shit off and the client will have to get it released. But for whatever they want to keep for themselves, keeping customs sweet is a must.

Then there's selling on what they've got. The smaller and more shady the client, the harder it is to shake money out of them. Cash flow is a constant headache—hence the value placed on regulars, from the Taliban to charities, Dow Jones 100 companies, and the UN. Because if Mickey's loose network of clients, charterers, airlines, and contacts don't pay their invoices on time, they don't get credit. And if they don't have credit, fuel, parking, maintenance, and overflight, permissions suddenly become unavailable. A twenty-five-year-old Il-76 drinks fuel like nobody's business— and without it, you're left with a useless metal sculpture in the shape of a plane at the end of some Central Asian or African runway, costing you thousands of dollars for every hour it sits there. Eventually, they just come and push you off it into the sand. Like the remote Afghan outpost where the crew dumped their crocked Candid, the dusty runways of sub-Saharan Africa and Eurasia are lined with rusting Soviet tin—some of it charred and twisted, but most of it just out of the cash it needs to stay airworthy and refueled.

It's this insatiable appetite for avgas combined with the pressure on costs that often leads airline bosses to skimp on maintenance and to "encourage" crews to fly with planes that shouldn't leave the ground. But the temptation to make savings they can trade, to make extra diversions for a little private business, and to fill up on unlisted consignments of their own can also tempt crews themselves to skirt the very edges of the possible when they fly.

The case of the Antonov-12 crew who simply ran out of fuel in midair on a run from Georgia to Turkmenistan because they forgot to factor into their knife-edge calculations the amount needed to start the engines on the runway at Yerevan has become legendary among these men, but only partly for its gallows humor. The sober truth is that it's a cautionary tale, one drummed into newbies: about how much fuel restarting your engines a couple of times will cost you (close to a ton); about how to eke the last bit of vapor from your tanks (raise the landing gear while you circle for landing); about talking to ATC so they don't keep you circling even when you divert to Baku for an emergency belly flop; and about keeping your eye on the money.

With the flights and their activities often shrouded in mystery, super-stition develops. Among the crews, some tell me they believe there's a mysterious sky-drunkenness, a narcosis that affects judgment and invites deadly errors, just as it does for scuba divers and the World War II bomber pilots who regularly saw "gremlins" on the wings at fifteen thousand feet, sabotaging their engines and giggling. In their accident-attrition log, Rus-sian aviation experts Dmitriy Kommisarov and Yefim Gordon reported on one An-12 crew who, running low on fuel high over Siberia, collec-tively and mysteriously "changed their mind" about stopping to refuel. "The available fuel was not enough for a non-stop flight to Irkutsk, and the captain soon had misgivings. However, inexplicably, he pressed on, wasting several opportunities [to land and refuel en route]. The result was as predictable as it was deplorable: 120 km from their destination, the outer engines quit, followed one minute later by the inboard ones with the air-craft at 5,250 feet."

Other reports tell of pilots, among them old comrades of Mickey's, who crashed into clearly visible hills or treetops despite clear and repeated warnings from crewmembers, ground control, and warning systems; or of sudden, extreme behavior that survivors find impossible to explain. In the crash reports, just as in the whispered gossip among survivors, it's a pat-tern that repeats itself again and again. Nobody really knows whether it's sky narcosis or just business that makes men go mad.

As we sit talking in the cool shadow of the giant plane while Sergei clumps about inside, the oral history gets another footnote: News comes down the grapevine that another crew has perished in an incident so far unexplained. Unexplained to everyone, that is, but men like Mickey who know how seductive the chances you take for the sake of getting the job done can be.

Overloading is blamed for the overwhelming majority of unexplained fatalities among men like these, though rumblings persist of aircraft fall-ing apart midair simply because they have become death traps, unserviced since the day they left the air force. Mickey says he's careful, but admits that the pressures, financial and otherwise, to take unofficial, cash-in-hand extra tons—both by overloading the stated cargo for tax-free bo-nuses from shippers and bosses in the know, or concealing their own shuttle-trade goods in the belly and in the escape holes—are constant. It is, he says, exasperated, part of the package. The fifteen tons is only a rule of thumb, so all sorts of things could affect that, especially weather conditions—Entebbe in Uganda is notorious for its slippery runway surface, a result of the way it was built and its position right next to Lake Victoria, for example. Bald tires and a ton too many on that and you'll end up underwater or in the terminal. Then there's how you plan and execute your takeoff. The more you have on board, the farther back you want to start—even if it means you get rolling on the grass fields before the tarmac runway. If you're in any doubt how fine Mickey can cut it, type "Il-76 takeoff" into your search engine and watch some of the home movies taken by stunned air-traffic workers.

Mickey's spooky ability to judge down to the last kilogram what he can take off with is illustrated by an anecdote I hear several times on my travels, from different sources and in different forms. Most swear it happened during a plane they were on, some tell it as a joke; that either means it's an urban myth or it happens quite a lot. It usually takes place in Africa or South Asia. The Il-76 is ready for takeoff: The crew have loaded both official cargo and their cash jobs, and the plane is stuffed to the rafters with exotic fruit and vegetables for export. The pilot begins taxiing for takeoff, and the plane gathers speed, but with only five hundred meters to go, they have no lift. Three hundred meters to the perimeter fence, and the plane still won't lift. One hundred meters, they're hurtling toward certain death. Fifty meters, and the front wheel finally lifts, as they just clear the fence. The pilot is furious. He turns to the loadmaster and shouts: "Idiot! I told you we could easily have loaded another punnet of cherries."

That's why Sergei's job as a loadmaster is so vital. He's not just some roadie, the guy with the trucks and the receipts, but the de facto physicist and safety engineer on every flight. With an Il-76, as with any of the Antonovs, he explains, you have plenty of room to maneuver if an engine fails or something—bad wind, or a rocket—knocks you. They're built to withstand that; it's what they do. Only when you're overweight and knocking right on the margin of being able to get airborne or not are you vulnerable. "Then you are like a man carrying a piano up stairs," points Sergei, marking a crazy angle with his arm. "It won't take much to put you right on your ass."

This is why, just as much as the pilot and navigator, loadmasters like Sergei are the ones they all have to trust. Together, their decisions about what extra tonnage fits where, and how much of it they can possibly manage this time, in these conditions, over these war zones, will see them make good money—and hopefully see them make it safely over the next set of mountains and with enough fuel, too—but only if Sergei gets the placements, the loading, and the numbers spot-on. More than one former Soviet source calls it "Russian roulette," with the loadmaster as the man placed in the insane, hugely pressurized position of having to try and stack the odds in the crew's favor with his sleight of hand and ingenuity before the trigger is pulled.

"Of course," smiles Mickey, though it's not much of a smile, "if he gets them wrong, we just have to be lucky."

But in the mid-1990s, Mickey's business antennae were already quivering again, looking for the next break. While the series of wars in the disintegrating Yugoslavia and borderlands of the Soviet Union were easy money, and Cyprus, Central Asia, and the Middle East were profitable strategic bases, the lure of Africa was harder and harder to resist for expert pilots and their ground crews. Word spread in the terminals and bars of the rich pickings to be made farther south, both on official business contracts and the potential for cash "extras" off the manifest. A strategic base like Sharjah was great, but sub-Saharan Africa had so much work going, there was almost no point being based anywhere but there for the moment.

Lke Starikov, Damnjanovic, Bout, and Hubert Sauper's weapons-toting *kamarads*, Mickey was about to find out just how well a little equatorial sun suited him. And the tricks and dodges he would learn there would be as vital for his survival as any military service.

CHAPTER NINE

This Is How You Disappear

West Africa, 1995–1999

AFRICA HAD BEEN A REMOTE PLAYGROUND for the superpowers throughout the Cold War. But as the face-off ended, Russian, American, and Cuban troops and supply lines to regimes and factions in places like Angola melted away too. Suddenly, power was up for grabs, and the spoils rich. U.S. commentator Karl Maier wrote of Angola: "Ideology is being replaced by the bottom line, as security and selling expertise in weaponry have become a very profitable business. With its wealth in oil and diamonds, Angola is like a big swollen carcass and the vultures are swirling overhead . . . lured by the aroma of hard currency."

He was right. Only the dark shapes circling overhead and scenting the rich pickings weren't vultures.

For a West that had been brought up to believe that any minute now the Russians were coming, the sight of a tidal wave of contraband-carrying, bar-destroying, free-market Soviet air force veterans screaming into the erstwhile "Free World" through the 1990s on giant army transport planes was a shock, to say the least. Indeed, it's difficult today to appreciate just how deeply spooked pilots and those few observers from Stockholm, New York, London, and Brussels who were watching must have been by the sudden arrival and proliferation of this new breed of crumpled Han Solos and loadmastering Chewbaccas in their deafening, battered, soot-pouring, low-flying *Millennium Falcon*s.

Even to the former Air America pilots whose barnstorming solo cargo operations they were quickly displacing over Africa and to a lesser extent Asia, the methods of the "flying legionnaires"—*avialegionery*, as they became known in Russia—appeared both insane and inscrutable. These established bush pilots throughout Africa, Central America, and Asia had reputations of their own as "anywhere-anything-anytime" DC-10, DC-6, and Hercules operators on God's own mission for the CIA. They were semimythical characters themselves, immortalized in Christopher Robbins's *Air America*, with names like Earthquake McGoon and Showershoes Wilson.

Seasoned charter agent John MacDonald, now only in his early thirties, remembers a family friend his mother and father would simply call Non-Sched Fred. "They called him that," laughs MacDonald, "because in all his years in aviation throughout the world, he'd never once set foot on a scheduled flight. He used to scare the pants off you for laughs, flying fully laden into tight canyons and trying to go under waterfalls. You'd look out of the cockpit window and all you'd see would be a wall of water, right up until the last second, when he'd just make it over."

These men, and therefore the CIA, had pretty much held the logistics of the developing world in their palms for years. But suddenly they had fearless, highly skilled competitors who were cheaper to boot. And within a couple of years, the old guard was on the ropes.

Russian émigré Evgeny Zakharov is a former pilot himself who left his home in Russia with a business partner named Yuri Sidorov in the heady mid-1990s and opened Volga-Atlantic, a cargo outfit in South Africa with a technical base in Namibia, chartering planes all over the continent for the UN and private clients alike. The operation is said to have had official blessing from the Russian authorities and set the standard for professionally run operations amid the chaos of a warring continent. Indeed, Zakharov is one of the *aviabiznesmeny* with a reputation among crews and technicians alike for successfully resisting the pressures to cut corners and push for overload.

Zakharov and Sidorov had different plans and split the company into two, with Sidorov going on to found his own start-up operating in the skies over Africa, and the employees choosing to either stay or leave with him. For his part, Zakharov now runs a leading, and highly respected, Johannesburg-based Il-76 and Antonov cargo outfit called, with a typical nostalgic flourish, Soviet Air Charter. We talk on the phone and I can feel his excitement as he remembers the men who flew for him in those first years. "This first generation were all ex–air force crews," he nods. "That meant they *thought* like a military crew, too—the order comes, they'll carry it out. Whatever it takes. No problem." Indeed, that military mind-set would soon prove crucial in landing big— and often highly dangerous—UN routes for companies like Zakharov's.

Still, these were early days, and to their chagrin, even these on-the-level fliers found themselves tarred with the same brush as their wilder comrades by a West struggling to come to terms with a culture, and with practices, with which it had had no dealings for three generations. And while Mickey shrugs it off today, in plenty of towns the pitchforks were most definitely out for these high-cheekboned, freewheeling, apparently anything-goes strangers.

Xenophobia played a part—how could it not, when their most closed of societies opened its gates and they marauded forth? These post-Soviet fly-boys, suddenly everywhere and dealing with everyone, whether they were in line with U.S. interests or not, were the Oriental Other—fathomless, fascinating, sinister, and semimythical men at one with their aircraft, descendants of the fearsomely skilled steppe horsemen mistaken for centaurs by the ancient Greeks. And the long-ingrained Soviet-style vagueness and aversion to transparency didn't help. Anyone looking to pin them down to definite answers about cargo, arrival times, place of registration, anything at all, was going to be disappointed.

"This smoke-screening instinct runs deep in the less official side of Russian business," says Mark Galeotti. "It was the Russian mafia who invented the so-called vampire phone at about the same time: a very fancy piece of kit, where every time you rang a number on this mobile, it would scan any nearby phones and clone one of their numbers. So that every time you phoned, you'd seem to be someone else's mobile. And that was particularly malign, because it was almost impossible to tap it, for the authorities. But for me that really encapsulates the modus operandi. If in doubt, your default is just to be a bit confusing. And I have a great fondness, bless them, for these well-meaning Westerners who think you can work in these terms and understand what the hell is going on. It's absolutely second nature."

In some ways, Mickey freely admits, war-torn Africa "seemed like home" to his crew for a while. The huge rewards on offer were hard to refuse, not just from armies like Angola's UNITA rebels but from the region's guerrilla presidents: men like Liberia's American-educated Charles Taylor, president from 1997 until 2003, when he was forced to resign and was indicted on a number of counts including his use of child soldiers during the conflict in neighboring Sierra Leone, campaigns of destruction and mutilation against civilians, and the use of slave labor to mine "blood" diamonds. Or the DRC's megalomaniacal Mobutu Sese Seko and his successor, Laurent Kabila. (The Congo's great hope, a former Marxist guerrilla who'd been friendly with Che Guevara, took power after the despotic Mobutu's overthrow.) Everyone, it seemed, had cash—often the plunder from territorial raids against their neighbors—to throw around. Together with the fat contracts on offer from humanitarian organizations, it meant the perfect storm of cash and conflict.

This was a prime stomping ground for some of the bigger beasts, too. Viktor Bout bought up a small aviation outfit in the DRC called Okapi Air and renamed it Odessa, coincidentally, after Leonid Minin's key home turf in Ukraine. In a move to give himself a measure of official cover, not to mention the protection of a "sponsor" on the continent, Bout then completed a masterstroke, forming a partnership with the wife of a lieutenant general in the Ugandan army who obligingly filed the flight plans for the ex-Soviet crews Bout sourced, just to make doubly sure they weren't scrutinized.

The move was typical, not of the *aviabiznesmeny*, but of the local authorities, who realized that these air outfits could be the answer to their prayers. Corrupt, covetous, and keen on keeping favor with strategic allies, they quickly became key partners, making up the bulk of any "secret" cargo shipments.

For businessmen, aid organizations, air-transport outfits, and mercenaries alike, it was every man for himself and follow the money. And while the world looked on and saw aid, people, explosives, ammo, and guns flooding in, money and diamonds flooding out, and Russian-made planes at every airport, joining the dots and trying to keep tabs on exactly who was flying what to where was impossible. This was a land in which the words *mercenary, aid transporter, trafficker,* and *businessman* were dangerously interchangeable.

For the pilots and crews, the money to be made flying between these newly privatized Soviet outposts was good. But the cost was often higher—between ten and twelve of these crews were shot down by rebels every year in Angola alone. Unfamiliar terrain and conditions took out just as many of that first wave.

"I've got many, many stories of very experienced pilots who have a lot of experience, but no experience in Africa," Evgeny Zakharov tells me in summer 2010. The former pilot from Volgograd saw and employed large numbers of these migratory airmen at the helm of his own series of companies operating Antonovs and Il-76s over Africa from his base in Johannesburg. "They come into Africa and crash because they don't know their job. Now all the captains are fifty-three years old because they're very experienced, they're from the Afghan war. But . . . you can build an operation, and you can have your ten thousand hours—some pilots think this is good experience. But that's nothing compared to ten thousand hours in Angola."

Through the 1990s, they gravitated in the hundreds to the West African former Portuguese colony, then in the grip of a bloody civil war between UNITA (a militia propped up by the U.S. until the end of the Cold War) and the MPLA (their rivals, backed by the Soviets). And while both sides had stopped officially backing anybody, Russian logistics and Secret Service operatives remained, alongside Cuban troops, until at least 1994, withdrawing only as the UN moved in. But as the official support ended, the knockoff-priced Soviet arms and ammo—and equally cheap transport for any cargo or troops either side had—flooded in. As in Serbia, they were fat times when illicit cargoes, both military and civil, were flown in and out of the combat zones. Many crews came to grief. But more thrived, whether by flying for shady, gunrunning, embargo-smashing operators like Bout, straight-up outfits like Zakharov's, or men like Mickey, who would double his official runs with his own cargo business within a business.

However they operated, there was one crucial ingredient to success down in Africa, the third *c* in that perfect storm of cash and conflict: chaos. Because while Europe and the Middle East were cluttered with air bases, radar positions, borders, and regulations—another Cold War hangover—in the vast, empty, and undeveloped spaces of Africa, no one could see anything. Planes, armies, cash, guns, gold could all seemingly teleport themselves from one location to another if you knew how. And men like Mickey quickly learned how to turn vanishing to a fine art.

The chimeric vagueness about location, ID, and cargo he cultivates is possible partly because of the lack of coordination between countries, agencies, and monitoring organizations. And for all the bold initiatives put forward by peace monitors and regulators, that opacity, that broken- ness, is baked into the system.

Like financial regulation, the close monitoring of cargo is something that's not really in the interests of a lot of countries to do well, especially if there's a benefit to the regime—financial, military, personal—in what's coming in and out on planes like Mickey's. This principle finds its most expert practitioners in Africa, in some ways the last bastion of freedom for such crews.

"In places like Africa, and to an extent Central Asia, because they're so porous and there tends to be quite a lot of corruption, it's very, very easy to fly whatever you want through," says one veteran South African pilot who hitched rides with veteran Soviet crews from Angola to Addis back in the 1990s. "And because there's no continuous radar coverage for most of Africa, let alone parts of Asia, you're invisible as soon as you leave the radius of whatever airport or airfield you set off from." From that point on, the position of the plane is whatever the radio operator says it is.

Even Uganda's Entebbe airport—the UN base for East Africa and the biggest, best, and busiest airport in the region—doesn't have any radar at all some weeks. There is a joke among Russian and Ukrainian aviators in sub-Saharan Africa:

Q: "What is the radar like at [name here] airport currently?"
A: "There? Oh, he's a little fellow, about sixty, and likes a drink in the afternoon."

It really is that ramshackle. For anyone who wants to monitor what the boys are doing—or what anyone's doing over large swaths of sub-Saharan Africa, the Caucasus, and South Asia—these flippant comments tell an inconvenient truth. Aviators in Africa could, and to some extend still can, get away with murder.

And they did. Throughout the 1990s, there was a sense of freedom bordering on gold fever in Angola despite its RPG fire and its live volcanoes spewing deadly lava and ash over airstrips and planes alike. The freedom came from a combination of remote landing strips—and Il-76s and An-12s were particularly suited to taking off and landing on unprepared or rough jungle airstrips—lack of official oversight and regulation, the almost complete absence of radar, and the interest of all parties concerned, from the crews to the regimes who hired them and the warlords and traffickers they did business with, in cloaking their activities in secrecy.

Veteran African freight pilot Terry Bonner is a U.S. native who's been flying cargo over South, East, and West Africa for over a quarter of a century and has developed a grudging respect for the ex-Soviet crews. "Whatever you say about these guys," he says, his gravelly East Coast voice catching with admiration, "these Soviets are the best pilots I've ever seen, period. They can get to places nobody else can land in, and they can do things nobody else can do with their planes."

Some pilots routinely flew arms, supplies, men, and cash for both sides, and for charities and international agencies like the UN in between. Nor was there any shortage of money. The ready supply of blood diamonds and precious natural resources meant that both militias could afford to pay almost any price for the right crew with the right plane.

One veteran pilot testified to the UN that he'd been approached to make sanctions-busting flights transporting weapons to Angola's UNITA rebel warlord leader Jonas Savimbi for a cool $100,000 a trip. The job was to fly the deadly cargo from Rwanda's capital, Kigali, to a clandestine UNITA base code-named Alpha One. There were to be no place-names or navigation aids at Alpha One, he wouldn't be on anybody's radar, and he would have no ground control. Instead, he would have to rely on his GPS to find the base and locate the runway at night. This pilot refused to make the delivery, he told the UN conference, because "it's not an easy place to get to at night, and they insist on doing it at night."

Others were less circumspect and paid the price, becoming jungle captives—creepingly aware as the days in captivity passed with no hint of ransom from their employers or pressure from their governments that, as cheap as the weapons they often flew were, they themselves were the cheapest and most expendable resource of all. Some were lucky— comparatively speaking, at least. On May 12 and June 30, 1999, two An- tonovs ostensibly under contract to fly aid into government-held towns in Angola were brought down by UNITA. The crews survived the crashes but were abducted from the wreckage by UNITA forces. One year later, five of the aviators—later identified by the Russian Embassy—were dis- covered half starved and raving in the Zambian jungle after having been loosed half naked into the bush by their captors.

But where many now feared to tread, Mickey looked at it coolly: It was a job, and all jobs have risks. You just have to read them right. And while many post-Soviet crews flew long, dangerous, and thankless missions there for clients like the UN wholly legitimately, for plenty more of his former Soviet military comrades used to flying impossible missions to poorly equipped landing areas, the kind of money they could make—not just from the cargoes they were commissioned to carry by their paymas- ters, but with their own cash businesses piggybacking those cargoes with side orders of arms, gems, booze, and whatever else they had a market for—was irresistible.

For the pilots, and business kingpins like Viktor Bout and his rival Leonid Minin, 1990s West Africa—Angola, Liberia, Sierra Leone—was hugely profitable. Indeed, so lax and corrupt were the legal and compli- ance regimes there that they had carte blanche.

One problem for anyone wanting to track down the gunrunners in a place like this is that, all too often, the paper trail leads nowhere. Cargo manifests need only appear to match what's in the hold in terms of ton- nage (and the amount of cash on the receipt). And the supposedly water- tight end-user certificate (EUC), which accompanies all arms shipments to certify the eventual destination and use of the weapons as evidence that they're not going to end up with any parties under arms embargoes or sanctions, is so easily forged I've made one myself on my laptop in a Ugan- dan hotel room, using a JPEG downloaded from the Internet, a ministry title I made up, the name of an official I got from the local paper, and the printer in the business center downstairs. It looks pretty good. It won't pass a full background check, like somebody calling the phone number on the government letterhead, or even thinking about it too much. Still, says one seasoned flight manager, "Nobody ever calls to check—why should they?"

In practice, so long as it looks about as good as mine, the cargo will be released, even if it's practically shouting, "Stop me, I'm dodgy." In 2009, for example, 103 sets of refurbishment kits for 53-65KE submarine attack torpedoes were authorized for export by Montenegro to Macedonia for a civilian project in Central Asia. According to the report of the International Peace Investigation Service (IPIS), "the table of exports states that the kits were ultimately for civilian use in Kyrgyzstan—which, one may recall, is at some considerable distance from the nearest ocean." (In the copious footnotes the monitor's voice deadpans: "It is also difficult to think of a civilian use for a torpedo.")

The problem is that a form is always just a form, and that means it's both official-looking and easily copied. When officials finally caught up with Leonid Minin as the 2000s dawned, they would discover just how much of a mockery these ingenious ex-Soviets had made of the entire EUC system. And who can blame them for trying when many countries' EUCs are in effect slightly glorified A4 letters; others' are full, multiple-field, serial-numbered certificates. There's no unified system, and so many flying around that hard-pressed, underpaid, politically appointed customs men in third world airports not only won't know what's genuine and what's not, but lack the resources, time, and will to check and chase each one up, especially given the time differences often involved and the pressure to release cargo and turn crews and aircraft around. More forms to be filled. Stamp. Next.

And if many experienced charter agents seem blind to the capacity for extra cargo ("They are great aircraft," says one, completely seriously. "One thing, though: If the pilots or technicians say they can fly, you always double-check. We'll work it out and we say, 'No, you can't fly that,' and they are like, 'Yes, we can fly it, of course we can fly it.' And we have to tell them, 'No you *can't*, you're five tons overweight, you bloody fool!'"), everyone seemed blind to the fact that without global standardization, EUCs were, and remain to this day, almost worthless.

All across Africa, planes were seemingly disappearing in midair only to reappear at impossible locations on the other side of the world. Flights that took off carrying food and shoes for disaster-stricken areas would land in Africa two refueling stops later carrying land mines, attack helicopters, or ammunition for rebel outfits like UNITA or Congolese warlords. These aircrews could—literally—be in five or more places at the same time. Then none at all. They were shape-shifters, masters of disguise and illusion.

Their cocaine runs used African stopovers in out-of-the-way backwaters like Guinea-Bissau and Angola instead of flying directly into Europe from Colombia and Peru because no African government had the planes or radar to detect and catch them, and because bribes were cheaper. And as for the journey there, most of the Atlantic is similarly radar-free, leaving them a clear run from the Cocaine Coast to West African bolt-holes like Sierra Leone and Liberia.

"The shit they pull is unreal, and radar coverage is just the tip of the iceberg," agrees Bonner, talking on the phone from his base at one of South Africa's own frontier airports. Before I finally caught him, we'd played an e-mail cat-and-mouse played out via one of the Internet's many unofficial message boards for pilots to share rumors—about clients, jobs, locations, aircraft movements, and other crews. I'd been lurking for weeks, and his posts—under a pen name more elaborate than the one he's requested here—had become increasingly preoccupied with ex-Soviet aircrews. The last one, the week before I tracked him down, claimed that "90 percent of all accidents in Africa are Russian-built aircraft. The question is, why? Most are poorly maintained and should not be flying at all." He claimed to have regularly seen "crews taking kickbacks to overload their aircraft. This is a fact: most of the Russian crews [over here] don't follow the rules of the air."

Now, with edginess in his voice and the clear, hesitant manner of someone who's not happy at all that he's been talked into an interview, but too polite to hang up and run, he explains what this "deadly bullshit" is. "They know the radar can't see them. We fly on a frequency called 1269, it's the air frequency and it's there for pilots to report their position. In the DRC, even over Brazzaville, they don't even have a transponder [devices fitted in planes as standard since World War II, which emit signals to help identify the plane's location both to air-traffic monitors on the ground and other aircrafts' automatic collision-avoidance systems], and what do you know, the Russians give erroneous positions! They'll radio different airports and tell *each* of them that they're just a few minutes away, and will be landing there shortly! They lie on their radio about their position. Unless something is done, more people will die."

The effect of lying about their position is that they get priority at their choice of airports. However, there are two side effects. One is the increased likelihood of midair collisions. But the other—and to Mickey this is a very nice side effect indeed—is that different airports will each note down the plane's position. And each time it will be different. So tracking a flight from, say, Entebbe in Uganda to Khartoum in Sudan becomes a strange game of find-the-lady involving all airports and ground-control centers en route, and plenty that aren't. Which of these positions, radioed to a control tower, contains the real "invisible" plane? And which are just ghost planes, positions reported and monitored, then lost?

So it is that our plane, taking off from, say, Southern Sudan, could appear in the night sky over Kenya, Uganda, Tanzania, Congo, Burundi, Somalia, and Sudan simultaneously. It will eventually land somewhere. But for most, it just fails to show up. So one plane becomes five, flying in different directions to different airports in the darkness, a kind of suspended Schrödinger's cat experiment in which all answers and outcomes are possible until the act of intervention, or until they land the plane.

Even when contact with ground control is established, it's laughably easy to fool. Mickey's most basic trick is so simple and effective it's almost unfair to call it a trick at all. "You're over Africa somewhere, listening to the air traffic on your radio," he says. "So you don't have any permission. Just tell them you're one of the other planes. They can't see what you look like. Maybe you know a British Airways flight is coming ten minutes behind, and we want to come through some airspace, we just 'borrow' that flight's permission. We radio and say, 'Hello, I'm British Airways flight number this or this, can I come through?' 'Of course.' Ten minutes later, when the real British Airways flight is coming, they say, 'Hello, I am BA flight so-and-so, can I come through?' Well, the control tower will know what happened. But you are already gone."

Indeed, using other people's call signs and flight numbers over Africa is, say insiders, "pretty standard—everybody's at it." And if your radar isn't great—if you have any at all—it's all down to trust.

"In any case, there's a lot of naïveté in places like Africa and Central Asia," says Brian Johnson-Thomas. "One of the reasons Kazakhstan was so popular as a plane-registration base for dodgy outfits—apart from the fact that they let anyone register—is that its call sign was always Unicorn November, meaning all Kazakh-registered flights began with the letters 'UN.' So all over Africa, the Caucasus, Asia, South America, a lot of ground staff who didn't know any better just let them do whatever they wanted, thinking they were something to do with the United Nations. They just would see 'flight UN-1234' or whatever, assume it was the United Nations, and welcome them with open arms!"

As it turned out, they needn't have worried. In addition to rebel militias and traffickers, there was no shortage of governments only too pleased to outsource some of their own dirty work.

CHAPTER TEN

Plunder in the Jungle

The Congo, 1997–2000

IF LATE-1990S ANGOLA WAS UNPREDICTABLE and dangerous for airmen, the Congo was another level of madness entirely—a fact that was reflected in the potential rewards. More than anywhere else in the late 1990s, the diamond-rich Democratic Republic of the Congo (DRC) had promised rich pickings for brave pilots, straight and *na levo* (meaning "on the left-hand side," the phrase is the Russian equivalent to "under the counter" or "on the sly") alike. Under the final, Caligula-like madness of President Mobutu, the DRC, then Zaire, also known as Hell on Earth, was falling apart. The man said to have declared his own country's currency void literally overnight simply because he'd taken a dislike to the necktie he was pictured wearing on the existing banknotes (thereby instantly plunging the economy back into a stone age of bartering, looting, and indentured labor) was finally being chased down by his own voodoo.

He'd had a good run. He had $4 billion deposited in a personal bank account in Switzerland (curiously, the exact size of his country's national debt); he'd been feted by American presidents from Nixon on (until the Cold War ended and the invites to canapés at the White House dried up); he'd canceled Christmas and declared December 25 his official birthday; renamed himself the Un stoppable Great Warrior Who Goes from

Strength to Strength by deed poll; demanded that the population wear his likeness on their clothes; and dealt with Western businesses only too glad to pay bottom dollar for his country's resources, no matter how they were mined, looted, or hunted.

Now his time was up. He fled in 1997 in a plane organized by none other than Viktor Bout and under heavy gunfire, prompting his son to say admiringly of the Soviet-made hardware, "If that had been a Boeing, it would have exploded!" thus giving ex-Soviet planes the kind of celebrity endorsement no money can ever buy. But by then the damage was done. Both Ugandan and Rwandan forces moved against the country, backing rebel groups and occupying large swaths of hill and jungle territory to the north and east. These groups' rulers, warlords, and the leaders of their loose, semiofficial paramilitaries relied on child soldiers, rape, and narcotics as instruments of fear and control.

For the Ugandan and Rwandan forces, there was just one problem. The Democratic Republic of Congo is nearly ten times the size of Uganda and nearly ninety times bigger than Rwanda. This meant neither army could hope to truly control the vast areas they eventually "occupied"; instead, they focused their energies and troops around strategic targets, like diamond-mining towns and airfields. And, having taken these targets, they quickly found new partners for their import-export start-ups among the commanders of other occupying forces and the rebels they'd been fighting. They quickly found themselves welcomed by rebel warlords, neither as foes nor as liberators, but as customers and potential global distributors.

The only problem the Congolese warlords had always had was the high-risk, high-cost, ad hoc nature of air transport for these things. It was nobody's idea of an efficient export process. So imagine the delight of these rebel leaders when they discovered that far from squashing their rackets, these UPDF and Rwandan forces, with their sudden monopoly—sorry, peacekeeperly control—over the transport infrastructure, mining towns, and air bases, not to mention their regular cargo flights to and from air bases back home like Entebbe and Kigali, were very much men with whom they could do business.

It soon became clear that rather than anything so gross as disorganized plunder, the export and resale of eastern Congo's natural bounty was a key part of Ugandan president Yoweri Museveni's funding strategy

for the military action in the first place. Indeed, one of the primary motivations for this Second Congo War (1998–2003) appeared to be the lust
for control over the country's most lawless and (not entirely coincidentally) most mineral-rich territory, with even the loosely allied Rwandan
and Ugandan forces clashing in a series of lethal firefights around the
diamond-mining center of Kisangani in 1999.

The result was war as it might be imagined by Werner Herzog: an arena
of charismatic psychopaths, brave leaders, visionary entrepreneurs, and
avaricious chancers loaded down with guns, cash, and their own demons,
toiling beneath a canopy of jungle foliage and strobe-lit by the regular
apocalyptic electrical storms that roam the hills and plains of Central Africa. Generals, privates, and guerrillas alike came to the Congo with their
dreams of riches, greatness, and dominion and saw them fulfilled; these
things made them monsters. Accounts circulated of isolated indigenous
pygmy tribes being hunted down by platoons of privateering troops and
eaten as food; of soldiers with get-rich-quick schemes involving the cultivation of narcotics out in the huge, unpoliced hinterland, with plenty of
money to go around for those who helped pack, transport, clear, and distribute the gear at the other end.

Just as in the crumbling Union back in the heady early 1990s and the
Belgrade of the red businessman, supplier had met consumer in the ultimate free-market party. And it went down just like any entrepreneur worth
his salt will tell you it always does: Once the warlords and rebels identified
their customer and smoothed out their distribution, all that stockpiled
DRC product started to, well, fly off the shelves. And fly it did—on the giant ex-Soviet aircraft flocking to the area as demand for their services
exploded.

"It was so different to flying in Europe," laughs Evgeny Zakharov.
"Short runways and no weather! In Europe you've got always your [re-
ports into] weather conditions: Here it's fog; here it's drizzle, there is bad
weather. In Africa, you don't have this, you never have a weather report.
And no radar. Plus, the runway conditions are very, very bad. And then
the manual will say the runway is two thousand meters, but really it's not
even fifteen hundred meters, because the other five hundred meters are
destroyed by bombs, by wars, or for some other reason—like in Angola,
where the runways kept getting destroyed by volcanoes."

But they were made of stern stuff. And among the respectable entrepreneurs were familiar names. Ukrainian Leonid Minin was busy homing straight in on the natural resources. Viktor Bout, having supplied the Antonov that had spirited the cancer-riddled Mobutu from his wedding-cake palace to asylum in Togo before the mob could get to him, had been operating in these parts for years already and was on hand now to supply the Congolese warlord Jean-Pierre Bemba's army of speed-guzzling teenage soldiers and rebel warlords with Soviet-built Mi-24 gunship helicopters in return for cash from Bemba-controlled diamond fields. There's a story told by Bout biographers Farah and Braun that the helicopters not only helped Bemba steal a march on enemy forces, skip arduous route marches, and travel without fear of ambush, but even became his own private duty-free shopping courier on the rare occasion that his militia found itself camped somewhere remote on a hot night without quite enough cold beer.

The chaos would—had anybody pre-9/11 given a damn what happened in Africa—have provided a useful historical lesson to coalition forces in Iraq and post-2001 Afghanistan on how not to handle their logistical support. Planes flew in and out like taxis, and while there's no suggestion that the crews, charter agents, or operators were doing anything illegal, the lack of system oversight their methods enabled was disastrous. The legitimate objectives of governments, armed forces, and even the UN (whose troops were implicated in 2008 in arms dealing, ivory trading, drug trafficking, and even counterfeit gold smuggling from the eastern DRC) became blurred and softened by their time in the jungle and proximity to so much precious plunder.

Still, financially for all parties, it was boom time: a win-win deal. Except, of course, for the ordinary locals, logged trees, protected species, and anyone the warlords happened to kill with the bullets and guns given to them as part payment by the Ugandan and Rwandan exporter-occupiers.

Well, maybe they weren't the only losers. After all, in late-1990s Congo just as in early-1990s Russia, when powerful, rich, and avaricious men played high-stakes games, it tended to be the innocent, the hardworking, the unwitting, and the unlucky who got caught in the crossfire.

Stray bullets and unfortunate accidents had an eerie habit of picking out Mickey's comrades. Stand on a runway in the DRC today, any potholed, dirt-tracked, litter-strewn, zigzagged, shell-holed runway. Look off to your left or your right, and there are the clues: everywhere, the fossil parts of these big, thundering, flying beasts. Panels and tires are halfway up trees, bolts and patches in ditches. Like the early aviators with their Icarus wings and multidecked canvas and flaming props, these new Magnificent Men in Their Flying Machines were falling, exploding, flipping over, nose-diving, breaking up, liquidizing locals, and flying by the duct-taped seat of their pants to get the job done. They were ex-Soviet air force, they'd flown through missiles into minefields and back out again before breakfast, and they didn't flinch from danger.

Sometimes maybe they should have, because the Congo has many ways of reclaiming the cargoes men try to fly out of there. The first to go was an An-12 that caught fire for no reason on landing at Bunia, forcing the crew to jump for their lives. Less lucky were the Il-76 crew that perished a couple of months later in June 1996, taking a chance on an overweight load and a ludicrously patched-up plane. They'd hit a telegraph pole earlier in the day, and the Candid was more tape than metal by the time they loaded up in the Congo. Not unusual, but the heat must have snapped it, and everybody died.

In 1998, Zimbabwe air force jets attacked and destroyed an Ilyushin belonging to Viktor Bout's Air Cess on the ground at dawn in Kalemie.

The next incident suggested one possible cause of the apparently spontaneous combustion in Bunia, when on November 10, 1999, a former-Soviet An-12 loaded to the gills with high-explosive (and now internationally banned) cluster bombs simply blew up on the runway at Mbandaka airport, killing six occupants and spraying the air base with wreckage. It was a disaster that would recur with distressing regularity. At 11:30 A.M. on April 14, 2000, sparks from an air base warehouse fire in Kinshasa spread to a cargo of ammunition, obliterating an Antonov-28 before spreading to other aircraft. Some 109 civilians on the ground are said to have been killed.

Dozens of fellow aircrews from the former Soviet Union were shot down by UNITA rocket and rifle fire over the jungle, and many more fell victim in other ways to their unstable phantom cargoes, with the seemingly spontaneous combustion caused by explosives in the hold, in midair or on runways, always given the benefit of the doubt by the possibility that it might, after all, have been an astonishingly accurate RPG shot that blew the planes up.

But as the 1990s progressed and first Angola, then Rwanda, Uganda, the Sudan, Somalia, Liberia, the Democratic Republic of Congo, Kenya, Burundi, and Sierra Leone all tipped toward chaos and war toward the end of the decade, Mickey admits the cold fact is that in some ways the dangers, even the deaths, helped anyone who wanted to play fast and loose.

For every crash site or shard of wing, just as many planes, crews, and illicit cargoes simply vanished, their fake ID, sketchy, ever-changing registrations and flickering paper trails making it impossible to determine whether they'd crashed or simply been repainted, and were now flying happily under an alias and new, heat-free ID. One Antonov downed in 2000 running arms to Liberia hadn't officially existed for some time, having been registered and deregistered on the very same day in Moldova—a phantom plane, written off as scrapped, flying on regardless through the African mist with its deadly payload, a ghostly *Flying Dutchman* with no home in the world and death at its heels. Rumors of collusion in the smoke-screening by governments persist. On October 30, 2003, UN investigators were turned away from the site of a Moldovan Antonov-28 believed to have been transporting illicit arms consignments that had crashed outside Kamina by "military officers armed with AK-47 rifles and people wearing civilian clothes." (The Moldovan operator later responded that they had conducted their own internal investigation and were "absolutely certain" they hadn't been running illicit weapons. So that was that cleared up.)

Even if people know where and who you are, there's a good chance in places like Africa you'll get away with it. Doug Farah and *Los Angeles Times* correspondent Stephen Braun reported that Gary Busch, a contemporary of Viktor Bout's, once found that three of Bout's own fleet of planes were using the same tail number and air-operations papers, noting simply that this was simply "the way it was" when trafficking in Africa.

One tail number, three planes, five different reported routes per flight per plane. With up to fourteen "phantom" flights per registered tail number at any given moment, the night skies over Africa, Eastern Europe, Asia, and the Caucasus are full of Mickeys. But which ones do you believe? And which ones do you follow? And how? Radar coverage peters out, leaving gaping abysses over the emptiest parts of the landmass—the mountains, savannahs, and rainforests, the parts least likely to be under government or police control. Borders are long, porous, and frequently unpoliced. "Once you're up," says Mickey, "you can come down and change things wherever you want, really."

"The Ilyushin Il-76, even more than the Antonov An-12 or An-24, is made for landing on rough, unprepared runways," says Brian Johnson-Thomas. And one of its special powers, and what makes it better than any of the American models the world had been using, is that it's designed to load and unload without ground assistance.

One former Il-76 pilot laughs as I ask him about the independence that buys. "If you really wanted to, maybe you could take off with whatever you like on board, wait until you're out of radar range, buy yourself some time by misreporting your position, divert somewhere to make an illicit rendezvous, land, unload your cargo, hand it over, take on something else, take off again, and resume your original flight plan. In the places these guys operate, nobody will notice if you're forty minutes late. Nobody can see where you are, and maybe you've already reported your position as close to your destination, so you might have just meandered a bit. That's how flights take off with one thing on board and land with another. Let's say for the sake of argument, food becomes something naughty, and that something naughty quickly becomes money."

All this may explain the apparent anomalies in the few media reports that make it out of places like the DRC when Russian cargo flights, legitimate or otherwise, come down.

Ernest Mezak is an investigative reporter and human-rights activist for the Komi office of Memorial, a Russian organization dedicated to preventing repeats of Soviet-style state brutality. He has followed the lives, and deaths, of Africa's Russian cargo airmen closely and points to the example of an Antonov-12 that caught fire at Mbuji-Mayi airport in January 2006. In the immediate aftermath, it seemed the plane contained first four men from Syktyvkar in the Komi Republic in Russia. Then it was not four but six men, from Syktyvkar and Ekaterinburg. It had flown in from Goma, except Russian news agency ITAR-TASS later claimed it had in fact taken off in Kinshasa. The weather was blamed for the crash, as was overloading and engine failure. At this point, a small media blackout appears to have descended, with the crew's names being protected—at their own request, it was reported to have been claimed by the operator, Evgeny Zakharov—and their repatriation being organized discreetly by suited officials.

It really is that easy. Jump on the plane, taking whoever you like with you. Take off. Then, once you're out of visual contact, do what you like. Carry on to your destination directly if you want. Or drop down into a field, make a rendezvous there, change your cargo, and take off again in a matter of a few minutes—nobody need ever know.

In those anything-goes years in Africa, Brian Johnson-Thomas recalls one ballsy pilot landing on a field with only the lights of a car to guide him down. The pilot was flying milk formula into Mogadishu in 1992 for Save the Children. Normally, the distribution operation would start at Mogadishu airport. But on this occasion, fighting meant the airport warehouse—now nearly empty—was too dangerous to get to. Not only that, but in the absence of any ceasefire, flying into the airport itself was out of the question. "So I drove out southwest of Mogadishu," shrugs Johnson-Thomas, "and found a nice big bit of flattish desert."

The Welshman then set about turning his "flattish desert" into a serviceable runway. He gathered up some sticks and lit a "pretty big" bonfire, then drove his Land Cruiser in a straight line for two miles, turned it back round toward the fire, and switched his headlights on to full beam, illuminating the other end of the notional runway. Then he waited.

"I spoke into the radio: 'Can you hear me, Dmitri?' 'Yes, I hear you, Brian!' 'Right, Dmitri, GPS coordinates are so and so, wind is from the southeast, and whatever else!'"

Slowly, the sound of engines tore through the still desert night. Johnson-Thomas lifted his HF radio. "I said, 'Er, left hand down, left hand down.' And after a bit, he said, 'I can see your fire!' I told him to circle over the fire and my headlights, then told him he was clear to land. I remember, we were both laughing and joking around: 'There is no other traffic in the circuit,' all that airport stuff."

Despite Johnson-Thomas's fears for his Land Cruiser, the landing was straight from the textbooks. It must have made for a bizarre sight, a Soviet-era superplane being guided round into position by a lone man on foot in the desert, waving as if helping a friend to parallel park. "He came in beautifully," beams the Welshman. "I did the whole thing, like at Heathrow . . . I wasn't sure, they've got lots of little wheels rather than big ones, so I brought him round facing back into the wind, and then signaled. He dropped the ramp, killed the engine, and we rounded up all these watching locals, just sort of part-time sheep shaggers and camel drivers, to help unload quickly. Then we just opened the front door and dropped the ramp and they walked in, up the steps, took everything down the ramp and onto our trucks."

Turnaround was, incredibly, quicker than he'd seen most cargo drops achieve with winches at international airports. "Dmitri was on the ground for something like five minutes, tops. Then he just took off again! That was it."

For pilots who want to go out of their flight path and make extra un-scheduled stop-offs for an undercover deal, the right know-how and a couple of contacts makes it incredibly easy to do. Mark Galeotti recalls instances of Soviet pilots stationed in Tajikistan making extra under-cover journeys from base to carry heroin over from across the Afghan border, "learning how to do the equivalent of turning back the mileage clock on a car . . . only on their planes," to cover their tracks in the event that anyone back at base ever asked for them to account for their jour-neys—or why they were suddenly so flush with drug money.

Even today, outfits like Mickey's adopt what's best described as a "can-do" attitude to identification and record keeping. One recent case saw an Il-76 belonging to a Sudan-registered outfit of what the local media had begun calling "mercs"—short for "mercenary aviators"–being stopped and inspected. The airline was a known one, and the tail number matched the number on its records, so the first instinct of the inspectors was simply to let it go. Then one of them spotted the problem: The airline had ceased to exist as a business three years earlier, after being struck off the civil aviation register and banned. Only clearly the guys operating the plane in the defunct airline's livery had other ideas.

With a creative approach to registration and paperwork, cargo planes can enjoy almost as many aliases and new identities as men like Viktor Bout. As I write this in late summer 2010, out on the rough scrubland of Entebbe military base, I can see three apparently abandoned planes whose future may yet be as colorful as their past. There's a white Il-76, registered in São Tomē & Príncipe, a tiny island republic off the coast of Guinea famed in aviation circles for its lax inspection and record-keeping requirements, and three Antonovs that according to one employee "the Georgians [another notoriously lax registration regime] were looking high and low for, for ages." All are looking suspiciously well kept, having been listed as unfit to fly.

"Them?" laughs one air base guard. "Oh, they will fly again, of that you must have no doubt. Today they are old planes, past their service life. But someone will fly them—you watch them disappear!" He laughs an expansive, jolly laugh behind his sunglasses and automatic and shakes his head at my question. And well he might. Owners, operator, and crews of planes like these have been witnessed "reviving" their registrations, paperwork, and even livery overnight with a bit of DIY know-how, resorting to self-adhesive stickers with logos rather than paint, because they're easier to change in a hurry—from blacklisted cargo airline or unknown independent operator to Kazakh air force or United Nations in as much time as it takes to peel, stick, and smooth over a few labels.

Mickey says it's an open secret there are outfits—he knows the men, though he's never flown with them—for whom quick-fix magnetic decals and even (should circumstances demand) matt emulsion are the product of choice. Emulsion because of the ease with which it can be washed off with water and a mop at the end of the day by man-with-van operators—while some networked airline groups interchange planes so frequently that anything more than a magnetic strip is an unnecessary encumbrance.

Needless to say, the application and removal of both can be haphazard, leading to bizarre games of mix and match on occasion, with planes appearing to sport the rear section of one operator's Antonov with the fuselage or wings of another. Today, other expat pilots openly trade mobile-phone snapshots on Internet chat rooms of Soviet-era cargo planes sporting game, but sometimes comically inept, attempts to replicate larger airlines' livery—even the famous United Nations logo and lettering on the wings and fuselage—in their attempt to escape detection.

"If they could misspell UN," one indignant expat British pilot tells me, his voice wavering between a shout and a laugh, "they would. And you know what? The authorities either don't give a shit, or they make money off them. Or they haven't got a fucking clue. Or all of the above."

Andrei Lovtsev, a respected former military and civil cargo pilot who now runs his own highly legitimate business and stable of planes from his headquarters in Moscow's Star City cosmonaut training camp, points out that checking, for those who want to check, is—theoretically, at least—easy. "If the plane has records done by bandits, I won't deal with them. You can always check [with the aviation authorities] when it was repaired. On the paper itself, the bandits put fake stamps. But there won't be any record [of those registrations, lifespan extensions, or repairs] in the factory. You can find it all out.

"It's not the pilots but those behind the business—those are the people who act without a conscience. Many are shot down in Somalia or Congo, but many crash through mechanical failure, and those pilots are betrayed!"

Indeed, as the 1990s wore on, it seemed more and more to Mickey that the pilots and crewmen were the fall guys; that they'd left one futile and badly run war in Afghanistan only to be catapulted back into one even worse. While the freedom to fly their own personal cargoes was welcome, the men making the real money behind the scenes, Lovtsev's "bandits," preferred the air-conditioned malls of Dubai, their luxury mansions in Sandhurst and Johannesburg, or their European retreats on the Med or in Switzerland or Ostend. And as for the rest of the world, it was just like Gary Busch said: Nobody cared. That was just the way it was.

But then, in 2000, quite by chance, the Italian authorities stumbled across a private party in a tiny hotel near Milan, and all that was about to change.

CHAPTER ELEVEN

Men of Wealth and Taste

Milan, 2000

IN THE HOT BLACK-AND-BLUE NIGHT of August 5, 2000, outside the open window of room 341 at the Europa Hotel, everything seemed to have stopped. The Saturday-night traffic was quiet, even for August; and in the long, lazy summer the outskirts of Milan, like the modest three-star, seemed almost empty. Here in the suite, though, things were definitely livening up for the occupant and his four hookers. While the utterly beautiful—and stark naked—Kenyan prostitute passed the freebasing pipe, the Italian girl held the heated rock of coke steady. The man inhaled, letting the rush of electric confidence spread through his body. Another whore, an Albanian, beautiful and wired, was distractedly watching the porno flick on the wall TV.

He looked down at his naked belly. At fifty-three, he couldn't deny he was carrying a few extra kilos, and, well, he probably shouldn't be doing this. But what the fuck—with a forty-gram-a-day habit, one more wouldn't hurt, and as a bona fide multimillionaire he could certainly afford it. He glanced over at the desk—he'd divided his two-room suite into "business" and "pleasure"—where the Russian hooker was frowning with concentration as she cut and diluted a few of the fifty-eight grams of cocaine for later disposal. Gritting his teeth on one more blast of euphoria, Leonid Efemevich Minin lay back on the bed. Life was good.

What happened next changed everything—for Leonid, for the three-star hotel of which he was part owner, and for international authorities baffled by the way their embargoes against war-torn regimes in countries as far away as Sierra Leone and Liberia seemed to make not one jot of difference to the number of weapons that found their way there.

The local police, having been alerted by a complaint—some later claimed it was a tip-off from another hooker who'd not been paid—knocked on the door, gained entry, and arrested the girls. They also arrested the man they initially assumed was just another hardworking business traveler indulging a few specialist peccadilloes courtesy of the local vice trade.

It took five weeks before they realized they'd stumbled across the prominent international gun smuggler, money launderer, and big wheel in the so-called Odessa mafia, a man wanted by the authorities in Switzerland, France, and Monaco for trafficking crimes, in Belgium in connection with the assassination of a Russian mafia boss—though nothing was ever proven—and in Italy itself. In fact, Minin, who produced an Israeli passport on his arrest, also had passports issued by the Soviet Union, Germany, Bolivia, Greece, and Russia under a variety of aliases including (to name but a few) Vladimir Abramovich Popela, Vladimir Abramovich Popiloveski, Leon Minin, Wulf Breslav, Leonid Bluvshtein, Leonid Bluvstein, Igor Osols, Vladimir Abramovich Kerler, and Igor Limar. He had been under surveillance by the Milanese customs and police authorities since 1992 for his involvement in laundering money earned from narcotics trafficking through the accounts of several prominent Italian businessmen.

But the real dazzle shots came from the party-loving businessman's suitcase. Despite being listed as the owner of a company called Exotic Tropical Timber Enterprises, investigators found a treasure trove of paraphernalia suggesting their portly prisoner was more than a businessman, more than even a common trafficker or a party-happy mafia kingpin. This was the paperwork of a serious international kingmaker: Alongside receipts for oil and timber exports were an inquiry by Minin about becoming the provider of Nigeria's mobile-phone network; a letter following up on his offer of a Ukrainian aircraft carrier for sale to Turkey; a letter from his Beijing office asking whether Liberian president Charles Taylor—then fighting off an insurrection and still two years away from his war-crimes arrest warrant—fancied establishing diplomatic relations with China; and correspondence between Minin and President Taylor's son Chuckie Junior.

Then, at the bottom, they stumbled across the arms deals.

Here was an end-user certificate for one consignment of thousands of small weapons, signed by ousted Ivory Coast dictator General Robert Guéï. An EUC is supposed to function like a fingerprint: Every shipment of weapons has one, unique copy, specifically about that deal. It's effectively a testimony statement guaranteeing that the shipment will only go to the people, and for the purpose, described at purchase. So far so good— except Minin's case was stuffed with copies of the certificate for later use elsewhere. (It gets even dodgier—Guéï later testified not only that he had signed just the one EUC—suggesting Minin had faked the rest—but that he'd been bribed to do so by Liberian president Taylor's offer of a share of the weapons.)

The prosecutors were on to him now—alert to the possibility that, while living right under their noses in a suburb of Milan, this apparently small-time operator was in fact indirectly responsible for horrifying militia uprisings and brutal regime crackdowns halfway around the world. The devil had, it seemed, been real all along, and he ran a cozy hotel on the outskirts of town.

Now feverishly looking for a smoking gun—something to tie Minin incontrovertibly to payment on one hand and trafficking on the other— they began sifting through his other possessions, where they found $500,000 in uncut diamonds; maps of the rebel-controlled Liberia–Sierra Leone border; a ledger filled with entries for small arms, including five million 7.62mm bullets; a fax to Minin requesting sign-off on a flight of 113 tons of bullets from Ukraine to the Ivory Coast; and the all-important money trail, via—you guessed it—a small Russian-owned aviation outfit.

It showed that Minin had paid $1 million to the outfit, an Azerbaijan-based operation called Aviatrend reportedly headed by a man named Valery Cherny, which not only brokered the arms purchase but chartered the plane and crew for delivery. A payment of $850,000 went to an Aviatrend account in that notorious mafia launderette that is Turkish Cyprus; the rest, rather more surprisingly, to Aviatrend's account at Chase Manhattan Bank, New York.

Investigative journalist Matthew Brunwasser, who followed the progress

of the bust alongside controversial Belgian UN arms-trade investigator
Johan Peleman, says Minin is far from the uniquely gifted criminal mastermind he's often painted as—not least in the Nicolas Cage Hollywood
action flick *Lord of War*, rumored to be based on (and fictionalized from)
the lives of Minin and Bout. "The timing of Minin's rise, and that of others like Viktor Bout, is not a coincidence," says the softly spoken San
Franciscan at his office in Istanbul. "Their power and success just would
not have been possible without the chaos, poverty, and disintegrating
state apparatus that hit the former Soviet republics."

Still, Minin's prosecution immediately hit trouble. Sure, they had the
vice rap sewn up, but as for the transnational trafficking stuff . . . who
the hell had jurisdiction over that? The evidence was top-drawer: faxes,
end-user certificates, all as close to conclusive as it seemed you could get.
The problem went deeper.

Like Viktor Bout's exploits, it appeared that many of the things Minin
was doing actually failed to qualify as illegal. Sanctions-busting is repre-
hensible and draws censure. Transporting illicit shipments of arms may or
may not break laws in the individual countries concerned, but all too often
those countries either benefit from the trade, have bigger fish to fry, or
have pretty weak, corrupt, and chaotic legal and enforcement frameworks
themselves.

Like the Muslim *hawala* system of money transference, or the peer-to-
peer downloading networks antipiracy groups find so tough to crack,
these arms deals benefit from their lack of central command—there's no
one bank that processes or approves payments, no central server, no accounts department in any one particular building in any one country. And
because they involve many parties in many territories, all working within
a framework of trust and loose allegiance, each country only sees a small
piece of the jigsaw.

It's the perfect camouflage: The picture is broken up, scattered, and hard
to detect. Only this went one step further: Even when the Italian police put
the picture together, not enough of it was within their jurisdiction.

Fighting seemingly chaotic trafficking networks like Minin's, in which
much of the evidence is scattered and loosely connected, through the
courts is always going to be hard, says Mark Galeotti: "We tend to think
of organized crime as a *Godfather* movie or whatever, disciplined, hierarchical, pyramidal, where orders go out from the Godfather, through the

ranks, and the foot soldiers at the bottom obey. In practice, it's actually nothing of the sort. Most of the time, your main men are out there hustling on their own account. The role of the gang is to set the turf rules, don't interfere, to mediate disputes, because shoot-outs are bad for business—it's to maintain security, to maintain a brand name that is valuable so that when people come along they know to fear you rather than say, 'Who the hell are you?' And in a way when there is some kind of systemic threat to the group as a whole, it represents the rallying cry."

I tell Galeotti he could be describing some of the affiliations that exist in the "gray" cargo world. He points out that a key strength of this network of loose affiliations is its adaptability, making it perfect for new environments. "In some ways a Russian or Ukrainian *mafiya* gang is more like a kind of freemasonry. If all of a sudden you've got some new opportunity, and it's not something you can do yourself, you get in touch. Someone will say, Look, I can get hold of a truckload of stolen sportswear. You think, Well, what the hell would I do with stolen sportswear? So the gang provides you with a network of contacts. The individual elements in this gang are often going to be a pretty stupid bunch of people. They might well be wily and have street smarts, but they're not thinkers, they're not intellectuals. They don't have business plans or mission statements. However, the organism as a whole and the economy that it represents is often surprisingly sophisticated. It reacts very rapidly."

After a trial in which his testimony was called *poco verosimile* ("scarcely credible") by the judge—Minin claimed he'd never known Cherny despite faxes and orders passing between them, saying he'd only ever bumped into him once in an Italian hotel bar—and despite a paper trail leading from Ukraine, Minin, and Aviatrend to the Ivory Coast and Liberia, Leonid Minin went to prison for just two years.

But while the Italian prosecutors were frustrated in their attempts to pursue the arms-running case, in other ways the bust was a success. Not only was the mother lode of documents and testimony something of a Rosetta stone—an unusually complete crash course in how to trace the movements of arms conducted across the globe by men like Minin and his network of cargo agents, pilots, quartermasters, and end users; as it happened, its coverage provided something of a wake-up call, too.

The bust's snowballing, high-profile nature—and make no mistake, cocaine, hookers, and diamond-rich rogue Liberian presidents were an irresistible combination for the media—called attention to the nature of these masonry-like networks and underlined the inadequacy of traditional law enforcement in stopping them.

From this point on, governments would at least try to work together, to keep tabs on what was coming and going, if not through their skies or their ports then at least through their banks. And if they were still no better at picking up or detaining these traffickers, at least they figured they'd found a new way to shut them down. As an associate of Charles Taylor, Minin had his assets seized, his accounts frozen.

For men whose sole focus is on making money, this approach promised much. But if anybody thought the tide was turning, they were wrong. At the turn of the decade, it wasn't just runways in out-of-the-way and unstable countries like Liberia or Angola that shook with the thunder of Soviet-era steel.

Genteel and decidedly developed, Ostend in Belgium became a traffickers' hub and the focus of a "Clean Up Ostend Airport" campaign, even as Viktor Bout himself acquired a place there; meanwhile, Europe's fringes from the Balkans to the Mediterranean remained open for business from utterly respectable and "rogue" cargo operations alike. But the cleanup campaigns had their work cut out, even with the invaluable help of the armies of dedicated, camera-toting plane spotters and cargo teams they recruited for the cause. Because stopping a loose trafficking network like this is a job that's difficult, if not impossible, even if you've got witnesses on the ground.

GENIAL, QUIETLY SPOKEN, and slight, Peter Danssaert is one of the men tasked with tracking this flow of so-called destabilizing commodities across the globe. As a leading light at the Antwerp-based International Peace Information Service and member of several UN Panel of Experts on trafficking, he specializes in the arms trade, providing expert services to the UN Security Council, the Organization for Security and Co-operation in Europe, and the UK parliament.

It's his job to monitor, and ultimately to stop, dodgy cargoes transported by men like Mickey in planes chartered by the likes of Bout and Minin. It's a tough task. But today, as he recalls one up-close encounter a few years ago on the smuggling front line of East Africa that proves first-hand exactly how swift these trafficking "organisms" are to adapt, even he can't help but laugh.

"I was checking into the hotel, up-country in Uganda, on some United Nations business," he says, "when I heard a Slavic-accented male voice talking on the phone behind me." Not Russian this time, he thought as he listened to the disembodied voice. Slowly he tuned in. His dealings with the arms-smuggling pipeline through Bulgaria in the past two decades had left him with enough experience to recognize a native.

"I turned round and saw a man wearing a pilot's uniform, complete with official United Nations insignia on the breast pocket," he says. "So, I waited, then I went over to him, exchanged a few politenesses, and then just came out and asked, as a UN pilot—as a colleague, really—whether he'd heard any rumors about the other side, you know, about illicit arms trafficking in the area. You could tell he spoke a very little English, and he clearly misunderstood my question, because he just nodded, smiled, and said to me in a low voice, 'No problem: You just tell me when, where, and how much.'"

Danssaert was surprised, and, without realizing quite what he'd heard, sought to clarify his question. "I said, 'No, no, I'm asking whether you *know* anything—whether you've seen any activity of that nature, smuggling arms, weapons, around here?'

"But he still didn't get it. He held up his hands like we had a deal, and repeated, 'Yes, yes, I tell you, *we can do it*. You just tell me: where, when, and how much. I will do it, no problem!'

"He scribbled a number on a piece of paper and told me to arrange the deal with his colleague, whose English was better. I looked up the number when I got home. It was a Bulgarian cargo outfit, sure enough—and sure enough, they've since been closed down for arms trafficking."

"Nobody knows *anything*," laughs another African flight manager. "Companies all get someone else to choose the planes and crew for them. And if there's a problem, you think they really wanna know they've got a trafficker on the payroll? No, thank you! I mean, it's always someone else's job. We all work like that. I think during Watergate, they called it 'plausible deniability': 'Oh, we didn't know. We'll fix it, we'll get rid of them.' In the meantime, they get to use the cheapest bidder, because they've got a budget to meet, overheads. What do you expect?"

Eastern bloc pilots touting openly for illicit arms-trafficking business while dressed in a UN aircrew uniform—business from someone in the employ of the UN no less—shows nothing if not a can-do attitude to business. This was Danssaert's own *Matrix* moment, when he says he began to understand just how pervasive and open the practice was. And it provides a tantalizing hint as to just what else, what other ad hoc deals and frankly air-bending cargo origami might be possible, when nobody was looking. Like everything in this shadow world of phantom airmen, arms traffickers in United Nations clothing, and disappearing two-hundred-ton aircraft, says Danssaert, you could get used to appearances being deceptive; if only you knew how they'd be doing it *next* time you tried to stop them.

But what Danssaert's Uganda encounter also means—apart from being very funny—is that the pilot was flying for the UN, wearing UN insignia, and taking orders for illicit arms deals on the side from anyone who approached him in a hotel foyer. This was a new pattern: no longer would the world be separated into good guys and bad guys, "clean" and "dirty" flights. The traffickers were intertwining themselves with operations—from peacekeepers to charities—that were so far above suspicion that they could do whatever they wanted with those extra tons, and nobody would ever know.

MICKEY, MOSTLY TACITURN (at least with me) and permanently beat looking, certainly doesn't look like part of an amazingly adaptable, agile trafficking organism. What he looks like is a working man from a regiment, or a factory: someone who would happily doze away his day in front of the television with a six-pack of beers at his side, given a chance at retreating back into the simple life. In some ways, it might just be the perfect–and completely unconscious–disguise.

There's another curious footnote to the many layers of disguise and informal camouflage connected to Leonid Minin's bust, though. Aviatrend, the outfit Minin had been using to transport weapons from Ukraine to Africa, and who had been accepting payments through Chase Manhattan bank as late as June 7, 2000, is listed on the Aviation Safety Network's database as having ceased to exist in 1998. Talk about adaptable.

And adaptability was the name of the game. By the time of Leonid Minin's bust, Mickey and his crew were flying the same routes in West

Africa as they always had anyway, only for the new clients in town: the UN, the global media, and the charity bandwagon.

Then, on a clear September morning in 2001, two planes hijacked by that other loose, agile global network, al-Qaeda, hit the World Trade Center.

And suddenly everything changed yet again.

PART IV

High and Wild: Afghanistan to Iraq

CHAPTER TWELVE

The Boys Are Back in Town

Afghanistan, 2001

THE COLORS BEHIND MY EYEBALLS are clearing. Mickey and Doug, my Canadian fellow stowaway, are already out and walking round the plane, Mickey stopping and idly kicking the giant plane's twenty wheels one after the other, with a roll-up on the go and a look of quiet satisfaction. I can't stand up without wanting to puke. Doug is having his own difficulties.

"Holy shit! Hey, Mickey! You'd better look at this, the tires on your landing gear are looking pretty thin."

"Let me see. You think those tires are thin? No. No. That's not thin."

"What . . . come on, man, I can see metal! Are you gonna change them?"

"No, no. Why should we change the tires? We will change them when they burst."

"You . . . oh, Jesus. And when do they burst?"

"Hmm. Usually when we land."

It's vintage Mickey. At least fourteen of the Il-76's giant tires are in the advanced stages of dangerous baldness, melting away or shredded to ribbons, but the pennywise logic of the small business says they'll make it just one more flight before they all blow out on touchdown.

Every man handles his near-death experiences in his own way. I'm focusing on stopping my lower legs from shaking, while the hitherto taciturn Canuck is in a state bordering on euphoria and can't stop talking. Around me, even the crew are rubber-legged and fresh with cooling sweat as they emerge blinking into the glare of the Afghan morning. Only Mickey himself looks like he's just finished a long, dull shift in a Moscow taxi, droopy faced and yawning. Having edged the Il-76 into the landing bay, past APCs and over gaping holes on an Afghan runway that would have been condemned and shut to air traffic anywhere else in the world, and while we gathered our brains together, he'd shaken on some suit trousers, taken his jacket from the hook, and stepped down the plank.

Out on the asphalt I pace the shadow side of the plane, eyeing the frontier runway's comings and goings. The bullet-pocked terminal building bears the sign WELCOME TO KABUL in meter-high red lettering, cracked and fading. Next to the lettering is a gigantic portrait of Ahmad Shah Massoud, local warlord and scourge of Taliban and Soviet invaders, blown up by suicide bombers on the eve of 9/11. Goateed and beatific in his ragged cap, he looks like Bob Marley up there. There's another Soviet-age giant to the left, a turboprop Antonov. All aircraft look far less impressive close up—check your favorite airline's bright livery from less than twenty feet, and chances are you'll be horrified by the mass of dents, rust spots, and missing rivets—but this An-12's rapidly passing from workhorse to knacker's yard. It's a patchwork of masking tape and rusting rivets with soot under the wings. Conscious of being watched by two clean-shaven young Afghans in drab green fatigues, I turn and head back to the Candid.

Mickey shuffles into view, blinking slowly at something on the number-four engine like a middle-aged builder preparing a job quote, and I call to him. "So what happens now?"

"Customs," comes back over the asphalt. Two impossibly young-looking types in shirtsleeves are padding toward us from the crater-pitted terminal. Behind me on the Il-76's cargo ramp, someone sniggers.

THE WORLD POST–9/11 was suddenly a very different place for cargo kingpins, straight and crooked alike. That's not to say it was worse. With the fall of Afghanistan to U.S.-led coalition forces in November 2001 and the invasion of Iraq in 2003, a huge, complex ecosystem of military, humanitarian, business, diplomatic, and media interests swiftly established itself in both. And they were ecosystems that required unimaginable daily quantities of supplies, personnel, and plant.

First came the coalition military, then NATO, the UN, aid organizations, and a tsunami of businesses in their wake, from Halliburton to the suppliers of the newly printed, non-Saddam Iraqi currency. Like Viktor Bout and Tomislav Damnjanovic, Komi-born technician Sergei Ivanov was one of the many who heard the clarion call put out by charter agents toting big contracts.

Just the wrong side of fifty, Ivanov comes from a small village in the Komi region of Russia on the northwestern slopes of the Urals. For twenty years, a decade on either side of the Soviet Union's disintegration, he was an airport-maintenance technician at a somewhat careworn cargo and military airfield in the backwater city of Syktyvkar. But in 1999, the Antonov An-24 and Tupolev Tu-134 cargo-plane repair specialist received an offer way too good to refuse—wages of between two thousand and three thousand dollars a month—and relocated to Angola, patching up planes for the migratory flocks of former Soviet crews drifting across the continent. But the occupation of Iraq was an opportunity too good to pass up.

"That was crazy work!" he recalled to Syktyvkar-based *Zyryanskaya Zhizn* reporter and human rights activist Ernest Mezak. "We were ferrying money across the country, notes of Iraqi currency—all the old bills with Saddam on them had to be removed, and we'd fly in and distribute the replacement cash."

And there was plenty of that cash flying about figuratively, too—the key reason Iraq and Afghanistan suddenly became so popular again as destinations, and even expat havens, for the lost boys of the old Soviet air force. "The food and living conditions there were brilliant!" said Ivanov. "Iraq's not 'starving Africa.' We got $50 a day per diems at that point— and by the next shift, incidentally, that figure had already doubled to $100, several times more than we got in Africa."

Things were looking up for Mickey at this time, too. Back in the world he knew—or at least close to Sharjah and the former Soviet Union turf of Central Asia and the Caucasus again—these Eastern European outfits seemed to have come in from the cold somewhat, at least as far as the U.S. was concerned. They enjoyed the free fuel laid on for suppliers to the U.S. military, and some respectable and established outfits like Byelorussia's TransaviaExport airline even made UN "preferred supplier" status.

Mickey recalls the swift-turnaround nature of the work. There was a permanent rush on: a whole series of new-build military and refugee camps needed supplying, equipment needed shifting, and among the rubble, revolution, and reconstruction, business was kabooming and new humanitarian imperatives were emerging. Everything needed transporting *now*. No wonder the pay was so good, whether you were working for a legit organization like Ivanov—these giant operations with august names like TransaviaExport, Volga-Dnieper, and Soviet Air Charter—or one of the paper outfits with resurrected planes and sketchy pasts that sprang up every day when times were fat.

As for Afghanistan, it was, after all, old ground for Mickey: There's a good chance he was coming and going from Kabul airport before the young men walking across the asphalt to check our papers were even born. And this time around, in 2003, give or take a few gray hairs, a paint job, and a sharp new dress code, he says that nothing much has changed.

And as it turned out, in Afghanistan I would soon get my own first experience as a buyer of "ghost" cargo coming in on another giant cargo plane.

I WAKE WITH a jolt. A watery dawn is breaking over the almond trees outside the window of our Kabul guesthouse. I can't stop shaking. I'm soaked head to toe, and at first I tell myself it's the terrors again, the night sweats that have been plaguing me since Mickey's dive-bomb through Missile Alley a few days back. But I'm freezing cold, and bloody. The sheets are covered in vomit, sweat, and, most worryingly, lots of blood. I stagger out into the hallway where there's a rudimentary bathroom and collapse on the floor, still and helpless under the washes of light-headedness and exhaustion, before the next wave slams my head forward with its force. And this is where the first of a series of revelations about Mickey's aid credentials hits.

The recent coalition invasion achieved two things in Kabul. One was the dissipation and regrouping of Taliban forces. The other was the final knockout blow to the local infrastructure. The city had already been stripped of its clerical class by Taliban diktat (since all questions of law

and civil rule were to be referred to a sharia council of mullahs for adjudi-
cation, the Taliban reasoned, there was no need to staff structures of state
and municipal power such as ministries, council offices, or courtrooms).
But with the coming of coalition troops, any remaining semicompetent
Taliban-side staffers were purged, and local warlords were invited onside
to become part of the new chain of command.

"That caused huge problems," says Hugh Griffiths. "It basically meant
that anyone wanting to do business in Afghanistan needed to pay off the
warlords first. I've heard of instances where organizations had to put relatives of these warlords on the payroll in order to be allowed to get their
job done unmolested."

So the government and civil infrastructure had been crippled. The
transport infrastructure, too. Then there was the power and fuel
infrastructure—the reason that ingenious Russian outfit's secondhand
Il-76 is still collecting dust somewhere in the Taliban-held badlands of
Helmand. But until this moment, I'd never really thought about the plumbing and drainage.

The chief reason for the waves of dysentery and diarrhea humanitarian
reports talk about is as simple as that. It's also one of the most visible items
on anyone's reconstruction agenda: People notice their toilet working in a
way they don't notice a new minister. The occupying forces were intent on
being seen to improve things, and quickly. That meant a huge, urgent call
for large cargo lifters to bring hundreds and thousands of tons of building
materials very quickly by air. At the same time, the sudden influx of military needed all their supplies in a hurry too—everything from rations to
batteries and fuel to bullets. Then there was the humanitarian emergency:
Refugees from the fighting needed shelter; mass movements into small
safe havens, out of the lawless countryside and into the cities, meant nobody had enough food. And as I've just discovered, the plumbing's shot
and people get dysentery or worse. All over the world, NGOs were scrambled by coalition governments keen—no, desperate—to ensure they didn't
end up footing the entire bill. They wanted, said Donald Rumsfeld, to
invite "nonstate actors" to play a valuable role.

Even before he'd finished that sentence, phones began to ring from
Belarus to Benin. The second Soviet invasion of Afghanistan had begun.
And this time round, the West and Mickey's crew were all marching in
together, under one big, green-backed capitalist flag.

You don't really "scramble" a cargo plane like the Candid—not unless you're trying to get it off some runway before an attack—but right now you could almost hear the thousands of combined tons of Uzbek and Ukraine-made engineering screaming as the payloads were hauled up the ramp and the engines went into overdrive. Like a dusty, landlocked Dunkirk, in that first headlong rush Afghanistan was the next stop for pretty much anyone with a piece of machinery that could get airborne, and the more cargo you could carry, the better.

Mickey's team found themselves at the front of the queue for aid work. They knew the country, the conditions, the runways, the places that could, at a push, be made to serve as runways. They knew the trade hubs and the Missile Alleys. And unlike a lot of crews, they were up for it. It was, shrugs Mickey, "*Nichevo*"—nothing at all. He's flown, he jokes, more over Afghanistan and Central Asia since 2001 than he did in the years he was actually stationed there. It was great—flying straight jobs on reputable charters—and the money was comparatively good, both with the extra payments and the money they made for Mickey Inc., filling the extra spaces in their plane with smokes, booze, and all the other stuff you'd sell your soul for in Afghanistan or out.

For coalition governments, the possibility that these airborne goods ships bound for Afghanistan and, just a few months later, for Iraq might hold a few plague rats was either far down their list of priorities or an embarrassing secret best not talked about, even though Peter Hain, a member of Tony Blair's own cabinet, had put two and two together back in 1999, and in November 2000 had thundered to Parliament about Viktor Bout, this "merchant of death who owns air companies that ferry in arms . . . and take out diamonds," and announced that "all the countries that are allowing him to use their facilities and aircraft bases to ferry that trade in death . . . are aiding and abetting people who are turning their guns on British soldiers."

He was talking about the cargoes which UN investigators reported his planes had been taking in and out of Sierra Leone and Angola. But even as the newspapers snapped up the story about this thrilling new bad boy of the international cargo game, then beat the drum for invasion, one of his planes was quietly transporting Taliban gold out of Afghanistan to a safety deposit box in the UAE.

By the time Baghdad had fallen and the second wave of the coalition-sponsored cargo gold rush had begun, nobody thought to ask whose Il-76s and Antonovs were collecting free "preferred supplier" fuel vouchers out there on the runways of Bagram and Baghdad. Then again, there was a lot to do, and quickly: medicine, rebuilding, security, shelter, and, of course, infrastructure like roads, communications, drainage. Plumbing. I understand that. Because curled up in a pool of my own blood and puke on the clay floor of a waterless bathroom in Kabul, I get just a small glimpse of the dilemma of an aid organization. And if this is what I think it is—amoebic dysentery—then I could use somebody's help, too, fast. And I'm not going to be too fussy about their CV.

By midmorning Canuck Doug and a young Afghan fixer named Haroun are awake and increasingly concerned. Haroun wants to get me treated fast. "My cousin's outside in his car," he says. "We'll get you some medicine." I'm half carried out to the front step and bundled into a car. The journey through Qala-e-Fatullah—formerly a middle-class suburb, now a dusty and rundown enclave still preferred by Westerners in the absence of much competition—doesn't take long but is still too long for me, and within seconds of starting out I'm retching and puking through the dust-caked window of the yellow Toyota taxi.

"Are we going to the hospital?" I moan, trying to keep control of my innards.

"No!" says Haroun, clearly horrified. "We need somebody who can help." I haven't the strength to argue and faint in the back, waking as we pull up outside a shop.

"This is good," says Doug the Canuck, a seasoned Afghanophile. "I think I know what's gonna happen next."

The ramshackle exterior is daubed in Dari's Arabic script. In common with seemingly all shops in Kabul, the shop sells the usual mix of snacks, Afghan pop cassettes, and hardware. Inside it's cool, but I can hardly stand. Haroun explains the situation while I lie in the doorway with a piece of plastic in lieu of a bucket. The shopkeeper looks at me and smiles. He has just the thing. He swaps glances with Haroun and signals for them to carry me out to the back, downstairs, and through a labyrinthine network of corridors, all lined with cardboard boxes and tea-chest-style crates.

We're led into the back, where crate after balsa-wood crate are stacked on pallets. Every one is stamped with the words HUMANITARIAN AID in

English, French, and a selection of other languages, and the logos of pharmaceuticals giants. One ticket says "UNHCR"—the United Nations' refugee service. He opens it with an eating knife and offers me a box of twenty-four high-grade antibiotic capsules stamped PROPERTY OF UN AID PROGRAMME—NOT TO BE DISTRIBUTED SEPARATELY. With shaking fingers, I hand him five hundred afghanis—about ten dollars. He thanks me and immediately wipes his hands with a wet cloth, assuring me the dose he's going to give me will begin to work in minutes. I tip my head back and neck a handful of pills, just like the shopkeeper says: three of the red ones, one of the ochre ones, and keep knocking them back—no water, so they stay down—until I stop vomiting. If I can do that, I will be okay.

Even weak and rambling, I'm curious about these UN packages lying around in a shopkeeper's back room. Haroun turns from concerned to shuffling and evasive. He knows all too well how the man came by this errant shipment of secure-stored UN aid, but I get him to ask anyway. After a brief chat, he turns back to me. "From the aeroplanes."

The shopkeeper looks at me. "God is great," he smiles. Yet if He moves in mysterious ways His wonders to perform, so does Mickey.

"None of what goes on should come as a surprise to anyone who's worked in international aid," says SIPRI's Hugh Griffiths. "Up to fifty percent of humanitarian aid in the Sudan and Ethiopia—to give you just two solid examples we know about—gets diverted to rebel groups, often via refugee camps. It's a mess. Even in places like Kosovo where there's a high level of international peacekeepers, [smugglers and aid black marketeers] operate."

And some of the names cropping up in Kabul, and Baghdad too, even in those early months of optimism and comparative peace, were already rather familiar. Viktor was there, for a start. And as early as 2003, wrote Hugh Griffiths in his UN report, "More than a dozen Moldova-registered, UAE-based companies . . . involved in arms smuggling with Tomislav Damnjanovic, began tapping into these booming, post-intervention economies, which were flush with foreign funds." From lords of war to valued partners in the reconstruction, it's astonishing the makeover a little bit of budgetary pressure from back home in London, New York, and Washington can give to any erstwhile bogeyman.

But there's the problem. Because focusing on the illicit activities of fast-and-loose outfits like Mickey's means stopping them—and if you stop them, you stop a good many of the only outfits with the capability, the know-how, and the balls to get your life-saving medicines, your refugee shelters, your own peacekeepers and their equipment, and the majority of emergency help to where it needs to be. Stop the sinner, and the saint vanishes.

Added to which, you risk catching plenty of above-the-board operators, planes, and crews in the same dragnet. Besides, as any ghost hunter will tell you, even when you find what you're looking for, it doesn't mean you can stop it from disappearing, or even that anyone will believe it exists. Even for dedicated trafficking monitors and plane spotters, these countless Ilyushins and the outfits and men who fly them are ghosts, drifting in and out of sight—almost unstoppable, untraceable, and unpunishable. Meanwhile, to the rest of us, these ghosts don't even exist.

Part of the difficulty is just how complex the web of private subcontractors and sub-subcontractors, all vying for lucrative coalition military and UN contracts in Iraq and Afghanistan, has become. And when everyone's outsourcing, the guy at the top of the chain rarely has any oversight of the agents employed further down. This is the explanation given in retrospect by the Pentagon for its contracts for outfits operated by Viktor Bout and other outfits about whose dealings questions have been raised. But really, by announcing that business rules apply in a military occupation scenario, just what did we expect?

In *War Games*, a masterful account of what happens when aid and military campaigns coexist too closely, Linda Polman describes the result as a new shadow state. She calls it Afghaniscam—the huge, aid-driven free-for-all that prevails in countries where military, humanitarian aid, and "local partners" combine, supposedly to achieve reconstruction and the efficient distribution of aid—in practice, to rip off as much as they possibly can in the melee. But it's not just aid consignments that get diverted, or whiskey that appears from nowhere in the false compartments below Kabul shopkeepers' meat refrigerators. There are far more valuable cargoes that have a habit of disappearing from Kabul International Airport and its military and logistics sister, Bagram.

The murk surrounding cargo suppliers in and out of the country that allows UNHCR medical supplies to go straight onto the black market—probably using the old transporter's trick of writing a percentage of the consignment off as damaged en route, just as Mickey learned to do in the

Soviet-Afghan war—is blamed by the U.S. military for the fact that over a third of all the weapons the U.S. procured for the Afghan government and its military and sent to the country are missing. According to the U.S. Government Accountability Office, some 87,000 weapons went AWOL somewhere in transit to Afghanistan because of "accountability lapses in the supply chain," with a further 135,000 weapons shipped from other countries also having vanished between December 2004 and June 2008. This is the U.S. military. Just think what happens in the case of nonstate actors.

BACK IN LONDON, I ask if anyone in the aid industry has any clear idea of the amount of "piggyback" cargo that is brought in and out with the humanitarian flights they charter—men like Mickey, delivering fifteen tons here, fifteen tons there. Not many do. Ask monitoring groups if anyone's ever audited the help-harm ratio of their flights, or the impact of these unofficial free-trade zones that spring up at humanitarian shipping hubs, and the silence is deafening.

"That'll be because the answer to your question is, probably not," sighs Amnesty's Oliver Sprague, who charts the movement of rogue air operators for Amnesty International from his office on a dusty East London side street. "Because the problem with answering it, if you think about it, is: Who's really going to want to start digging around in that? It's one of those questions; you would be a very brave organization if you wanted to start opening those hatches."

It's not necessarily that they don't want to know what else the crews they employ are carrying, he explains, pointing out that agencies like Oxfam "check every time they want a charter aircraft that they're not propping up some gunrunning empire." Indeed, Oxfam's own logistics people proudly point to the fact that they have a responsible procurement policy that alerts them to known "dirty" planes. But even they accept there's a limit to what they can do, and that the hidden stuff, by its very nature, is much harder to steer clear of.

"The way it works for humanitarian flights is this," says Sprague. "You do an ad hoc charter, you pay for everything: You pay for the fuel, you pay for the crew, a fixed price to deliver you from A to B.

"Now, that's fine and dandy. But if you have something like the Il-76, then obviously you've got quite a lot of space to play around with. See,

most humanitarian goods aren't actually heavy—you are actually shipping pretty light: stuff like piping and sheeting. You very rarely ship
food—you do if you go regional to regional, but you don't ship food from
the UK to Sudan. So that gives you quite a lot of space to put other stuff
in—it's basically cash in hand for the crew. And, well, what can you do
about *that*? Because even if you say that they only had [your cargo on
board when they left], they're probably on quite long runs, and they're
always going to stop off in Benghazi or somewhere else, and you can't
really control what they take on there."

Still, when the recent paper prepared for the UN by SIPRI names the
International Committee of the Red Cross, Concern Worldwide, Action
la Faim, and the Swedish Free Mission as humanitarian aid organizations
involved in the hiring of arms-trafficking operations to deliver their aid
and personnel in Africa, it's clear more could be done. Indeed, Gerard
Massis, director-general for logistics at MSF (Médecins Sans Frontières),
unwittingly echoed Viktor Bout in his response to the allegations, declaring that these flights were "like taxis," and that there was no way of
knowing what else the outfit would be doing either before or after they'd
dropped off the aid cargo.

While Oxfam's Tricia O'Rourke insists that it's wrong to assume
"dirty" airlines are necessarily cheaper than reputable ones, Sprague
points to a huge cost differential. "Let's say you want to fly something
from Manston in the UK to Al-Fashir in the Sudan. You need to use an
Ilyushin-76 because not only does it have the capacity you're after, it can
land and unload without any help from ground staff. So you look around.
If you're prepared to use a Moldovan-registered outfit and claim a humanitarian waiver, you'll get the job done for $70,000, maybe $80,000.
But if you're going to say, No, I need a reputable, silencer-fitted, and thus
EU-airspace-compliant Ilyushin-76, then it'll cost you closer to $150,000.
There's huge pressure on cost for aid organizations, and a lot of their
money comes from government, so you can imagine the kind of questions
that might get asked when you spend double the lowest quote on a flight.

"We all know that there are cash-in-hand things, contraband that they
want to deliver, but it's also about positioning the aircraft," says Sprague.
"There's an incentive for certain companies to want to fly those kind of
flights—even if they know they are not the world's greatest in terms of
money, it puts their aircraft in a decent place to go somewhere else next.

It makes commercial sense: Sometimes these flights don't really pay anything, but [it's next to] an area that could well pay quite a lot."

There's also the problem—and it's a big problem—that in Mickey's
business, work is so unpredictable and competition drives wages down
when the jobs do come. The pilot of that East Wing Il-76 recently impounded by Thailand on its way from North Korea on a sanctions-busting
run was, his wife explained to the media, on his first paying job for some
time. He'd sat at home for weeks without a flight and was desperate to
bring back some wages. Even Mickey, whose own connections keep him
more than busy, still doesn't exactly look like a man dripping in cash, and
he's one of the lucky, flexible, business-minded ones. While the Bangkok
crew were released uncharged by Thai authorities, who would blame
them if they found an extra way of making those odd flights pay?

As Mark Galeotti says: "For these guys, business will go to the lowest
bid—people don't care how you do it. And particularly when you're traveling to places where there are hidden virtues—let's say you're flying
something in and out of Burma or the Philippines. It gives the flyboys a
chance to do a bit of drug trafficking on the sly while they're at it. And
because of that, their rates will be extraordinarily competitive."

And so long as the rates are extraordinarily competitive, plenty of
people on the side of the angels aren't about to go looking any two-
hundred-ton, Tashkent-made gift horses in the mouth.

Even monitoring groups like IPIS find the silence around the subject
deafening. "We hear about smuggling happening on aid flights," says
Peter Danssaert when I tell him what I've witnessed. "But we have to be
careful about saying anything in our reports—there's the feeling that
there should be more of it discovered than there actually is."

O'Rourke accepts that even the oversight allowed by the best monitoring systems doesn't rule out illicit cargoes making their way in with aid,
or, exceptionally, dirty airlines being chartered. "We have to balance the
need to deliver lifesaving equipment into a disaster area as quickly as possible with the availability of a 'clean' aircraft or freight company," she says.
"This is a moral and ethical dilemma that Oxfam is not alone in having
to deal with. We have the systems in place to help us make informed
judgments, but unfortunately the nature of the air-freight industry and
the countries in which we work mean it is very difficult to eliminate
altogether."

Many aid groups counter with some justification that it's difficult to know what other goods have been transported in planes used by them. Indeed, the more I learn, the more the very ideas underpinning some monitors' efforts—dirty and clean flights, rogue airlines, good guys and bad guys—start to look impossibly quaint.

YOU HAVE TO feel for the big NGOs, the Oxfams and the Red Crosses. They're clearly playing catch-up—able to track and avoid where possible only those outfits that have already been busted, or in some cases those that have shown a disregard for their own standards of blurriness, subtlety, and outright invisibility.

Yet this is where the beauty of the taxi-driver or postal analogy really comes into its own: It allows everyone, not just Mickey, room for denial should they wish. And where there's room for denial from authorities charged with some form of regulatory oversight, from customs to aviation authorities to some of the less reputable or experienced NGOs, there's space for complicity. This is especially true in places like Kabul airport, Entebbe, Kinshasa, and Mogadishu, in which, to use the words of SIPRI researcher Hugh Griffiths, "the monthly payrolls go missing more than they ever actually go missing, if you know what I mean."

"Two or more parties are always involved in accepting these ploys," says my no-name pilot informer, who was involved in the campaign to clean up "dirty" illicit-arms-dealing airports like Sharjah and the old Ostend airport in Belgium. His most recent approach to Sharjah airport was par for the course, he says. "There's a complicity [in creating just enough doubt] so that people can say, 'Oh, really? I wasn't aware.' I went to Sharjah last February, and I told the authorities there about the things that were going on there with one airline in particular that I saw. The person I spoke with expressed astonishment that this company could be involved in something illegal. Since then, I've tried corresponding with him, but he refuses to reply to my e-mails."

This sense of "complicity" he mentions crops up again and again, from the blind eye turned to profiteering during the great Soviet arms sell-off to the NGOs prepared to do whatever it takes to achieve their stated goals, and the "don't ask, don't tell" policy adopted by crews and some operators toward illicit cargo.

It seems a strange, pervasive force, like the creeping madness of which Kipling and Conrad wrote: damnation one tiny compromise at a time. But perhaps its causes are neither psychological nor moral.

Perhaps it's just what the balance sheet says you need to do. Having any empty plane standing on a runway somewhere is a hemorrhage in the wallet you just can't live with, not unless you're prepared to write off thousands of dollars a week just for the pleasure of having the thing sitting there. And the huge cost of fuel when you do fly your quarter-century-old, soot-belching superplane means that while you can't afford parking charges, you can't afford to fly it empty, either. It's an odd idea: that Mickey, Viktor Bout, anyone working the gray side of the cargo trade might just have become slaves to the plane they hoped would liberate them, forced into deals they'd rather not do by the demands of their vehicle itself and the pressures of the only business they know. Indeed, Viktor Bout himself talks of being forced to register his planes under flags of convenience and operate in sketchy countries simply because his aircrafts are either banned or encounter paperwork difficulties in more respectable regimes.

On the plus side, he jokes, at least Mickey's not in charge of an Antonov An-225—code name Cossack—a plane so large and with such a monstrous appetite for fuel that its carrying ability and fuel capacity alike remain unknown. According to one seasoned British-born loadmaster and flight manager who's flown both Il-76s and Antonovs into the world's worst trouble spots, including military, aid, and commercial missions to Baghdad, coalition logistics to Kandahar, peacekeeping forces to Kinshasa, and set-transport job for Michael Jackson's *HIStory* tour, "No one's ever actually been able to find out for sure how much fuel the Cossack will hold. They've got the manufacturer's calculations, but they're always out by a bit. And the An-225 is so massive that no one's ever managed to completely fill the fuel tanks up before departure! In any case, no one's ever going to have the money to fill up with that much aviation fuel either."

Built for the Soviet space program back in 1988 to hold the USSR's space-shuttle counterpart until it was high enough to fly solo, only one of these monsters of the skies even exists; a second was started on three separate occasions, but all three times the factory ran out of material, time, or cash and abandoned work. Another Briton, thirty-year-old Aaron Hewit, remembers traveling on it as part of a small detachment ordered to accompany some "heavy kit" to the top-secret Operation Jacana offensive by combined Royal Marines, Australian SAS, Norwegian FSK, and U.S. Special Forces in 2002. "It was so big, the first we knew that we were airborne was the aircraft listing to aft and we all fell about the place," he recalls. "Then on landing, I remember seeing Bagram directly below, but the following three to four minutes are somewhat lost on account of the fact I lost all bearings and possibly even consciousness. The nose dropped, the aircraft fell at an alarming rate, and suddenly we were on the floor."

With its caving ladders between floors, ocean-liner-size compartments, and flip-top nose, the 225 is the butt of plenty of jokes—from Sergei especially, who finds it an excellent thing—but the jokes mask a stark economic reality for the whole business: The bigger your plane, the less picky you can be about the kind of thing you let on board.

Then again, for crewmen on the lookout for a little extra personal cargo unknown to charterer, client, or anyone else, a big plane can make the contraband a very tempting line too. Especially in a place like Afghanistan.

CHAPTER THIRTEEN

Afghan Black

The Drug Pipeline, 2002–2010

THE SOVIET WAR that taught him all he knows is long over. But like a modern-day Lieutenant Hiroo Onoda, the Japanese soldier who evaded capture in the Philippine jungle until 1974, still unaware that Japan had surrendered in 1945, Mickey and all the other men who haunt Afghanistan's dusty streets and snowcapped mountains still inhabit a world long past for the rest of us. Some of the same bandits and mujahideen fighters haunt the airport perimeters and the dark, chaotic edges of town, shooting at the same giant, screaming silhouettes as they come in to land. Inside those silhouettes, the same group of old comrades watch the place they know better than their own hometown rise up in front of them. Just as they did back then, they can hang that left at the valley, then straighten up and climb over the mountains, even rise and fall, pretty much in their sleep.

Meanwhile, on the ground, the guys running the show might have a different flag, but the ones really keeping the place together, the local business wheels, the shopkeepers, the officials, well, they're the same too. Governments change, wars start and end and start, but business is always business. Mickey lists the places in town where he knows for a fact that you can buy booze in this dry Islamic country, because he's spotted his own booze turning up there. The list is long, enough of the names familiar—from tea shops whose refrigerators have false bottoms housing cases of Smirnoff to street hawkers whose lemonade bottles are selectively spiked for the right customer, and restaurants who've got themselves designated as charities, the easier to take delivery of important "medical supplies" that may or may not be of a fine French vintage. For Kabul is essentially a Prohibition-era Chicago—one with worse cops, better-armed mobsters, and a bigger racket in City Hall.

This is where personal relationships with regulars count, claims Mickey. "He can sell a bottle of Johnnie Walker for up to two hundred dollars here," agrees one regular customer, a European expat who asked me not to name him or give any clues as to the location of his discreet—even disguised—drinking den. He's understandably afraid of police reprisals in a month that's already seen three city-center "Westerner-friendly" establishments, including the famous aid-worker hangout L'Atmosphere, shut down in a series of heavy-handed raids by the Afghan police. The violent raids shocked many of Kabul's foreign contingent, used to the blind-eye policy of local law enforcement. Each time, the raids followed a mention in the international press. "Last time it was *Newsweek*," says the owner, "which everybody knows President Karzai himself reads closely. You have to be careful who you talk to."

He explains the supply pipeline. "We get it flown in from the United Arab Emirates—Ajman, neighboring Sharjah, sells pretty cheap alcohol because they know that while Sharjah is Islamically conservative enough to ban alcohol sales, the aircrews can fly as much as they want out through Sharjah airport without any checks at all. And when you get to Afghanistan, customs might find it, but they'll ask for a bottle here or a bribe there—a lot of Afghan officials, whatever their stripe, are drinkers on the sly—and they'll take their cut and your aircrews will get their contraband through. Further down the line, we'll be serving it to Westerners, and to some Afghans, very discreetly, having paid off the police; then every so often they'll raid us and confiscate the booze. And then they'll sell it back to us, or they'll drink it themselves or sell it elsewhere. The whole circle is complete, and everybody gets something out of it, starting with the aircrews, and nobody's interested in stopping it."

Running illicit booze is just part of it. The coalition-backed Afghan government has inadvertently made it increasingly attractive to smuggle small arms into the country, too. "Back in 2002, a lot of firearms made their way into Afghanistan, and it was all legal," says one former NATO soldier. "But then the Afghan government decided it didn't want foreign companies making money from selling guns in Afghanistan—it wanted to make the money itself by selling confiscated weapons and granting licenses. So now whoever wants a gun has to get one brought in illegally. And that's where ad hoc runs by ex-Soviet crews like yours come in."

But there are even bigger-paying opportunities here for any crews enterprising enough to make use of their invisible overweight space and old connections. Narcotics are the one cargo that's always illegal, never simply illicit or gray, and in an environment controlled by an American-led coalition, it's almost impossible to catch a trafficker red-handed. But Afghanistan is also the world's heroin-production giant, circumstantial evidence suggesting illicit air-cargo export is everywhere.

"The real story at the moment is how much drug money makes its way from Kabul to Dubai in cash every day," says NATO spokesman Dominic Medley, tracing the Kabul-UAE route flown more or less daily by Mickey during his Afghan air-bridge stints.

"Heroin makes everything else, even put together, pale into insignificance," agrees Pakistani journalist Ahmed Rashid, who's lived with the Taliban and seen Afghan cultivation and its supply lines at close hand. "When you're talking about trafficking in Afghanistan, if you're talking about arms or bootleg alcohol, you're talking about relatively small figures nowadays. I mean, there's a lot of it, but the real money is in heroin. It started coming in and going out again with the Russian cargo planes around the mid-1990s, as well as with passengers on Ariana Airlines and people crossing the porous land borders by road and on foot. But since the invasion, with more planes coming in and going out, the sheer bulk involved is astonishing."

Indeed it is. In 2009, Afghan finance minister Omar Zakhilwal finally (and reluctantly) confirmed estimates by U.S. officials that around $10 million is smuggled out through Kabul airport every single day on planes. Indeed, that amount is just the actual cash that's trafficked illicitly: as for heroin itself, reliable estimates, he confessed, are hard to come by, partly because of the fug of chaos and misdirection surrounding the airport. Meanwhile, figures obtained by independent Afghan-focused news agency Skyreporter.com suggest that since the coalition invasion in 2001 and the sudden explosion in flights—passenger, cargo, and military—coming in and out of Kabul, the Afghan heroin export trade's black-market value has risen from around $1 billion to more than $6 billion—60 percent of Afghanistan's entire economy.

Afghanistan is not just the world's biggest producer of opium, but the world leader in cannabis, too, with a yield of 145 kilos of charas—high-grade Afghan hashish—for every hectare farmed. Like the fruit Afghanistan exports, it's a summer crop with a shorter shelf life than opium, but it yields more cash, grows easily, and, crucially, far less visibly. And for crews whose motto is not just "never fly empty" but "never fly without filling every cubic centimeter of hidden space"—even to the point of painting over the glass rear-gunner bubbles on military models to make it look from outside like a solid-metal aerodynamic feature, while inside it's big enough to store many thousands of dollars' worth of charas—the answer doesn't take too much to fathom.

With the NATO-led occupation, history is repeating itself: In September 2009, an investigation was launched into claims that British and Canadian soldiers had found a way to smuggle opium out of Camp Bastion and Kandahar on huge troop- and logistics-transport planes.

For their part, some Russian diplomats accuse the CIA of complicity in the flow of heroin, in an attempt to "flood Russia." How, they point out, would the U.S. react if Russia had occupied a country on its doorstep like Mexico, and promptly oversaw a cocaine boom?

As I lift the stones around Kabul, it slowly emerges that forces at work within the Afghan airports facilitate a regular large-volume opium-smuggling cargo operation, too.

Whoever's smoothing the way, the risks are high; but with the profits Afghan heroin makes (plus no transport costs, and friendly ex-Soviet military faces all over Uzbekistan, Tajikistan, and all the way up to Europe), the upside is attractive enough to make the same pipe that Mickey began working twenty-five years ago a popular choice.

This informal system of allegiances and acquaintances is just one of the things that makes the jobs of men like Danssaert, Hugh Griffiths, and Brian Johnson-Thomas much harder, not to mention the in-country military and NGOs who must try to chart and trace a network of flights, connections, onward routes, cash jobs, and verbal agreements that looks, to the outsider, like pure chaos. In the same way that Leonid Minin's and Viktor Bout's paperless "networks" of planes were chartered on nods and winks and paid for in cash—or the Islamic *hawala* loans that enable money laundering in Sharjah— they work on the basis of a community of trust and shared allegiances.

Still, for some time it was a mystery how so much of it was getting through, along with the cash that buys it, from the poppy fields of Afghanistan, through the UAE of all places, back to Mother Russia and Moscow, gateway to Europe. If it's a simple drug mafia or smuggling operation, it would seem to be an unusually influential one. It took an investigation by the British newspaper the *Independent* in 2008 to reveal to the outside world what everybody in Afghanistan already knew: that the flooding of Afghanistan with guns and ammo smuggled in from the former Soviet Union, the influx of foreign businesses and private security companies to Kabul, and the flow of heroin to Russia and Western Europe were not coincidental.

Russian smugglers told the newspaper's reporters how they were facilitating rendezvous between Russian arms dealers and Taliban drug lords at bazaars in the Tajik desert, the huge no-man's-land that was once the Soviet-Afghan border and is now an unpoliced wasteland—albeit a wasteland dotted with the same landing strips once used by the Soviet air force's air-transport and bomber regiments to fly into Afghanistan during the Soviet occupation. Landing strips now used once more by Mickey and the boys, back on their old stomping ground in the same old plane, to refuel, load, and unload. The brokers claimed absolutely no money was involved. "We never sell drugs for money," boasted one of the smugglers to the newspaper. "We exchange them for ammunition and Kalashnikovs."

In fact, these Tajik bazaar rendezvous between Russian gunrunners and Afghan drug lords have their own exchange rates, with one kilo of heroin equal to thirty AK-47s. The deal done, the guns will be brought over the Tajik-Afghan border in parts—either in small consignments or in fifteen-ton bulk shipments, in the cargo bellies of overloaded Il-76s, typically marked down as spare auto parts and machinery.

In the course of his investigations, Russian secret service investigator Andrei Soldatov has found evidence that the smuggling pipeline Mickey reminisces about from the Afghan war, complete with old boys from the intelligence network on the ground pushing kilos onto cargo planes, is still there and has been anything but dormant in the intervening years. Only the background he paints is even more curious. Because it turns out some of this smuggling during the Soviet-Afghan war wasn't quite as se-cretive as even Mickey had imagined.

"In the late 1980s, the first guy who organized heroin traffic through the Soviet Union to the West was not military intelligence but KGB," he says. "In Uzbekistan there were some special [-service] guys who decided that it would be good to undermine Western consciousness or Western morality by smuggling heroin and all these things to Western Europe. [The heroin smuggling pipeline then] was a special operation, protected by people from the KGB in Uzbekistan and here in Moscow."

The pipeline typically runs up into the Urals in Russia, then on to Moscow and St. Petersburg before working its way by land or air through the Balkans and on to Western Europe—90 percent of the heroin injected in Frankfurt, Edinburgh, and Barcelona comes via this route from Af-ghan fields. But if that pipeline, and the heroin-smuggling network out of Afghanistan toward Russia and Europe, was originally part of a grander scheme, then one day in 1991 it cracked apart just like the Soviet air force, its masterminds simply losing the state agenda and going private.

"Some of [these KGB agents] were still involved in this business in the 1990s," says Andrei Soldatov. "Only in the 1990s it was not ordered by anyone, it was just corruption—some guys inherited something from the Soviet time. So they just turned it to profit."

When, in April 2002, authorities in Tver, about one hundred miles to the west of Moscow, arrested an army veteran whom they suspected of be-ing head of a "small but competent" group of four alleged to have sewn up the local heroin market by using "old connections from his military days stationed down in Tajikistan" to import high-grade heroin by air trans-port, they hit the tip of the iceberg. Now Vasiliy Sorkin, chief narcotics officer in the Moscow administration for internal affairs, claims everyone's in on this most profitable act—private entrepreneurs, warlords, cargo traf-fickers, and even their comrades currently serving Russian military—in a way that makes it almost entirely risk-free for the delivery men. Only an estimated 6 percent of all Afghan heroin coming through the Russian Fed-eration is intercepted by police or FSB agents.

Unsurprisingly, witnesses are reluctant to come forward, says Soldatov, with everyone having their piece of the pie to protect. "One colonel de-scribed this system in Uzbekistan and the old Soviet channels being used now for smuggling heroin. He served in this unit [which he's accusing] in

Uzbekistan, and he now serves in Moscow, so it looks like he knows something. When I asked him for information, he produced some names. It could be some kind of vengeance against guys who were more profitable than him."

Perhaps the fear is justified: With former KGB agents and Afghan drug lords combining to fund the trafficking of heroin on planes like Mickey's, it's not just General Aminullah Amarkhel and his allies on the Afghan side, or journalists for *Moskovsky Komsomolets* with exploding briefcases, who have to go into hiding if they poke around the wrong air operation once too often.

One aviation expert and illicit-cargo tracker I interview about it not only asks not to be named at all, even with a pseudonym—"in case people guess"—but wants his countries of residence and origin withheld.

"I'd rather not correct the impression people have that I live in the country I'm most associated with," he says. "I've spoken to people before, even the guys who wrote the Bout report, but I asked them to keep my name out of there. Because I've had requests previously to meet me from certain parties who would invite me to meet them for a flight in their Il-76. I had the distinct impression that they were going to open the door for me at thirty thousand feet, without a parachute."

That sounds like paranoia, and I dismiss it. That is, until I meet a UN investigator one summer morning in the long, platform-side champagne bar at London's St. Pancras station, hub of the high-speed Eurostar train service linking London to Paris and Brussels. He's on his way to a NATO conference in Brussels and agrees to meet for breakfast beside the platform. We talk for an hour or more in the high-up, open, glass-sided bar, beneath the vaulted ceiling and Victorian clock, and when I mention the expert's fears about meetings with some of his quarries in the plane, he chuckles with me over coffee and croissants. But he waits until my tape recorder is switched off at the end of our chat before laying a hand on my elbow and guiding me over to the side of the concourse.

"Now that that's off, I can talk to you about this," he says. "A couple of years ago, it seems a guy fell out of a plane like your friend's, about thirty thousand feet over the Arabian Peninsula. Someone at the destination knew the number of men who had got on, but didn't see quite as many get off, so he challenged them. The airmen just said, 'The door came open and he fell out.' Now anyone who's been on one of these planes knows that it should be very difficult to just fall out. But still, that's just what happened. Let's just say if I were your friend, I'd be very wary of going up in an old plane with anyone who might bear him a grudge. But you certainly didn't hear that from me."

And with that he's gone, leaving me on the platform, wondering about my contact's invitations to high-altitude meetings. I think about the uncanny efficiency of the Afghan drug pipeline, and I wonder who's behind it all. Then, for the first time in months, I remember the ski-masked, armed spooks proliferating across the Surcin crash site, wiping away all traces of the men, the plane, and their cargo; the FSB and GRU men haunting Cyprus, the Middle East, and Africa. And I think: I really want, just once, to see the faces of these faceless men, to find out just who, or what, these mysterious forces are.

And then, almost immediately, I catch myself. Really, I'm not at all sure I do.

CHAPTER FOURTEEN

There Are Huge Forces

Afghanistan, 1995 and 2010

THE ARTIFICIAL LIGHT FIZZLES as another colleague leaves the office, switching his monitor off, grabbing a stout overcoat, and calling a brief "Good-night" toward the few desk lights that are still illuminated before hunching his shoulders and tasting the first wet blusters of the Swedish autumn night.

The angle-poised lamp, the occasional flicker of a screen reflected in the tall windows and the odd tap of a key or rustle of paper—SIPRI's own Non-Proliferation and Export Controls report, some dog-eared printouts of recent JPEG photos from the UN, perhaps—are the only clues the security patrols have that the long, pale building overlooking a black expanse of parkland in Solna, just north of the capital, is still occupied. But it is. Because this is the headquarters of the Stockholm International Peace Research Institute. And at this moment, someone here is sifting through databases, reports, and flight records. And just like me, they're trying to picture the faces, movements, and motivations behind the results this avalanche of information keeps throwing up.

"The British government even had a specific department that checked out aircraft registration numbers," says SIPRI's Hugh Griffiths through the tinny echo of a cell-phone line. He's working late again, and one of the reasons he's working quite this late rankles. "They had that department precisely because they recognized that these numbers can tell you a lot about planes, and therefore a lot about who's taking what where. But they've now shut it down, leaving it all up to the likes of us to try and follow these flights and match up the records and figure out what's going on." He lets out a short, bitter laugh. "And the reason they gave up is, ironically, that there are *so many* very distasteful people out there operating these illicit flights."

While the responsibility for logging and checking aircraft registration, along with airworthiness and safety checks, should lie with an individual country's civil aviation authority, the reality, especially in developing economies and states with high levels of corruption, is never quite that simple. He sighs, clearly frustrated at the task faced by the monitors in nailing even the worst, most cocksure smugglers. "They're everywhere, and they're unbelievably confident. I mean, these are people who'll offer you raki and slivovitz at ten in the morning when you go to see them for a meeting about their activities. And they're all getting around any attempt to keep tabs on them by registering their planes in lax regimes like Kazakhstan, where there's no transparent, consistent, and reliable record keeping. So all the global databases, like the British one, are being utterly defeated by the lack of transparency in these unregistered countries. It's crazy—we know what they're doing, but they're always one step ahead."

I can understand the frustration of men like Griffiths, and even more so those like Peter Danssaert of Antwerp's International Peace Information Service, whose concern—and research on behalf of clients like Amnesty International and the U.N.—has taken him deeper, into covert government involvement in the gray economy these flights serve. "As I explained to the European Commission," notes the Belgian researcher, "many of these illicit transfers, and/or diversions of weapons, could not take place without at least one government knowing about them, and another turning a blind eye." He adds drily: "That's most likely the reason funding can be difficult to secure. Government involvement, or at least turning a blind eye, is the second taboo in our little world, after the connections between aid flights and arms smuggling."

This makes a difficult job into one constantly threatening to become impossible. I find Mickey hard enough to pin down, even in close conversation over a beer. The idea of trying to tackle thousands and thousands of planes, consignments, crews, clients, and cargoes every day more or less forensically seems positively quixotic.

But as Danssaert describes the slippery customers and the brazen operations; the wormholes that keep opening up and swallowing them without trace again and again, just as the net is closing around them; and the obstacles faced by researchers at IPIS, Amnesty, and within governments, I can't help thinking it seems more than merely crazy how the traffickers are always "one step ahead."

No, not just crazy. Somehow, it seems positively uncanny—almost as if there are more powerful forces at work, throwing a spanner in the works of the monitoring and policing agencies.

And if that's the case, then the idea of poster boys like Bout and Minin as public enemies—lords of war, striding round the globe engendering chaos and destruction all by themselves—starts to seem not merely misguided but like a hugely successful red herring.

After all, Leonid Minin's coke-and-girls party was a present to himself, celebrating the successful shipment of 113 tons of small arms to West Africa. That's a lot of guns, enough to get noticed by law enforcement, even the remaining Ukrainian military.

But then, it wasn't as if nobody back in Ukraine had noticed long ago. In the mid-1990s, Ukrainian president Leonid Kuchma ordered a parliamentary commission to investigate the rate at which arms went missing from his bases. The report found that of Ukraine's $89 billion in military stocks in 1992, by 1998 $32 billion had mysteriously evaporated.

No sooner was the report ready, however, than the commission was mysteriously closed down. All seventeen volumes of work disappeared. The head of the commission, General Oleksandr Ignatenko, was court-martialed and stripped of his rank. The only publisher willing to go public about the findings, a Kiev newsletter editor named Sehry Odarych, was ambushed one night outside his apartment, shot in the leg as a warning, and told as he writhed in pain against the wall of the block, "Stop getting mixed up in politics, or we'll eliminate you." The attackers simply vanished and were never found. The police informed Odarych he'd shot his own leg in a bid for attention, though he didn't have a gun.

The secrecy around the upward connections of operations like Mickey's is often so deep and tightly enforced that it's only when things go wrong, as they did in Belgrade for Starikov and Damnjanovic, that a crack appears for a brief moment and we gain a glimpse of the forces at play.

Indeed, but for one incident, involving an Il-76 flight into Afghanistan in the mid-1990s, even the little we know about the smuggling routes from coalition- and NATO-occupied Afghanistan might never have come to light. And if the flight had gone as planned, it's possible we may never have heard of Viktor Bout or the men with no names for whom he may or may not work.

But the flight did not go as planned. And the story, even as it continues to emerge today, is one of the more curious tales in gunrunning history.

It is a sunny Sunday in Moscow. Young, successful, fresh-faced, and sharply dressed, film producer Ilya Neretin is the guy behind 2010's Russian record-smashing, true-story action blockbuster *Kandahar: Survive and Return*, about a gunrunning Il-76 crew's kidnap and escape from the Taliban in 1995.

The film's great—a swashbuckling, hyper-real yarn full of grit and suspense. I'm not surprised it went down so well in a resurgent Russia, just as the Rambo films did in a gung-ho 1980s America determined to reclaim some of its self-confidence even at the expense of factual report-age. But I'm interested in the story, and in its background. The men were flying a mission for Viktor Bout, but there has always been talk of darker dealings about their run to Kandahar that day; and if I can understand who these other, publicity-shy forces are with an interest in Il-76 missions like this, then perhaps I can begin to put Mickey's work in context.

We chat at length—about the film, about the state of the country then and now, about Neretin's recent private travails, about the pleasures and pains of filming in Morocco (Kandahar's body double), and about the long strange trip Russia has been on since 1991. I like Ilya a lot: He's great, easy conversation; he pulls mother-in-law stories and wisecracks out of no-where; and though I've been chasing him for weeks for this chance to speak with him, he's got that rare ability to make you feel as though he's been bursting to get together with you for a chat for ages. And while he's telling me about the film—and the challenges involved in getting a full Il-76 and crew over to Morocco—he laughs all the time.

He likens the crews he met—the original guys, on an arms-smuggling mission for Viktor Bout to Afghanistan, and the team of Byelorussian daredevil cargo dogs he had to call to fly the Candids on film—to cowboys.

"What happens to these guys on their missions, and the captured crew especially, it's just like a western," he says. "In westerns, the heroes say, 'This is my land. There is no government, no police, nobody can help me—only I can do it, alone.' Our Ilyushin-76 crew on this flight came to understand that. Look around: Taliban, arms dealers—there's only enemies. In that situation, we might say the Taliban are the red Indians. So if I want to keep my freedom, or my land, as they say in westerns, I have to do it myself."

It's a picture of crews like Mickey's I'll encounter time and again—called cowboys as an insult by those who believe they cross the blurry line between business and criminal activity too often, and as a compliment by those who know them for their self-reliance and toughness, like real-life High Plains drifters. But Ilya's words are also a shocking summation of the post-Soviet mind-set that spawned Mickey. No government, no police, and it's help-yourself time: Call it anarchy or call it Reaganomics.

Ilya is a breath of fresh air in a lot of ways. After months of wrestling information from insiders who'd rather not talk at all, I find him charming, irreverent, and wisecracking, and his interest in the crews mirrors my own. "The human story is . . . interesting, I think," he agrees. "We're talking here about the taxi drivers." Then he goes off on a tangent about a visit from his mother-in-law. There's a lot of laughter.

We've been talking for a while, and I'm feeling pretty comfy with him. I mention that I'm actually looking into the story of these crews—not just their lives but their role in spreading humanitarian aid, peacekeepers, guns, and drugs, hope, and darkness around the world.

Then I tell him it's an interesting connection in the film, that the Il-76 there was chartered by Bout.

Ilya stops me, but doesn't say anything for a moment or two. "Matt, you and I, we know what kind of world we live in, I think," he says, finally. "Look, Matt, I will tell you this. There are so many 'Mr. X' figures ruling this world. And Mr. Bout is a prince. But there are *kings*. If you sell arms, you will do it, if some high-up guy will cover you. My aim wasn't to get to the truth about all that. That's for prosecutors." Then he adds: "And journalists."

Then, suddenly, he has to go. I contact him again, but—apart from a few dating-scam e-mails obviously sent by a Trojan virus on his computer—I never hear back from him.

So I do some more digging. And that's when I discover the other side of the story of this crew's daring escape. Because the whispers are true: There's more to the story of the captured crew than his script, or he, is letting on.

Yes, this recently privatized crew of former Soviet pilots were forced down in their Il-76 and diverted to Kandahar by the Taliban back in 1995 while making an illicit arms run to the Northern Alliance—just as in the movie. And just as in the movie, they were kept hostage by the Taliban for over a year.

It's all correct, just as it happened in the film. The Russian government tried to negotiate at first, but the negotiations stalled. As the weeks became months, hope began to fade and the crew began to take matters into their own hands. They hatched a plan, talking to their captors themselves and convincing them that, as well as the cargo, the plane itself—now simply gathering dust and peeling on the airfield runway—was quite a catch, worth millions on the open market, and more as the Taliban air force's very own military-cargo transporter. But, they said, without regular maintenance and the occasional firing of the engines, it would be useless. A complex, regular maintenance regime needed all seven crew-members, they said. And, for the first few check-ups—all conducted under armed guard—they showed the Taliban just how to do it.

By Friday, August 16, 1996, after more than a year of captivity bordering on slavery, the guards had become relaxed enough for four of them to disappear for prayer, leaving only three guarding the crew. The pilot, Vladimir Sharpatov, saw their chance. Saying only, "We need to start the engines," the crew pushed past their captors, locking them out of the Ilyushin and starting the jets to taxi down what, by any estimation, was nowhere near enough runway for takeoff.

This is where the plane and its air force–veteran crew showed their true mettle, lifting the wheels just as runway became rock and heading not north to Russia—Sharpatov knew the Taliban would have fighter planes patrolling the air corridor by now—but west to Iran, and then on to their home away from home, Sharjah, flying just meters off the ground to evade Taliban radar. Less than three days after the heavily bearded, dazed, and exhausted crew landed at Sharjah, the fed, rested, shaven, and medically treated crew arrived home in Russia to a heroes' welcome. Three days more, and the crew were decorated with Order of Orange and Hero of the Russian Federation medals by Russian president Boris Yeltsin.

That's what happened, and it's all true. In Russia, indeed, the action film's portrayal is fast taking its place in the canon of historical fact. Dmitry Rogozin, formerly leader of Russia's Narodna ("Homeland") party, now Russia's ambassador to NATO, even calls the film a "documentary"; he has become friends with Sharpatov, whom he calls a national hero, "like a pop star." Well, like Mickey, Sharpatov's a brave and resourceful man. He deserves hero status.

But the truth is a complex, multilayered thing. And so what I am about to tell you could also be the full story. It may also be what really happened.

By August 1995, relations between Russia and even the northern Afghan government were tense, Russia accusing the Afghans of fomenting unrest in Tajikistan. Still, with a nod and a nudge from the security forces, Viktor Bout was commissioned to fly munitions into Kabul under the radar, on the quiet, for the more moderate mujahideen of the Northern Alliance.

Bout knew the pilot, Sharpatov, who'd been flying for him regularly since they met in a Sharjah hotel bar. This was not the first time he and his crew had done the arms and ammo run from Albania through to Kabul in the Candid, and Sharpatov knew exactly what he was carrying and how careful he would have to be to avoid detection. Normally, it was fine—*nichevo*. But not this time. The radio operator failed to maintain radio silence, and the Taliban air force's MiG-21 intercepted them.

According to investigators Farah and Braun, when news of their captivity reached Bout, he hit the cell phones. Bout himself told *New York Times* journalist Peter Landesman that he called the Taliban commanders, attempting to kick-start solo negotiations with them by phone, then flew to Kandahar himself but was denied access. The commanders were convinced that the flight had to have been an official Russian air force mission and would only go through the government, but their negotiations also stalled. Quite why the Taliban's men should have become so convinced of that fact is an intriguing question that's never really been fully addressed. Was it simple paranoia? The inability of a highly politically committed group to see a simple private arms deal for what it was? Marshal Shaposhnikov's flat "No comment" when I press him on the issue, even years later, of whether this was indeed in some way a covert state mission raises the tantalizing prospect of a black op of some kind through a deniable middleman like Bout.

For many months, nothing was heard. Then, behind the scenes, Bout, whether alone or in consultation with the cash-strapped Russian military, reportedly came to an agreement that both he and the Taliban could live with. They'd allow the men and their plane to "escape" if Bout would agree to supply them with planeloads of arms and ammo from now on. Everybody was a winner. Within days, the crew were allowed to fly home.

One source at the UN who actually knows Bout and prefers to remain off the record claimed to me in the spring of 2010 that Bout had once told him that he'd just been doing what he'd been instructed to do by "someone much further up the food chain." Just who that person is has never been fully established—and if Marshal Shaposhnikov knows, he isn't saying—though there are claims Bout's father-in-law is a former KGB grandee, and these days is one of Vladimir Putin's staunchest backers.

And while he was freer with his hints in the old days, since the heat came on, Bout's lips have got tighter too. Once, when he was asked outright, he said, "They didn't escape; they were extracted. There are huge forces—" and then promptly clammed up. In an interview with the *New York Times* shortly before his arrest, he appeared on the verge of saying more, then backed down once again: "[My clients are governments, but] I keep my mouth shut," he said. Then, pointing to the middle of his forehead: "If I told you any more, I'd get the red hole right here."

Indeed, the FSB were not averse to reminding cargo operators who held the whip hand. In 2000 the Russian secret service, perhaps embarrassed by Bout's increasingly high profile, perhaps as a friendly warning across the bow, appeared to make a terrifying example of one of his Il-76 operator peers. In September of that year, masked FSB men announced they had seized an Il-76 carrying twenty-two tons of hidden cargo unlisted on its documents, then raided the offices of its operator, a Moscow-based cargo outfit called East Line working out of Domodedovo airport around thirty kilometers from the city, whose regular patterns of flights to Pakistan, the Arab Emirates, India, China, and South Korea seemed to have flagged what they had long suspected: This was a major smuggling operation, with one goal being the evasion of customs on contraband from China. Despite the protestations of the director general, Amiran

Kurtanidze, the armed, balaclava-clad FSB agents trashed the office, pulling out drawers and filing cabinets, and walked out with all the company's computers and paperwork, effectively paralyzing East Line's entire cargo operation.

News of the bust spread fast: Two more of the company's planes were found idling on remote runways in Siberia and Nizhny Novgorod, their crews, having got the news on the radio en route from China with twenty-nine tons of illicit cargo hidden "beneath the floorboards," tried to turn and head back to China before running low on fuel. They then promptly landed their planes and fled into the steppes and the villages, leaving them *Mary Celeste*–style, to be discovered hours later, radios still crackling.

But there was a twist. Kurtanidze claimed to the press that the busts and charges of wrongdoing were, first of all, mistakes that could easily have been rectified—and then part of an elaborate setup orchestrated by a shadowy group he called the "Reconciliation and Accord Foundation" that was trying to control routes to China as an air-cargo operator for its own dark purposes, and to snuff out any "competition."

Some of the braver Russian newspapers went further: the FSB, they said, was harassing one of the precious few good companies. East Line had set up in the tough days of 1993 at Domodedovo, and, it was claimed, had refused to pay the mafia groups who were crawling all over the airport. This was, it was whispered, nothing but a shakedown by *mafiya* elements within the Russian state itself. Russian business paper *Kommersant* speculated that a strengthening of control over customs clearance, or a personal business interest from a member of the government, were behind the raid. While the investigation dragged on East Line's fortunes plummeted, and by the time it was quietly dropped, after a succession of government statements reiterating their claims about the airline but not one prosecution, Kurtanidze was gone, and aviators, exporters, and charterers across the former Soviet territories were in no doubt as to who the real players were.

To Russians at the time, the rumors of official skulduggery were all too believable. If anything, the FSB seemed to be treading unusually softly. The raid, well-publicized and dramatic as it was, was very little, very late. It would certainly send out an obvious warning to other crews and middlemen that they knew exactly what was going on. But by that point neither Mickey nor any of the other crews, charterers, or business-men in on the world's richest smuggling scene could stop trafficking—even if they'd wanted to. The money was simply too good.

To this day, the FSB—if it was indeed the FSB who ordered the bust, and not private interests working within the security service—has never acted against these airlines or their crews again. Nor has any more been heard from the Reconciliation and Accord Foundation.

Certainly, covert influence in the affairs of cargo operators is not un-known. As Grigory Omelchenko, the former chief of Ukrainian counter-intelligence, told Peter Landesman of the *New York Times*, "Traffickers like Bout are either protected or killed. There's total state control." Per-haps, then, Ilya Neretin's claim is not quite true. Maybe whoever was covering the arms shipment was watching all the time. Perhaps the crew weren't, after all, alone without help from any quarter.

Slight, mousy-haired, and leather jacketed, Andrei Alexeivich Soldatov looks more like the bass player in an indie band than the scourge of the Russian secret service's more maverick tendencies. And like Mickey's op-posing angel, he's also something of a Zelig, popping up at the scene at the most crucial points in the post-Soviet story. At just twenty-one, he became a reporter for the newspaper *Sevodnya* and paper-hopped, cover-ing the Beslan school siege and massacre and the Moscow theater-hostage crisis. He's met defectors, followed spies, and uncovered Kremlin com-plicity in criminal behavior. But now aged thirty-four, it's as an investiga-tor into the black ops and extrajudicial activities of Russia's secret service networks, past and present, that Soldatov is best known.

"A lot of these flights in and out of Afghanistan are clearly enjoying some protection," he agrees. He explains that his suspicions run to the idea that it may in fact be in Moscow's interests to keep a pipeline for se-cret cargoes open, and to know what's in other people's. He also suspects that a little visible heroin trafficking into Russia itself, with the odd care-fully managed seizure here and there, plays into the hands of a Kremlin keen to point out NATO's inability to stamp out the smack trade at Rus-sia's back door—perhaps works even as a pretext for greater intervention in Central Asia once more. "There's a new stage of the Great Game going on," he smiles, recalling the covert jockeying for military and commercial

influence in Afghanistan and India between Britain and Russia in the nineteenth century. So much for disorganized crime.

But if someone is killing, protecting, raiding, or controlling all the traffickers using these flights, and if someone's letting just enough heroin into
Russia to put pressure on NATO to exit Afghanistan, well, the question is,
who? And just how high up do you need to go in order to find them?

"I always say to everybody, I'm not the police," laughs Peter Danssaert
when I call on him again, at his office in the dockside quarter of Antwerp,
Belgium's historic diamond hub. This time I need help understanding
what looks more and more like secret state collusion and less like a few
freelance bad guys. "I'm not in this line of business to put people behind
bars or whatever else."

For Danssaert, these questions are part of what attracted him to the
job of researching trafficking flights. "For me it's a puzzle—you have a
problem to solve. If someone tells you there's an arms flight over here, or
some arms are being sent there, for me the motivation is to find out how
it's done, who's doing it. How does it fit into the bigger picture?

"You see, many times, these arms brokers and freight forwarders who
are doing illicit and gray stuff are also doing legitimate stuff. And in a lot
of cases, they're being hired by the same governments to do the same
thing legally that they're doing illegally, or at least the same thing openly
that they're doing illicitly! So, what I try to find out is, how? That's the
puzzle that keeps it interesting for me."

But Danssaert is one of a small group of people—too small, he'll readily
admit—at shoestring-budget organizations in different countries, each
attempting to monitor the migrations of arms and other destabilizing
materials across the globe. It's a hard job made harder by the conflicting
demands of funding organizations who want certain reports "out there"
while their particular topic's hot—but they all want the reports to stand up,
so they need to be methodically watertight. Danssaert says he's "working
right now on one that started out twenty pages long, and it's now already
two hundred pages. Amnesty are asking for it, but we've got to get it right.
Hopefully we'll publish it in the summer. Or, uh, just after the summer."

The job's also made harder, he says, by people who write about it.
"When people write articles about it, they make it sound very easy, or at
least much less complicated. But the world's a complicated place, and this
business is far more complicated than it sometimes seems."

And just how complicated it can be—and just how "licit" and "illicit" can become dangerously blurred—is perfectly illustrated, says Danssaert, by the thick, cultivated murk that always tends to envelop not just the operations but the attempts by governments and law-enforcement groups to stop them.

"For example," he smiles, "my personal problem with a lot of these reports into [Bout's activities] is that they're completely self-referential," he says. "I've even known a case where an author wrote an article with some suppositions in it, then the intelligence agencies used that article as the basis of one of their reports, and eventually leaked that internal report back to the journalist, who quoted 'intelligence sources' in reporting it as fact!"

Indeed, it's the suspicion of underhanded dealings—along with the inability or disinclination of the CIA, Washington, and some investigators to respond when questions are raised about their claims—that plays into the Bout apologists' hands. Most famously, one of Danssaert's predecessors at IPIS, a Belgian investigator named Johan Peleman, has become something of a favorite target among Bout's camp, fairly or unfairly, for the perceived "sexiness" of his reports. "You can tell the ones with a hard-on to pin stuff on him easily," says one investigator with amused contempt.

The punch line is supplied by the man himself, who, with typical flamboyance, acknowledges—even perhaps encourages—this diffuse infamy, seemingly delighting in playing jokes on those who've made Merchant of Death–watching into a lifetime pursuit. On his Web site, under "Contact Details," it simply says: "Postal address: History book, intelligence files, and people's imagination."

But Bout is only the most visible poster boy for the whole phenomenon of "merc" outfits—these maverick aviators who've been playing a large, unacknowledged part in world affairs.

So how hard can it be for the authorities to clean up the skies—especially in countries under lockdown like Afghanistan, Iraq? On paper, blacklisting should work, or at least extremely close performance management and observation. So should searches. So should a lot of things.

The twist is, in the worst places on earth, for the most dangerous, crucial jobs, Mickey and his comrades, with their screaming, taped-up Ilyushins and Antonovs, not to mention their low rate cards for a job, were often the only game in town. As one airman I call to check a few facts in spring 2011 jokes with me, laughing as he ad-libs to the tune of *Ghostbusters*: "Who you gonna call? Byelorussians!"

Still, as the 2000s progressed, Viktor Bout's role in Liberia and Angola was becoming more widely known. In late 2000, when British government minister Peter Hain made his impassioned speech to parliament in which he coined the nickname "Merchant of Death" for Bout, he succeeded in scaring the horses, and the subsequent pressure from monitors, NGOs, bloggers, intelligence services, and investigators would see some—though by no means all—of the wildcat crews' operations for the U.S. military come under fire. By 2005, names like Bout and Damnjanovic came under increased scrutiny.

As the spotlight shone brighter on the illicit movement of guns, people, money, and resources around the world, some cargo outfits would move on again, looking for happier, more discreet hunting grounds—places where the skies were still free and where their services were once again in urgent demand. Places they had friends.

For some, that meant a renewed focus on empty, wing-and-a-prayer Africa; for others, the equally radar-free skies of South America.

Only this time, for Mickey, I couldn't escape the feeling that it looked increasingly like a last bolt-hole. In fact, for many of their comrades, these outposts would be the end of the line. And for at least one very high-profile former Vitebsk colleague, this is where the international law-enforcement net would begin to close in.

PART V

Back to the Jungle: Central America and The Horn of Africa

CHAPTER FIFTEEN

High Times on the Costa Coca

Central America, 1999–2008

As IT EMERGED THAT al-Qaeda had been funding itself with knockoff CD, T-shirt, and DVD sales, the penny began to drop that terrorism, drug-trafficking, illicit arms, the vice trade, and even copyright infringement might be full and integral parts of a global economy, just as the different parts and divisions of the "straight" economy are.

As eureka moments go, it was a little late, coming to the capitalist West a full decade after Mickey, Viktor Bout, and Leonid Minin had seized on it. But there it was, at last. Post–9/11, the world suddenly began feverishly trying to put the pieces of the international terror puzzle together.

To anyone who'd seen the Milošević regime in the last days of Yugoslavia funding guerrilla armies and paramilitary organizations with bootleg cigarettes and illicit weapons smuggled aboard Soviet-era cargo giants, it shouldn't have been a surprise. But a surprise it was. So was the fact that the Taliban was nowhere near running short of money because they controlled the heroin trade, justifying the rather un-Islamic practice of drug trafficking by pointing out that it was for the greater good of bringing the infidel to his knees, using the old tactic of the passing Afghan "well-wishers" who used to throw the odd wrap of heroin or bag of weed into tanks and over garrison walls for the occupying soldiers, hoping it would addict and debilitate them.

Narco-terrorism, a term coined in Peru in the early 1980s, was the new buzzword, and the rise and proliferation of organizations like al-Shabab, the Janjaweed, Somali pirates, and the Colombian left-wing guerrilla organization FARC began to seem more like a global issue than a local one.

Suddenly, Mickey's flights were no longer simply the concern of aid agencies, businessmen, warlords, and the odd monitor or plane spotter fortunate enough to have a desk in Washington, Antwerp, or Stockholm. Like it or not, even these radarless expanses were plugged into the global ecosystem—albeit an ecosystem overheating on its own wild, freewheeling energy.

These planes may have earned their narco-smuggling stripes back in Mickey's Soviet-Afghan war days, but their route networks have grown, taking in cocaine from Colombia, Peru, Venezuela, and Mexico. As early as 1992, authorities right down through Central and South America had begun noting Central American cocaine cartels forming what one U.S. intelligence report called "formal alliances with Russian organized crime groups." That year, Colombian authorities had begun recording contact between a Colombian known as "Caliche" whom they suspected was one of the main couriers for the Orejuela cartel, and a man he called "Sylvester" from Russia's powerful Moscow-area *mafiya*, the Solntsevskaya Brotherhood. The two men, it emerged, were setting up a "large-scale distribution network" with the West African states—in which, coincidentally, a large ex-Soviet aviation infrastructure had quickly established itself—turning into popular transshipment points.

By 2001, an intelligence report by the Colombian Administrative Department of Security found that "Russian and Colombian criminal groups have been negotiating shipments of drugs that were paid for with short- and long-range weapons, that were later sold in Central America or directly to subversive groups of the country."

All this high-volume trade with subversive and criminal groups—meaning, essentially, FARC—would be impossible, of course, without help and official collusion. Which is where FARC's Cold War contact book came in. Through the 1980s, the guerrilla army had sent soldiers abroad for training, commonly to fellow revolutionary communist lands, from the Soviet Union to Vietnam. By the 1990s, the lines of communication and transport between their soldiers and their now-freelance ex-Soviet comrades-in-arms was bearing more profitable fruit.

Moisés Naím, for whom as Venezuela's minister for trade and industry in the 1980s and 1990s, FARC's activities had presented an almost daily challenge, compares the era's Colombian drug-trafficking kingpins like Pablo Escobar explicitly to Viktor Bout. Both, he says, were "Mr. Big" characters in their own particular nascent industries; industries which would quickly become so highly evolved that they would no longer need Mr. Big figures at all.

With the mid-1990s decline of legendary Colombian cartels like Escobar's, the components in the process—shippers and producers—saw they could work in more agile, less public ways and effectively sidestep these powerful middle men, and Latin America buzzed with strange new kinds of sea and air traffic. In Mexico, reports surfaced in 1998 that the Russian mafia was "supplying Mexican drug traffickers with radar, automatic weapons, grenade launchers, and small submersibles in exchange for cocaine, amphetamines, and heroin," while DEA agents found posing as members of the Russian mafia with three hundred Kalashnikovs going cheap was suddenly an effective way to draw Mexican *narcos* out for a sting.

But an investigation by MSNBC in 2000 not only revealed the extent and richness of the network that made up the South American Connection, but proved to anyone harboring doubts just how mind-bogglingly profitable the business was for the airmen prepared to work the routes.

Recalling Andrei Soldatov's cryptic words about protection for smuggling flights from Afghanistan, U.S. intelligence uncovered "an alliance of corrupt Russian military figures, organized crime bosses, diplomats and revolutionaries" flying regular consignments of weapons to Colombia and returning to the former Soviet Union with their payment—up to forty thousand kilos of cocaine a trip.

According to U.S. intelligence sources quoted in the MSNBC investigation, throughout 1999 Il-76s began taking off from air bases in Russia and Ukraine bound for Amman in Jordan packed with surface-to-air missiles, guns, and ammo. They would refuel in Jordan, "bypassing customs with the help of corrupt foreign diplomats and bribed local officials," then head off, tracing seemingly crazy routes via the Canary Islands and Guyana to Iquitos, deep in the Peruvian Amazon jungle. There, they would land and unload at remote airstrips, or in some cases even parachute-drop their cargo to Colombian FARC guerrilla detachments. These were lightning operations allegedly coordinated by a committee of men: a rogue officer in the Peruvian army; a notorious fugitive Brazilian narcotrafficker, Luiz Fernando Da Costa, also known as Fernandinho Beira-Mar—or 'Seaside Freddie'—living in Paraguay's "smuggler city" of Pedro Juan Caballero; and a Lebanese businessman. Despite heated denials from Colombia, in August 2000 the Peruvian government confirmed the smuggling ring's existence, and that each parachute drop to the guerrillas had included around ten thousand Russian-manufactured automatic rifles acquired on the black market in the Middle East.

At the jungle airstrips, the weapons would be unloaded and replaced with cocaine—some of which would be given as payment for the weapons to the Jordanian middlemen; the rest flown back to Russia and Ukraine "for sale there, in Europe and in the Persian Gulf," at up to fifty thousand dollars per kilo. The sums were staggering. "While most of the weaponry goes directly to FARC," wrote MSNBC's reporters Sue Lackey and Michael Moran, "a smaller amount is parceled off to other guerrilla groups [including] Hezbollah, the Iranian-backed movement best known for its guerrilla activities in southern Lebanon [via] Arab immigrant communities of Paraguay, Ecuador, Venezuela and Brazil."

The subtle sophistication of the arrangement—in which every party to the deal was kept remote from almost every other party to make detection more difficult—echoed the loose agglomerations favored by networks like Bout's and Minin's. One U.S. intelligence agent told the reporters the weapons came from ". . . organized crime and the military. There is a tremendous gray area between the two in Russia and the Ukraine." Indeed, the scale of the operation, not to mention the sheer nerve, took even the intelligence officers who uncovered it by surprise, drawing comparisons with the scale of "straight" manufacturing businesses. It was, said one in admiration, "a big operation . . . there are a lot of people involved. It's literally an industry."

Around this industry, like any other, grew networks of suppliers, secondary service providers, and bottom-feeders. Up and down Central America's coast, the flight paths traced by Mickey and his fellow pilots in their Candids and smaller Antonov turboprops nurture small economies of prostitutes, bent cops, and fixers. But perhaps the most curious of all are the legions of fishermen and farmhands who set out into the wilderness daily before dawn in the hope of finding off-target or jettisoned bales of cocaine from a wayward illicit drop.

"Good morning to you all. Ha-ha! It's a beautiful March morning. That was Bob Marley, and this is a message from our sponsor." There is crackling as someone covers the microphone with a hand, and the sound of the local radio DJ arguing with someone off-mic about which button to press to start the ad. Then they locate the button, and here it comes over the airwaves: a woman's voice, matronly and with a soft Caribbean lilt, urging hungry Belizeans to come to her chicken diner. In the bright coastal sun, the Bakelite radio on the counter of the boat-repair shop loses reception for a moment, and the only sounds are the waves. Then it comes back on as the DJ introduces a comedy song called "I'm Just Another Gringo in Belize."

It's just the start of another lazy, sun-kissed day on Ambergris, one of the tiny, sandspit-and-swamp cayes—pronounced *keys*, like the Florida archipelago they resemble—off the mainland of this Mayan-Caribbean state. Belize is a tiny coastal country nestled between Guatemala and Mexico on the Central American coastline. Accordingly, the former British Honduras is part coastal paradise, part Mayan hill-and-jungle backwater, and projects the kind of quaint, slow-paced charm we all remember from childhood visits to elderly aunts by the seaside. The waters this side of a long coastal reef glow bright blue, and farther out, where the peasant fishermen ply their trade and the occasional launch zips by on its way up the Central American seaboard toward Florida, they are calm and reassuringly hushed. It genuinely is the last place I'd ever expected, quite literally, to fall over the slit and dissolving remains of a twelve-kilo sack of uncut cocaine someone had left lying on the sandspit beach of the long caye during a dawn walk.

If I'd been able to read the local papers for the couple of months before my arrival in March 2003, I might have had an inkling. On a cloudy Wednesday morning in February 2003, Belizean drug-enforcement agents on a tip-off stormed a field on the Mexico-Belize border and stumbled upon a still-smoldering torched aircraft. But if that was genuinely their first clue that all was not entirely as it should be on the sunny shores of this tiny Central American paradise, perhaps it shouldn't have been.

For years, fishermen and farmers up and down the Mosquito Coast have been doubling up as cocaine salvage men, pushing out early in the morning to see what they can rescue from the fields and waters of Belize and neighboring countries like Mexico, Guatemala, and Honduras. Locals here earn a matter of pennies a day—yet a handful of those industrious or well informed enough have long been living a Central American rewrite of *Whisky Galore* (Compton Mackenzie's book and subsequent film about a small Scottish island community onto whose beach fifty thousand cases of scotch from a wrecked World War II cargo vessel are washed). Only here, the flotsam comes in the form of shrink-wrapped bales of 100 percent pure cocaine, not bottles of booze.

On a sandy, shark-encircled caye a few kilometers along the Costa Coca just weeks later, I was a passenger on a local fishing boat whose skipper explained to me as he sped right past his fishing waters and into the deeper ocean that it was always worth his while scouting around for the "taped-up plastic sacks of cocaine that the *narcotraficantes* drop into the water at night." Sometimes, he explains, the *narcos* whose job it is to deliver the drugs to the planes come round the coast at night and attempt to rendezvous with the plane's crew. If they are disturbed, chased by law enforcement, or just paranoid, the easiest thing for them to do is push the cargo over the side, carefully wrapped so that it floats discreetly, in the hope of doubling back and retrieving it when the danger has passed—the big-money equivalent of throwing your joint from the car window. The air trapped in the sacks makes them float, semi-submerged or just below the surface, glinting as the light bounces off the plastic. Often they do return and retrieve their cargo, but there are often stragglers, bales washed away from the rest. These are, says the skipper, "the bales the fishing boats find, mostly. Sometimes from a plane too, though, I think."

By now it was late morning and my skipper and I were no longer alone: A handful of small dinghies could be seen combing the reef waters and the deeper sea beyond, packed with fishermen hoping to land their own twelve-kilo, plastic-wrapped golden ticket. Up and down the beach, meanwhile, were the sacks that hadn't made it—punctured on impact with the ground, swept out, torn, and washed up again, their precious contents either a dissolving bubbly residue or gone forever.

Back on land, the caye is awash with the stuff, young teenagers selling cocaine—or a hurriedly home-cut version of what the boats or 4x4s brought in—for as little as ten dollars a gram on jetties, beach bars, and up and down the sand in a way you'd normally be offered cheap souvenir beach towels or hair braids. One can't help but notice how, among the rows of hovels, rusting pickups, and wooden boats, the occasional spanking-new, tinted-glass Humvee sits incongruously; or the odd rococo home extension with pool among a cluster of poor-but-proud shacks at the end of a dirt road. This is just one of the bizarre local economic glitches—along with a series of microbooms to the cash economy whenever a shipment falls—that attends this particular delivery method to the local arms-for-drugs traders.

The idea of spiriting large quantities of Colombian-grown drugs out of rural Belize by cargo plane is not new. In July 2000, British paratrooper Ken Lukowiak wrote a best-selling account of a successful marijuana-smuggling operation he masterminded from his British garrison in Belize in 1983, using military-transport aircraft to spirit large quantities of grass to Europe. Successful until he was caught by the army and jailed, that is.

Yet the Belizean police do seem incredibly unlucky to keep narrowly missing an arrest despite the tip-offs they receive from local witnesses. Just months later in August 2003, enforcement authorities in Blue Creek, a mile and a half from Quintana Roo, Mexico, arrived just too late once more and found another ditched Antonov. This time the gun was smoking: On landing, the An-12's wheels had become stuck in the thick mud of the field, crippling it. Just like the Candid team who left their junk plane to rust in Afghanistan after having dropped their generator for the U.S. military, this crew knew what to do. The plane itself had cost just $1.5 million; it was expendable. The cargo wasn't. Witnesses reported seeing men arrive at the plane by car, pick up the crew and a suspected ten bales of cocaine, and speed off in the direction of the Mexican border . . . where they vanished forever.

And then it all went quiet.

Still, for all the lack of visible activity along these shores—and the smart money was on the smugglers keeping a low profile after two delivery SNAFUs in one summer—the world seemed to be under a blizzard of cocaine. Even as I walked along the sandy Belize beach looking for ripped sacks, a German laboratory was discovering that nearly nine out of ten euro notes tested positive for cocaine traces. When disposable incomes began rising again on the back of an oil and gas boom, Russia itself began to catch, then incredibly to eclipse even the U.S. as the primary market for Colombia's most famous export. According to a contemporary report from the Russian Embassy in Bogota, cocaine profits from the Russian market alone exceeded $600 million a year in the early 2000s, with a kilo of cocaine costing three times as much in Moscow as in New York.

It was all coming from somewhere. But these were pieces of a puzzle, still too few and too scattered to make sense. There were no more stranded planes seized in Belize after that summer, nor were any reported the following year. Aside from a few isolated cliques of plane trackers, the Latin American connection seemed to have slipped back off the international radar. In retrospect, perhaps some of the traffickers should have been alerted by just how quiet it had gone. Because someone, it turned out, was watching very closely indeed.

The day was perfect. The Caribbean sun shone, the radio played, and I shuffled through the sand past the ripped sacks on the shoreline and the police station with its public telephone hanging off the hook, toward my hotel. I passed a large sign facing out to sea, and glanced up. It read: DUE TO PREVIOUS INCIDENTS AND MISINFORMATION, WE FIND IT NECESSARY TO RESTATE THAT DRUGS ARE ILLEGAL IN THE ENTIRE COUNTRY OF BELIZE. I stopped, took a photograph, walked on. And all the while, the bales of carefully packed cocaine kept falling from the skies and over the sides of rendezvous boats into the coastal waters of Central America for the occasional enrichment of local fishermen and farmworkers.

CHAPTER SIXTEEN

Welcome to Little Minsk

Africa, 2003

THE AFRICA IN WHICH MICKEY—NOW SPORTING a permanent "Gulf tan" that ended at the neck and wrists—touched down sometime in late 2003 was a far cry from even the Wild East of Central Asia and the Balkans, or the organized chaos of South Asia. Even in the late 1990s, before the Balkans went quiet for once and while the really big contracts were to be won in Afghanistan and Iraq, Africa was once again a reliable place to make good money.

A series of conflicts had left swaths of Uganda, the DRC, Somalia, and Sudan lawless but naturally rich no-man's-lands, while unrest continued across West African states like Sierra Leone, Angola, and Liberia. These conflicts had also destroyed much of the continent's transport infrastructure. So by the time Afghanistan and Iraq ops came under the spotlight, Mickey was back, striding through the rainy-season downpour and across the treacherous Entebbe tarmac. Things were heating up for pilots with time on their hands, bills to pay, and an Il-76 to fly. Soon the skies shook again with the roar of former Soviet giants, overloaded with cargo.

Fleets of buccaneering Il-76 crews flew in from Byelorussia, in clear breach of the international Lusaka Accord, which now qualified any technical aid to Angola as military. *Belarus News* reported in 2001:

The invitation, issued by the Angolan Ministry of Defense clearly shows what role the Belarusian aviators will play there. Ahead of the looming presidential elections in Angola, the state army badly needs additional reinforcement of their capital. The only way to get the military contingent there real quick is by air. The pilots run great risk, but, due to the lack of job at home, they usually accede to the offer. Remarkably, all 18 pilots and technicians have first to resign from [their current employment] and sign individual contracts . . . All contracts used to pass through a special exercise in the Belarusian Foreign Ministry. So if some emergency happened, the government was responsible for bringing back the jet crew or locating them abroad if they are unaccounted for. However, with the private contract everything is different—the inviting side bears no responsibility for tragic occurrences that might take place. Nobody seems to care about human casualties.

With nobody watching their backs, more than ever the airmen, the technicians, and their network fell back on each other for support. In many cases, they carried out their own maintenance, hustled spares and extras, and paid with an apparently basic but in fact very sophisticated system of favors through contacts. What went around came around, even when the company couldn't back them up.

In fact, everything I discover about Mickey's journey from his Siberian and Byelorussian homes to Afghanistan, the Emirates, Africa, and beyond seems to illustrate how nothing happens in a bubble—the ripples felt by even the most seemingly unrelated incident back in Russia or Sharjah can be felt in Uganda years later. How else to explain the way tens of thousands of dollars' worth of jet fuel can appear in the middle of a third world field at night, seemingly unbidden, on a tanker that just rolls up to our plane, parked on an abandoned runway?

It happens at night, in 2009. We're standing in near-total darkness on an airfield in the middle of a small African country that I've promised under threat of retribution, legal and otherwise, never to name. The fuselage pings and pops quietly and clattering echoes from the hold. Leg-stretch time, and it's freezing outside. There's a pair of headlights in the blue misted distance as dawn creeps in—a long way off, but you can hear the rattle of a motor, faintly, approaching and then fading. On a dirt road, with nobody else for miles. Mickey passes me his coffee. It's disgusting. Standing behind me, Sergei's hand is reaching for his jacket pocket, digging and twisting deep in the misshapen cloth.

The engine noise is back, and louder now. A truck lurches upward from the ground and rattles and bounces and squeaks toward us over the waste. It is followed by another covered tanker, headlights yellow-filtered but still bright enough in the beam to dazzle us momentarily and send Giacometti shadows splashing back across plane and runway as the vehicles stop and five fair-skinned men jump out. At least two have little rifles and are wearing casual fatigues. Wordlessly, they begin pumping fuel. Less than twenty yards away, the nozzle sloppily feeds the giant plane, splashing fuel on the floor and down the side. The night is thick with the heady scent. I give it a couple of full-nostril breaths, and the flammable air is cold in the nostrils.

Sergei, cigarette in his teeth, has stopped pulling at his pockets, has found his lighter, and is attempting, one-handed, to flip it open and spark a flame without spilling beer from his can onto his cigarette. The panic propels me far into the darkness until I'm aware that there's been no explosion. The sound of laughter carries through the gloom, and I guess I'm chicken. Still, I think I'll hover on the edge for the rest of the stop-off.

"Very good feeling for survival," frowns Sergei later, having explained for the umpteenth time to me that he's smoked around fuel before, and how safe it is so long as you're experienced and judge it right and keep the beer can handy for your butt and ash. "But maybe you worry too much."

The refuel rendezvous is a regular assignation, and it's just one way of getting tax-free petrol from someone else who's in a position to write off a percentage of their own stock as spilled, lost, stolen, or damaged and collect on the insurance or the favors. That's the way business gets done out here. Because for all the wonderment, frustration, fear, and sheer dumbfoundedness they engender in other aviators, wherever they are found, these men are a tight, organized community of contacts. Still, it's a surprise to learn just how much sway their Soviet military past still holds over their apparently mysterious movements, if not how much it accounts for their seemingly uncanny abilities both in the air and on the ground.

"With a lot of these guys from countries like Russia, Ukraine, Kazakhstan, and Belarus, it's the old squadrons at work again," says Hugh Griffiths. "The logistics, air defense, and surveillance squadrons based in places like

Vitebsk, well, that was a massive air force town, and a big base for them during the Soviet-Afghan war. And those connections have endured. The smarter guys, from GRU, military intelligence, the pilots, they all set up their own operations in the UAE and just attracted and recruited all their ex-colleagues who gravitated to them. There are plenty of colonies of them now—UAE is one, South Africa is another, Equatorial Guinea. They're like these Soviet outposts, frozen in time."

By the middle of the decade, many prodigiously talented Russian, Ukrainian, and Byelorussian airmen—often survivors from the first wave of aviators who arrived in the early 1990s—had, by and large, settled. Many now had families, often relocating loved ones from back home. They lived regular lives, grateful for the stability and the paycheck-price differential. Others put in six-month shifts, or just flew here and stayed until they got a job flying out, the same way as they flew anywhere. Some continued to live as they would have in the army. They were the ones noticed, and treated cautiously, by locals: barnstorming, smoking, smuggling, laughing, brawling, wheeling, dealing, boozing, and romancing their way across the continent.

From Somalia to Angola, South Africa to Sierra Leone and all points in between, they continued to roll into air base towns like tropical storms, whipping up mini–economic tornadoes of cash, carousing, contraband, and chaos wherever they landed.

Everyone has a story to tell. For every jilted boyfriend whose girl has fallen for these work-hard-play-hard mavericks of the skies, there's a bar owner like the one I meet in Kampala who recalls the night the roaring-drunk Il-76 crew got into an argument, started cracking each other's heads on his restaurant's fittings, plates, bottles, and furniture, completely wrecked the joint, and then, when the police arrived, saw the funny side and freely dispensed more cash than the owner had ever seen "to pay for the damage, plus a bit extra for you, for giving us a great night out."

The headlines in these cargo-outpost towns are full of aviator-related incidents like the 2009 heart attack during a bout of postmission coitus—enhanced, says the local tabloid press, by fake Nigerian Viagra. Iain Clark, Africa director of global charter agents Chapman Freeborn, remembers the time a few years back when "one former Soviet republic actually banned its cargo crews from flying in direct from Mwanza in Tanzania." This infamous "party" stopover for Russian airmen that filmmaker Hubert Sauper had witnessed was becoming overrun with prostitutes catering to cargo crews, and the republic—Clark will only say it was in Central Asia—choked off the direct flight route back home in order to prevent cases of HIV and AIDS flying in by Il-76.

But for all the stories of dissolute lifestyles, there's a side that gets reported less regularly: touching acts of generosity toward an "adoptive" local family, or lifelong business partnerships struck up. For every incident like the one in 2009 in which Entebbe police were called when a local woman was ejected from an airman's rental apartment the morning after in an unedifying full-volume argument over "whether she was still a hooker or now a pilot's fiancée," there's been a genuine love affair and a future together away from the business—after just one more big-paying trip, of course. Half-Russian, half-African children aren't unknown, and across Africa wives, official or common-law, can be seen waving crews off on another flight, to another part of the world. And sometimes they wave as they come back, too.

The guys were popular; every time these boys were back in town, from Angola to Kenya, they were flush with cash, dressed to the nines, and looking up old friends and new, sweating off the life with good times and cold booze.

They stay six-deep in rented company houses, sleep on their planes and in off-season hotel rooms; one "Little Russia" is a smart suburb of Entebbe town just uphill from the lake known by locals as Virus, partly because of the research institute there, partly because of the sexual shenanigans that soon made its shared crew huts legendary.

The expat network is wide and enduring. "I've got a lot of [aviator] friends in Africa," remembered Sergei Ivanov— a technician who worked at an Angolan base known as Volga, after the Russian river, throughout the freewheeling, conflict-torn late 1990s and early 2000s—when he was tracked down by a Russian newspaper after another crew plummeted to their deaths. "There are literally masses of airplanes from the Soviet Union out there. On a single airfield in Angola I once counted thirty An-12s, plus a lot more Il-76s, An-72s, and other aircraft.

"[My bosses] had this great plan," said Ivanov, "to create a fleet of aircraft across Africa operating from Namibia, with technical bases elsewhere—officially authorized by the Russian authorities. They brought equipment: ladders, lifts, and so on. Parts were bought, experts were hired from Ekaterinburg and Kirov. All just to serve the Angolan aircraft."

These surreally located Slav-speaking communities and dozens like them from Iraq to Uganda became, for many technicians, pilots, and crew, homes from home, with crews, technicians, admin guys, and security living and working together for companies with good old Russian names like Volga-Atlantic and Troika-Link. Roll up at any air base's gates, or the network of warehouses, shops, and houses that form around them, and you'd be as likely to hear a Russian- or Ukrainian-league football match blasting through the thin walls of the prefab huts as the engines of an approaching Candid.

Like the Englishmen dressing for dinner and sitting down at mahogany tables in jungle clearings in Conrad's *Heart of Darkness*, these men transplanted their unit, their skills, their hardware, even their culture out to sub-Saharan Africa, Arabia, South Asia, and the Far East.

And though it seemed Sergei Ivanov was keen to point out that his bosses, of which Evgeny Zakharov was one, refused to take sketchy cargo or even servicemen, not all of them were quite as fussy.

"Sometimes you'd see six aircraft from the former Soviet Union a month come down," said Ivanov to the Komi, Russia–based reporter who tracked him down. "It was mostly Ukrainian crews who crashed. They were shot down, basically. We used to call them *bezpredelschik*—'the lawless ones.' The devil only knows what made them carry the kind of stuff they used to carry.

"Militants from UNITA used to put us under pressure too, when they wanted to fly," he said. "They knew us quite well, but we would never take military. We never took weapons either. It got to the point, when they threatened us with handguns and tried to force us to take some general on board, that we actually used to pretend we'd 'broken' our plane! And the difference is, we lost only one plane over Angola."

These lawless, doomed Ukrainians Ivanov used to watch fall flaming to earth across Angola were Mickey's old *Afghantsy* comrades—war tested and steely nerved. Like the Air America boys from whom they'd inherited the mantle of winged white devils, they lived by the credo, "Anything, anywhere, anytime, professionally." They were also crack flyboys, airmen who, as the Kazakh president used to say about his personal pilot, "could land upside down in a cave." They came, they played fast and loose, they took money to fly whatever you have, and having come through the hell of Afghanistan, they thought they were immortal.

But here, out over the savannahs, the forests, and the mountains of an Africa dissolving into a dozen different wars, the rich rewards to be gained from flying arms and even members of different fighting groups made them targets. The paydays were potentially massive, but so was the cost as these Icaruses burst into flames from Luanda to Kinshasa. Dozens were shot down, blown up, or killed by Mickey's old demons, bad luck, bad timing, bad weather, tiredness, and "the life."

But even more aircrews from places like Siberia, Ukraine, and Byelorussia who came flooding into the world's tropical chaos zones fell victim to their new environments.

"I knew one An-26 crew that was virtually wiped out on one assignment because most of the crewmembers got malaria," says one veteran cargo pilot. "This crew lived together on the plane, ate together, did everything in close confinement, in their bubble, and the malaria just swept through them. Quite a few of them got killed because of lack of proper understanding of the illness and lack of treatment in time. It wiped out more than fifty percent of the crew."

But even that won't stop the plane flying the next job "the very next day," he says. Then he adds something that startles me, something that echoes Viktor Bout's dark warning about the nameless people who will "give him the red dot right there" if he says too much: "There are forces who bring other people to the aircraft, and it flies again."

Wherever the pilots and their crews flew, in their wake there grew whole cottage industries of Slavic émigrés, Afghan war vets, technicians, trainers, fixers, import-export agents, charter guys, middlemen. Because while the Soviet air force and army had been wound down, the intelligence services and secret police weren't immune to the pinch either.

Suddenly, the "gray men" began appearing—former KGB agents with phones full of numbers, lines on plentiful cash, and heads full of questions about the local rebels and their diamond mines. It was straight from a Graham Greene novella as these exotic colonial outposts became the haunts of wealthy businessmen with no CVs and well-connected émigrés with vague pasts in intelligence. For some company pilots, they represented a chance to grab a piece of the pie, to go into business.

"Just think," they said in dirt-floored bars and makeshift offices all across the continent, "with your cash and connections, and my flying ability, we could clean up."

Cash appeared, planes were registered, and that's exactly what they did. Where did the cash come from? What strings were attached? It was anybody's guess. Those who knew weren't telling, and the flyboys weren't about to look any gift horses in the mouth.

Africa was Viktor Bout's stomping ground too. He bought up a small aviation outfit in the DRC called Okapi Air and renamed it Odessa. Leonid Minin, meanwhile, was building his African import-export empire, holding court with Liberia's Charles Taylor, and putting his crews up at the infamous Hotel Africa in Liberia—also a favored stopover for smugglers and traders, including one who reportedly used it as a convenient place to rest on Pakistan-Netherlands hashish runs.

Those were high times indeed. But now those men are gone and the skies over Africa are ruled by others—some good, some bad, and not one of them doing anything that anyone will arrest them for.

"There are all kinds of people out there, from Tajikistan to Angola," laughs Mark Galeotti, whose work for the British Foreign Office saw him become persona non grata in the CIS for a while, "and a lot of them are former intelligence professionals. In the 1990s there was a massive running down of the intelligence networks. Under Putin a lot of it crawled back, but a lot of people by this point had already cut their connections and, frankly, were making a lot more money outside. So in plenty of places, you've got your former local military-intelligence resident, the sort of chief officer in a country, who's married a local, settled down, and is now the go-to fixer for Russians wanting to do any kind of business."

The result, a network of consular teams, businessmen, and expats—many left there by the receding tide of Cold War politics, others heading out to the furthest reaches of the old sphere of influence in search of work—means wherever you are in the world, and whatever you, your crew, and your mammoth Ilyushin aircraft need, you're never too far from a friend of a friend of Mickey's.

And nowhere was the so-called gray area dividing Russian and

Crew lounging in the shadow of the Il-76 on a "pizza run."
(*Doug McKinlay*)

ssian cargo crew relaxing by a bomb crater during the first wave of coalition flights into Iraq. Such
ews were invaluable partners to the U.S., NATO, and UN's combat and reconstruction efforts. (*From
 archives of Zyriansky Zhizn/zyryane.info*)

Cache of Polish-made, Soviet-era weapons. With what was the world's biggest stockpile still not dry, there are more where these came from. (*NATO*)

Dangerous and costly, the decommissioning of weapons such as these, from an arms stockpile in the Ukraine, is the only way to keep them off the black market. (*NATO*)

"Certain steps had to be taken": Marshal Evgeny Shaposhnikov in 1992, with General Colin Powell. (*NATO*)

The smoking remains of Starikov's doomed Candid in a Belgrade field. In the days following the crash, a cordon of military and secret police guarded the wreckage. (*Igor Salinger*)

UN arms trade experts Brian Johnson-Thomas and Peter Danssaert inspect a seized cache in the DRC. (*Brian Johnson-Thomas*)

A lone helicopter patrols the northern Afghan borderlands. Long, porous, and only patchily monitored, such borders are an open invitation to smugglers. (*Matt Potter*)

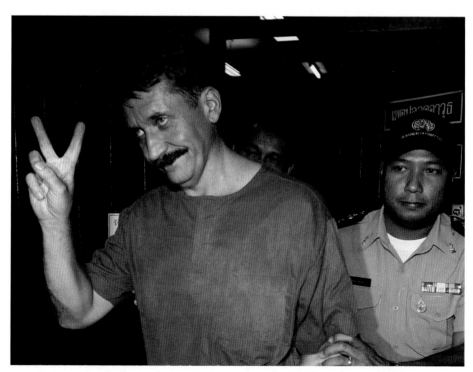

UNITED STATES DISTRICT COURT
SOUTHERN DISTRICT OF NEW YORK

UNITED STATES OF AMERICA   )   CASE NO. 08 Cr. 365
)
          v.   )
)   AFFIDAVIT IN SUPPORT OF
)   REQUEST FOR EXTRADITION
VIKTOR BOUT,   )
     a/k/a "Boris,"   )
     a/k/a "Victor Anatoliyevich Bout,")
     a/k/a "Victor But,"   )
     a/k/a "Viktor Budd,"   )
     a/k/a "Viktor Butt,"   )
     a/k/a "Viktor Bulakin,"   )
     a/k/a "Vadim Markovich Aminov,")
)
          Defendant.   )
)

AFFIDAVIT IN SUPPORT OF
REQUEST FOR EXTRADITION

CHRISTINE A. HANLEY, being duly sworn, deposes and says:

1.   I am a citizen of the United States and I reside in the State of Virginia. Since 2002, I have been a Special Agent of the Drug Enforcement Administration ("DEA").

2.   I submit this affidavit in support of the request by the United States of America for the extradition of VIKTOR BOUT, a/k/a "Boris," a/k/a "Victor Anatoliyevich Bout," a/k/a "Victor But," a/k/a "Viktor Budd," a/k/a "Viktor Butt," a/k/a "Viktor Bulakin," a/k/a "Vadim Markovich Aminov" (hereafter "BOUT") from Thailand to the United States for the purpose of prosecuting him on the charges contained in the Indictment, Criminal Docket Number 08 Cr. 365 (the "Indictment").

3.   In the course of my duties with the DEA, I have

A DEA affadavit supporting Viktor Bout's unprecedented extradition to the U.S. A non–U.S. citizen, Bout had never set foot in the States before his extradition. (*DEA/Courtesy victorbout.com*)

The talented Mr. Bout shortly after his arrest in Thailand: Even in custody, the legend of "Viktor B." continued to grow. (*Apichart Weerawong/AP/Press Association Images.*)

"This isn't starving Africa": A Russian airman sitting on billions of new, Saddam-free Iraqi banknotes in the hold of an Antonov. (*From the archives of Zyriansky Zhizn/zyryane.info*)

"These flights are clearly enjoying some protection": Andrei Soldatov, scourge of the Russian secret police. (*Andrei Soldatov*)

An-12 on a reconstruction run: Aviation boards buzz with conflicting reports of the history of many such planes. (*NATO*)

Sacks of the kind used to pack cocaine are jettisoned into the sea off Belize, where they are "caught" by fishermen. (*Matt Potter*)

Bricks of Mexican cocaine recovered in a DEA raid. Like legitimate business, the illicit side has its own brands and logos. (*DEA*)

The post-Soviet "cataclysm" is over, but in Russia's little-known Ural region, discarded and second-hand military hardware is still a common sight. (*Matt Potter*)

Lenin, Putin, Roman Abramovich, or Osama bin Laden? Fake IDs for sale in the bazaars of Central Asia. (*Matt Potter*)

e stuff of James Bond movies: Dropping twenty-million-dollar ransoms to Somali pirates is just
other paycheck for these men. (*Getty Images*)

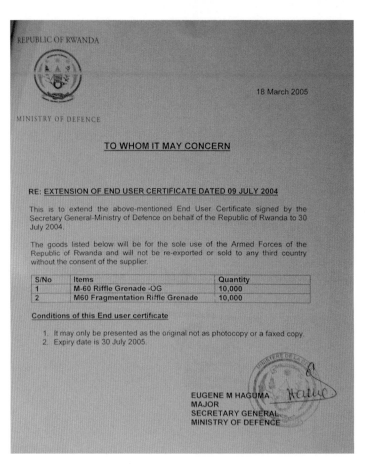

REPUBLIC OF RWANDA

18 March 2005

MINISTRY OF DEFENCE

TO WHOM IT MAY CONCERN

RE: EXTENSION OF END USER CERTIFICATE DATED 09 JULY 2004

This is to extend the above-mentioned End User Certificate signed by the Secretary General-Ministry of Defence on behalf of the Republic of Rwanda to 30 July 2004.

The goods listed below will be for the sole use of the Armed Forces of the Republic of Rwanda and will not be re-exported or sold to any third country without the consent of the supplier.

S/No	Items	Quantity
1	M-60 Riffle Grenade -OG	10,000
2	M60 Fragmentation Riffle Grenade	10,000

Conditions of this End user certificate

1. It may only be presented as the original not as photocopy or a faxed copy.
2. Expiry date is 30 July 2005.

EUGENE M HAGUMA
MAJOR
SECRETARY GENERAL
MINISTRY OF DEFENCE

This sample end-user certificate from a legitimate arms export to Rwanda shows how basic—and potentially easy to copy—these cargo "fingerprints" really are. (*Peter Danssaert/IPIS vzw/Transarms*)

Hotel Ilyushin: The author catches some sleep on the wing. (*Matt Potter*)

Ukrainian commercial pilots and mercenary activity grayer than at these far-off, disease-riddled outposts in the sun.

Even Mickey's old commanders from the air force were in on the action: While Mickey had left the military and gone into business, his former comrades had been marketing their own services pretty energetically, too. Through the mid-1990s, Mickey's old commander in chief Marshal Evgeny Shaposhnikov had become Boris Yeltsin's personal representative on the board of a firm called Rosvooruzhenie, a wholly state-owned arms-sales and export company set up by the Russian state itself to bring in cash.

By the early 2000s, the business of arming, supplying, and transporting to East Africa was booming, literally, with men and hardware flying off the shelves once more—this time *above* the counter.

Sales of attack helicopters and MiG fighter jets to disreputable regimes like Sudan, where they were just as likely to end up in the hands of the Janjaweed militia's "Devils on Horseback" troops as responsible COs, put Russia in the firing line of international peace monitors, but they had the happy effect of giving the country semiofficial on-the-ground military presence in some of the world's least stable trouble spots: Every regime's air force across Africa, Asia, and the Near East equipped with Russian planes suddenly also found it needed the men to maintain them, repair them, oversee their use, and train the country's own airmen (indigenous air force pilots in places like Sudan are chosen primarily for their loyalty to the regime, not their skill, and are legendarily, tragicomically inept).

"The main point, it's not that Russian pilots are replacing American pilots," says Evgeny Zakharov. "The reason is more to do with Russian planes—Antonovs, Ilyushins—are better for Africa. These Russian aircraft, the Ilyushins and Antonovs, have replaced American aircraft. That is the reason. And so there's a lot of demand for pilots. For example, there's a very, very big shortage of pilots for Antonovs. I tell you, these Russian pilots are really in demand because it's easy to find somewhere to train to fly a Boeing, but there is no place you can train to fly an Antonov-12."

The humans followed the hardware wherever it was the only thing that could do the job—the Candid's twenty giant wheels made it perfect for rough airstrips; the Antonov-12 could land anywhere; and in the empty spaces of the third world, they could all fly well past their official airworthiness had expired—until, and in some cases *after*, they simply began to fade away. The result was the spread through the third world of de facto Russian, Ukrainian, and Byelorussian air bases, compounds, and communities. Just like the old days, the businesses had branches everywhere: trained air force men, instructors, military intelligence, technicians. Only this time someone else was paying and none of it cost the exchequer, the armed forces, or the people back home a single cent.

The existences of any state-sponsored arms-running operations are shrouded in secrecy, but tantalizing glimpses into their workings show just how blurred the lines between instructing another country's pilots (legal under international law), maintaining their aircraft (also legal), and fighting for their air force as mercenary forces (very illegal) can become.

In May 2008, a Russian fighter pilot was reported "killed in action" in Sudan—a country in which, despite the trade links, there was no Russian military involvement, let alone action. Both the Sudanese and Russian authorities first denied all knowledge, then that any such incident had taken place. Then, in the now-familiar routine I first saw at work on Belgrade airport's molten tarmac, they ordered an immediate media blackout: Sudanese government troops raided local radio stations who reported the incident, shutting one down; Russian state media censored the story.

But pictures leaked out via the Internet, and finally Russia—having denied that "any Russians whatsoever were in Sudan at the time"—claimed the pilot was an instructor at a MiG fighter air base outside Khartoum.

Just one problem. The "instructor" happened to be flying his MiG-29 into battle against a two-hundred-vehicle assault force of over twelve hundred heavily armed Islamic Justice and Equality Movement rebels from Darfur, marching on the capital. As the armored column headed toward the presidential palace, the MiG came in for the kill, only to be hit by 12.7mm and 14.5mm machine-gun fire. And when the pilot's parachute failed to open on ejection, his secret mission as a mercenary pilot almost died in the dust with him.

And it wasn't just "decommissioned stockpiles" of pilots and aircrews who ended up putting deals together in the sub-Saharan sun, but former Soviet secret agents too—those ex- KGB and FSB men who'd opened up shop here for whatever services they were in a position to provide. Indeed, even today much of the South African secret police is made up of Mickey's old compatriots.

Andrei Soldatov remembers how former KGB men in South Africa met with Nelson Mandela's newly installed ANC government in the mid-1990s to discuss the provision of a ready-made secret service for South Africa—one that was not tainted by having worked for the previous apartheid regime. "Mandela's people asked this one former KGB officer to organize the transfer of thousands of [former Russian KGB] people from Moscow to South Africa. So that's what happened. And now the former KGB guy who arranged it, he's quite comfortably off, and he's come back to Moscow. His son's still out there working on it."

This fact makes all the more intriguing a March 1998 daylight housebreak and assassination attempt at Viktor Bout's $3 million Johannesburg mansion by phenomenally well-armed, masked paramilitary raiders who have—incredibly, given the audacity of the crime—never been caught or identified. Bout's mansion, in the exclusive Sandhurst district, was so heavily fortified some locals mistook it for a VIP detention center: walls five meters high were crowned with high-voltage wire fencing, while heavily armed security guards and attack dogs kept up a twenty-four-hour patrol of the grounds. On paper, the house itself, not to mention its two swimming pools, fountains, tropical garden, and separate accommodation for guests, should have been impregnable. It also provided Bout with a very comfortable lifestyle. Yet one March afternoon, as his elderly Russian housemaid was chopping fruit in the kitchen, the door was kicked in by masked paramilitary-style raiders who knocked her unconscious, beat her son, and stormed through the house, making off with $6 million in ready cash but, oddly, leaving all other valuables—including paintings and antiques—where they stood.

That was the first "warning," according to Richard Chichakli. He claimed the message was clear: "You're vulnerable. Get out." When just days later Bout's car was peppered with bullets by a gunman on a motorbike, then a henchman was beaten on the street, he took the hint. As with the KGB/FSB's masked-raider bust of East Wing, and the subsequent claims of involvement by a secret society, rumors of South African secret-police involvement in the Bout raids persisted. This was partly because, by this time, the discreet influence of former Soviet secret service men, and particularly those from the GRU, the old counterintelligence networks abroad, had become so pervasive—with Africa a particularly popular haunt.

"The sort of people who were abroad anyway tended to be the smart guys or the ones who had skills," confirms Galeotti. "And until the late Gorbachev years, they tended to be those who played the game in the Communist Party and everything else—not because they actually *believed* in it, but because they wanted the cushy job. The number of KGB I've spoken to who say, 'Why did I join the KGB? To get a cushy job! Joining the party was the only way I was ever going to get to live abroad!' So now you have these very smart, amoral people out there, still working off the same skills and knowledge base."

They work on the legitimate side, mostly—businessmen whose networks from the old days are useful for contacts and suppliers. These people, says Mickey, will know the outfit he flies for, and will often know him personally; they'll know he can get a job done. They might even request him by name. It is, he says, no different than belonging to a football club.

It's a small, tight-knit community, all right, just like any pioneer group. And when a crew is lost, which is often, everybody knows at least someone connected with the disaster. Which makes me wonder how they can be so fatalistic; how even when it's so close to home—the same kind of plane, the same airport, the same client, a friend—men like Mickey can accept the same fuzziness around the crash as they accept in their business dealings.

So I make up my mind to find out. And that means getting deeper inside the minds, and the remaining outpost communities, of this exotic and increasingly endangered airborne species.

CHAPTER SEVENTEEN

Russian Rain Keeps Falling

The Congo, 2005–2009

IT'S BEEN AN ODDLY COLD, dark midsummer 2010 in East Africa, chasing Mickey's crew, friends, and contacts around, catching the odd flight, and keeping up with Sergei's drinking. I'm getting over a fever, fed up, and, more than anything, increasingly claustrophobic—I'll never know how it is Mickey and company still haven't tried to dice each other up. I've got so much Nile beer coming out of my pores that nowadays even the mosquitoes look the other way when they see me coming. This is, Mickey tells me, what you get from the Life—though I can never get to the bottom of whether he just means "from life" and he's adding the definite article because that's what Russians (who don't have them) think you do when you speak English. Or if he really means something called *the* Life—the way you live when you're in the gang.

We make a motley handful about town in Africa: an ever-fluctuating number of giant, spindly, gangly, fat, tanned and pale, old and young Slavs dressed to the nines, trailed by one incongruously scruffy little Brit. And here, as dollar-spending *mzungu* and airmen to boot, we are a target market. Like sailors' dens in a port town, the local economy, from restaurants and bars to tattoo dens, hotels turned bordellos, and casinos, is geared up for these crews and their dollars. Hassan, the stocky, flashy boss of the

Simba Casino in the belly of a giant mall in Central Kampala, has even started hiring Kazakh girls as dancers. "We had a lot of old Soviet airmen in when we got the dancers last time," he says. Another pilot says there's recently been a whirlwind romance between a Ukrainian airman and just such a dancer. "This time next month, they'll have their own cargo airline," he laughs. "And guess who he'll have doing sales."

Then Mickey and I split—partly because they were flying somewhere I'd actually need a visa for rather than the standard fifty-dollar bill at immigration, but mostly because I'd had a bellyful. I spent a couple of days sobering up and chasing leads across the country. Then one afternoon I went to a place called Kampala Casino to meet with some off-duty Moldovans who never showed, and instead got talking to the manager, Peter. Once he was absolutely sure I wasn't a crooked revenue man trying to shake him down, he summoned a slender-legged waitress to pour me a cold Club on the house and slipped me the number of someone who—if I didn't know her already, which he clearly couldn't believe—I should speak to.

This contact would, he said, give me a deeper understanding of the curious communities of displaced ex-Soviet aviators in Africa. Having seen only Mickey's rootless drifting, I could use it. The woman was, he said, pretty much the social organizer of that community in East Africa, known for sorting out any aviators who got into trouble out here. I said she sounded like a Slavic Lara Croft with a pilot's license and laughed. Peter didn't laugh; he just nodded. "Call her. She knows everyone," he smiled, and left to tend the tables.

And that's how I met Katya, Aviation Queen of the Jungle.

Katya Stepanova can fly a plane herself, and after talking to her for just a few minutes, you realize she knows her way around not only an Il-76 but more aircraft than the designers know they've made. These days she runs her own highly successful Kampala-based travel firm, taking tourists, dignitaries, and businesspeople over the country's hills, cities, and jungles by light aircraft for safaris, nature trails, hiking, sightseeing, meetings, and kicks.

But that's only half her story. For a whole generation of honest, hardworking aircrews from the former Soviet lands who've washed up in Africa and, unlike Mickey, have decided to linger, to try and put down roots and carve out a life for their families, she's something between a social hub and an oracle, and her insider status gives her a unique perspective on the pressures, dangers, and temptations many of these crews of *Afghantsy* Lost Boys face.

With her long red hair, ready laugh, action-girl past, and one-of-the-boys wit, it's not hard to see how she's become the center of a whole social group and support network for marooned ex-Soviet flyboys zooming back and forth across the dark, radarless expanses of sub-Saharan Africa. Now in her early thirties, Katya is the aviator daughter of a Russian Il-76 pilot who'd moved from his base near Moscow to the Congo when the opportunities for honest, skilled, and hardworking ex–air force men like him dried up back home. She grew up in and around her father's Candid, flying with him on missions across Africa and further afield.

"Nowadays they're not so young anymore," she says, "but when we arrived out here the youngest pilot was thirty-four, thirty-five." She remembers that 1990s generation of newly arrived jungle pilots, bound together by common experience and mutual respect.

This was, she says, back before "the UN began controlling it all," when a pilot and his Il-76 was the closest thing many shelled, roadless areas had to a local bus, and military, ministers, civilians, and crates would jostle and bid for space on board. "At the beginning, all the crews here were nice, and everyone helped each other." She confesses she yearns for those times now. Times when the business of flying your Il-76 or your Antonov around Africa was, she says, "just a lot simpler." Still, even then they found themselves being scapegoated, hustled, and worse. "But it's always been risky. Crews kept getting arrested in the Congo in those days— they arrested crewmen, not the airline bosses. I remember one crew I knew, they got arrested and had to disappear pretty quickly. I had the Russian Embassy asking me if I knew what had happened with them, but I didn't."

It only takes the mention of my connection to Mickey and the others for Katya's memories of life among the first tidal wave of ex-Soviet aircrews in Africa to pour out. There were the times she and the crew had to deal with amphetamine-fueled child soldiers whenever they landed in jungle airstrips controlled by some of the wilder Congolese rebel warlords. "You hope nothing will happen," she says, "because it's just a ten-year-old. But then, you know, a ten-year-old with a gun, anything could happen. Those child soldiers are totally fucked-up, they don't really know any better. They're scared little kids, really, trying to be tough."

Once, a girlfriend of hers, an Eastern European crewman's daughter, pestered a crew to take her on a mission over rebel-controlled DRC territory. She got her wish, and the girl spent half the trip flattened, terrified, against the fuselage as rebels in the Congolese uplands loosed a hail of machine-gun fire without any warning, bullets smashing through the glass and ripping into the cockpit, missing her by inches and smashing the plane up inside and out. She got back okay, says Katya, and shrugs. Technically, "they probably shouldn't have done it. With me it was different: The crews never took me on military flights, just commercial runs. They looked after me, they made sure I was safe, and I wasn't really scared; [as a teenager] it was a case of, Nothing to do today, so I'll go up. It was interesting. The guys would never have let anything happen to me. Seriously, they all looked after me. I went with them on missions back then; they're my family."

Such are the bonds of expat language, culture, and common interest that the ex-USSR aviator "family" extends to pretty much everyone in the beat-up Soviet cargo-plane business over Africa. "They all come through Uganda at the moment," she says. "I've met most of them, I think." Russian aviation magnate Evgeny Zakharov is an acquaintance too. He is, she says, not just one of the few genuinely well-known post-Soviet movers and shakers in these parts, but one who's "not full of shit" either—the highest compliment.

I grab my chance—I'm interested to hear the view of the wider expat "family" on the shadier side of the cargo industry, people like Mickey and that thorn in the side of investigators Viktor B. So I ask her about Viktor Bout, just because he's been on the news today. She weighs up my question before exhaling a jet-powered plume of cigarette smoke into the night air. "He wasn't doing anything that everybody didn't know about at the time. It's all politics."

Also counted as extended family are the casualties. "A few months ago, an Il-76 went down in the lake here," Katya says. "All crew were killed. And I knew them." The community was already in mourning at the time of the lake crash for men it had lost the month before. In February 2009, a Ukrainian Antonov-12 en route from Kisangani, DRC, to Ukraine, with Entebbe and Luxor as refueling stops, crashed on takeoff from Luxor, coming down half a kilometer from the runway, catching fire, and killing all five occupants: two Ukrainian citizens, two Byelorussians, and a Russian.

"The pilot was a friend of ours from back in South Africa in 2002," she says. "He was called Yuri Matveenko: a good guy, and a fucking great pilot. I dunno what he was thinking—the plane was junk. Shit condition. And the pilot was one of the best, most well-known pilots. When he stopped in Entebbe he stayed with my dad. He knew the condition, why the hell did he fly it? Probably he thought he could just make it for that last leg of the journey home, even though his plane was junk." She shrugs. "Well, he made it halfway home."

The reason for the An-12's dive could be incorrect loading of the aircraft or pilot error, according to an interview on local TV given by Egyptian civil aviation minister Ahmed Shafiq almost immediately after the accident. Yet according to subsequent crash reports, the plane was indeed less than airworthy. Even Luxor airport's technical ground staff had warned the crew not to take off because the plane had a fuel leak. But this was no mysterious lapse of judgment, no hallucinating narcosis: The killer, she says, echoing almost everybody connected with the business out here, is money—as usual. It's what encourages risks like that, encourages overloading, encourages crews to take invisible cash cargoes unknown to their paymasters. "The pay is not bad, but if you are making money, you wanna make more money; you're thinking, 'Okay, well, if I can make more money, why not?' You know the problem is: You don't know how long your contract is going to last. That's the problem. So you are trying to make as much money as you can, because you don't really know how long you are going to be making *any* money for."

In the days that followed, Russian aviation forums were no less affecting. Messages from fellow *avialegionery* and former comrades paying tribute and offering help, witnesses describing the event, aviators appalled at the waste of life and looking for answers, and loved ones across the world in their hour of grief all served as a reminder that these are not just pilots and loadmasters but men: "Half my heart burned together with Dad on that plane," read one. "And what to live with survives, I would not wish on my worst enemy."

Another spoke of the psychotherapy she'd had to undergo to get over the loss of her father years before; the wives, brothers, and children of other fallen *avialegionery* joined the condolences. Meanwhile, the Russian Orthodox Church in Johannesburg held a memorial service to mark the forty days of mourning. Everywhere, messages ended with the words, "Come in to land now, crew."

It's a reminder that in some ways, Katya is not unique—there are hundreds of crewmen's daughters propping up communities like this one from Afghanistan to Angola, as well as back home in Russia; family members who travel in their dads' planes across continents, living action-packed teenage years and young adulthoods their counterparts back home can only dream of—or else wait, anxious for news from cities they'll never see.

Yet the remarkable combination of Katya's junior Il-76 aviatrix experience and her connections among crews, air industry, and locals here in East Africa have made her something of a go-to among old hands and new arrivals in Africa from back home. Only recently, her mobile phone rang with a number she didn't recognize: It was one of two Russian pilots on a mission in the eastern DRC who'd apparently been passed her details as a contact who could help them out of any tight spots, and he was in one. He told her he and his comrade had fallen very ill. They'd noticed their skin was turning yellow, and as they'd heard she knew people, and his English was almost nonexistent, could she help?

"Hepatitis," says Katya. "We got them out of the bush and over to Kampala, and got them seen by an English doctor. Don't ask me how they got my number."

She got to know people really fast when she arrived, she says. The daughters, wives, and girlfriends who wanted to come out and tag along while their men disappeared for weeks on end "all had time on their hands and didn't know anyone either, and the guys were never there, so they formed quite a big community in the end, everyone helping each other out." Nowadays she plays unofficial human SatNav for new arrivals, too. "I get a lot of new arrivals, you know, pilots asking me about runways, and fortunately I can usually tell them, 'This one you've got to watch for the holes on the left-hand side,' or, 'They bombed the hell out of the end of that, so stop short.'"

Just for the hell of it, I test her. I tell her I'd expected Rumbek airfield in Southern Sudan to be better, what with it being the biggest city in the southern half of Africa's biggest country. "Ooh! That's bad," she says. "There's hardly anything, it's still all dirt and bushes." Which is spot-on.

She reminisces about her days as a twenty-year-old at the end of the 1990s, when the skies were so full of Soviet-made metal you could grab a ride in an Ilyushin or Antonov like getting on a bus; then she recalls lying on her front watching the warlord-held jungle of the Congolese frontier whooshing past below in an endless, cinematic kaleidoscope of greens and browns, and says she appreciates how lucky she was. Only now, like everything, thrills like that are sort of drying up. It's getting more ordered. The rules are getting tighter. The UN is in town now, calling the shots for all the cargo ops. It all goes through the UN, over at the military base.

There's a sense of things closing in on the old networks of former Soviet air force guys, for sure. You can feel it everywhere. Every week, news feeds come through to Entebbe, reporting on yet another aviation authority somewhere that's banned yet another kind of Antonov plane, or another company, or another whole country of registration. Currently there's not a single airline registered in the DRC that you can even think about flying anywhere over Europe without scrambling God knows what forces intent on keeping you and your noisy, teetering agglomeration of metal away from their lovely expensive buildings, roads, and people.

For the first time, there's competition out here now, too. South Africans are moving in. "They're the only pilots who can do anything like the things that your ex–Soviet-Afghan war guys can do with these planes," she laughs. "Those pilots are just as crazy." She likens the sudden competition to the frontier-style atmosphere among aircrews and their old comrades on the ground way back in the 1990s, when her dad came over.

The world she describes is in many ways similar to the one Mickey encountered when he washed up first in the Balkans and Central Asia, then the Emirates, all dirty-nailed and dusty-mouthed, and ordered his first freelance beer in an air-conditioned hotel next to the hangars. Only like everything in Africa, it's both instantly familiar yet essentially different, too.

Before Uganda, her family had moved around with the flying work her cargo-pilot father could pick up, she says. She'd lived in Cyprus, among other places. But in the mid-to-late 1990s, Russia was still seen as a dead end for many émigrés. And over in Africa, business was really picking up. There was plenty of flying to go round, plenty of cargo to shift, and a fair bit of money to be made. And while pilots like Katya's father were relentlessly law-abiding and aboveboard, like any wild frontier, East Africa had its attractions for those who were prepared, like Mickey and the boys, to take things just a little further.

Just as it had in the 1990s, what the locals called the "Russian rain" kept falling over the resource-rich, rebel-patrolled Congo, with another Antonov listed as carrying aid equipment simply falling from the sky, presumed shot down, over occupied, diamond-rich, rebel-encircled Kisangani.

Then in May 2003, some 120 people were sucked to their deaths in an unexplained incident when the giant loading-bay door of an Il-76 owned by Hermes, a small Russian-operated outfit contracted to the Congolese military, mysteriously opened forty-five minutes into its flight at ten thousand feet over Kinshasa, loaded with soldiers and their families. After the pilot's successful landing of the stricken, depressurized, and unbalanced plane, he and the other surviving crew members were immediately visited by the equivalent of the Men in Black, sequestered by Russian authorities in a room at the Grand Hotel, Kinshasa, and ordered not to discuss the incident.

Something was clearly very secret, in any case: Later that year in October, a tense face-off ensued when a crashed An-28, just eight hundred meters from the runway at Kamina airstrip, was immediately surrounded by Congolese military, who refused to allow UN military observers access to the wreck or the cleanup.

January 2005 saw a cargo flight for a French NGO crash outside Kongolo, injuring all ten occupants, seven of them unlisted: The flight was not authorized to carry people. It later emerged that the plane had been grounded twice before for infractions, but cleared immediately on both occasions to continue flying humanitarian missions.

In October 2005, two passengers—Congolese army soldiers en route from Kisangani to Bunia—were turned into soup by an An-12's still-spinning turboprops when a crash landing on a dirt strip caused the wheels to smash their way into the cabin and, in the panic, all one hundred passengers burst through the doors and ran blindly in all directions—including right through the props. (Seeing the first two becoming human smoothies and the limbs of the next three flying off in many different directions apparently slowed the rest down somewhat; the evacuation proceeded in a more orderly fashion after that. An interesting idea for passenger airline safety drills, perhaps.)

Weeks later, an An-12 broke up in the air for no reason. Then in January 2006, yet another "just fell apart" on the ground, got struck off the aviation register, and was towed away for scrap. It was spotted again a few months later, back from the dead and in the air, blithely sporting a new paint job and a recent Kyrgyz registration.

One Russian crew landed their cargo plane only to have the wings literally fall off as they touched down. One simply flew into a hill outside Goma in July 2006; days later, another hit the side of a mountain in Bukavu in thick fog. Someone else's Antonov smashed into a parked 727 on the runway when his brakes failed. One Ukrainian Il-76 crew's plane "just exploded" at Pointe Noire, Congo, in May 2007. Then, at the same spot on the same runway in September, so did an An-12. On August 26, 2007, an An-32B carrying nine tons of freshly mined cassiterite, or tin oxide, experienced engine problems, hit tall jungle trees, and crashed. On September 7, 2007, two Georgians, two Ukrainians, and a Congolese crewman died when their junk-status An-12 carrying palm oil crash-landed in a Goma volcano field and caught fire. Another was shot down over jungle on the Rwandan border.

Then there was the showstopper, the one everyone talked about—that is, October 4, when a 1979-vintage, Ukrainian-operated An-26 crashed shortly after takeoff from N'djili Airport, Kinshasha, fireballing at high speed into a packed market square just after half past ten in the morning, spinning turboprop blades simply atomizing everything in their path. In addition to between nineteen and twenty-two fatalities among passengers and crew, a further twenty-eight to thirty-seven bystanders on the ground were literally mown down. Reports circulated soon after that one Congolese occupant had survived the initial impact, but that enraged locals had dragged him from the wreckage and beaten him to death—without, of course, waiting for the crash report to find for or against human error as one of the causes. Not that there would have been any point in waiting for the crash report: Some claimed the "black box" flight recorder was either one of the items looted from the wreckage, or had already been removed before the flight.

As I wrote this chapter, the news came in that an An-24 (NATO codename: Coke) had inexplicably nosedived into Nganga Lingolo cemetery on its final approach into Brazzaville, Congo. All five Ukrainian crew and one Congolese passenger killed. I'm no conspiracy theorist, but that sounds like a run of terribly bad luck for anyone.

It does get better away from the Congo, and away from the gaffer-taped planes themselves, but not much. Because while East and Central Africa have a great many things going for them, they aren't always world leaders in health and safety. So instead of asking how these things happen and trying to protect the poor Joes they tended to happen to (and usually at altitude) by, say, going after whoever wanted to hide a conscription of cluster bombs aboard a civilian aircraft, people started taking aim at the messengers.

The way Mickey tells it, and we're translating roughly here, "It's always the same, just with a different visa." Coming back from the Afghan war in the eighties was just the same, he says; like America's Vietnam vets, the Soviet Union's grunts got back from their unwinnable, sun-parched, booby-trapped, guerrilla-war hell only to find they were the whipping boys. "It was, 'We don't know what you were doing out there anyway,'" he recalls. "And, 'We heard you did some bad things, plus you did not win, and it was all a big mistake, so you will get nothing from us.'" And now, twenty years on, he's still wearing the mark of Cain: uprooted, demobbed, he tries to steer a course through the daily, hourly drip-drip of compromises his new third world homes test him with, and to stay alive. But even down here, the term "mercenary pilots"—shortened to *mercs* by the locals—has become the buzzword favored by firebrand politicians wanting to be seen as cleaning house and African nationalists who believe the continent would be just fine if they could get rid of white troublemakers. The mercs are everybody's favorite whipping boys.

Meanwhile, in New York, Stockholm, London, and Ostend, governments and arms monitors rage against "dirty airlines," "dirty planes," and "traffickers."

Some powerful voices are beginning to speak up, though, including the former World Bank chairman. "Note how, in our narrative, the criminals and the deviants are always the suppliers," sighs Moisés Naím. "It's never the consumers, even when it's the consumers who are creating the profit opportunities, and who are behind the market that creates the people we now call criminals and deviants."

Naím suspects looking to scapegoat the deliverymen is a more attractive option for many within the business and political spheres than tackling root causes. "The EU, the U.S., Russia, China—we can all keep on churning out weapons systems and land mines, snorting cleaner, meaner drugs, buying our way into brands on the cheap and DVDs in the pub; this way, when people get hurt it's not our fault, it's the guy at the other end.

"It's estimated that eight percent of China's GDP is associated with export and production of counterfeit goods, from car brakes to Prada bags," he says. "And when you have eight percent of an economy like China's involved in that, it means that literally millions of people wake up every day and can only make a living and bring food to the table because they are involved in what *we*, here in the West, call 'illicit'—and *they* call a normal way of making a living.

"To use a more cruel analogy: For us consumers in the West, we are told by our governments that these are all 'illicit acts.' They are 'criminals.' 'Underground.' 'Deviants.' There's a lot of deviancy in the conversation. Now, you go tell that to the Afghan farmer whose only way of making a living for his family is to plant poppies for export. And you know that he's not getting a lot of money. The big money is never at the beginning or end of the chain—the big money is in the *middle* of the chain. But we call him a criminal, right? He's a 'drug grower.' Or the woman who leaves her family in Guatemala and is beaten all the way and is an illegal worker, and ends up working as the nanny of an investment banker. Blame them? No. The consumer creates the market—every time."

"Our businessmen are at fault, not the crews," nods former pilot Andrei Lovtsev. "They have gone there to Africa, and to be truthful they're working there for kopecks compared to the foreigners. I speak to the Americans and they say, the Russians—even though it is more Ukrainians, Kazakhs, and so on—in the business rent out the planes for kopecks, and the crew get even less. For an An-12, they only charge around $1,000, $1,200 an hour whilst an American Hercules will cost $6,500. The crew get $5,000 or $6,000 a month. It is very low, yet they fly to difficult places in difficult conditions and are met by Kalashnikovs and taken away, and they don't know if they will be shot or not."

Indeed, the airmen themselves are now often more valuable to local thieves and warlords than the cargo they carry. In August 2010, three Latvian-Russian pilots flying food in for international peacekeepers in Sudan were heading from Darfur's Nyala airstrip to their rented villa downtown. Suddenly, several 4x4s swerved into their route, blocking the road, and gunmen forced them to the floor, kidnapping them. It was the second such incident in Sudan in a month: In July 2010, the "horseback

devils" of the Janjaweed militia had abducted and beaten a Russian pilot
shipping supplies to UN/African Union peacekeepers in Darfur, having
forced his aircraft down at gunpoint during takeoff and dragged out and
pistol-whipped the three rebel commanders he was also secretly transporting. From being expendable, among rebel groups airmen like Mickey
are now highly prized both for their ransoms and the bargaining power
they represent.

Unusually, in both these instances the airmen were recovered swiftly,
before any public ransom demands had been made; and though news
reports are vague as to how or why the men were released, a deal with the
militias seems likely. The flight boycott of Somalia that followed the
deaths of an entire Byelorussian crew in 2007 meant a lot of cargo never
got carried and a lot of money never got made. And in Darfur right now,
there is simply too much cash at stake to risk a kidnap turning into a
murder.

There is, however, another possibility. Viktor Bout hinted that "huge
forces" were behind the recovery of his gunrunning Il-76 crew captured
by the Taliban in the mid-1990s; indeed, it's widely believed that a quid
pro quo deal was struck to begin supplying the Taliban with arms in return for their release. And with Russia supplying arms and mercenaries
to the Janjaweed's backers in the Sudanese government, it would be all
too easy to see both incidents as simply ways of hurrying up the next delivery or putting pressure on price. They certainly wouldn't be the first
Islamist militia to wrap cash and kidnapping up into an offer that ex-
Soviet cargo operators just couldn't refuse.

If you're wondering why airmen would take the risk with jobs like
these, whoever's prepared to fly over Africa gets fat bonus commissions,
and Mickey admits with a shrug that the rewards from government contracts, humanitarian aid, raw-material transport, and ad hoc business
make even the risk of kidnap and violence worth taking. And meanwhile,
the men and the metal and the extra tons of overloaded cargo just keep
falling from the sky and disappearing into the bush at gunpoint.

IN A LOT of ways, Katya Stepanova is Mickey's opposite—a live wire, a
respectable businesswoman running a successful business according to
the rules. She pays her taxes and has a landline and a postal address; she's

great, runs a transparently honest company; and most of all, she's full of infectious lust for life where Mickey is often downbeat, obscure, vague, and comfortable with his silence and his worst-case scenarios.

Still, the picture even she paints of that generation's progress across the continents after the motherland set them free without a paycheck or a pension is a sobering one. She talks me through a lineup of her family friends and what's happened to them since they first came out here to fly cargo. There they were, young and strong, smart cookies and crack aviators, mechanics, loadies, and navigators. And then, like Iggy Pop's Dum Dum Boys, they begin to fall in a grim roll call of casualties. Bad luck, bad calls, and the wrong plane.

"There's this guy, he died in the Antonov crash in Luxor a couple of years ago. He's one of the guys at the bottom of Lake Victoria—yeah, that was one of Evgeny's crews. Some got kidnapped in the DRC, nobody ever paid the ransom. Another one's dead, another just disappeared, I don't know what happened to him . . ."

The crews all know one another from way back, she says. From the same towns, they've all been colleagues, and friends, flying the same planes for years all over the world. Then they came to Africa and worked as hired hands—different planes, different crews. A huge number are dead or missing.

I'm stunned for a moment, recalling Mickey's first conversation with me, the way he counted these devils down on his fingers, like a man biding his time here in this world before bowing to the inevitable and heading off into the water, the fire, and the hereafter with one of them. Here they are, his brothers gone before. It's like a family tree in horrible, inverted negative, in which instead of one common ancestor multiplying to produce generations of offspring, the logic is reversed and a whole generation of men produces a single heir, the sole survivor of twenty years of flying these foreign skies.

It pisses Katya off, she says, that all this work can be done and all these sacrifices made by good men in the name of getting their job done, and at the end of it, "all people want to talk about is gunrunning, like that's the only thing they're carrying."

She reminds me that nobody ever wants to investigate these air operations, or the crews' fifteen tons of cash cargo, when they're using them to take more food to more starving refugees than any other crews, aviation outfits, or airlines, big or small, could ever hope to match; or that without their constant flights here and there, on- or off-record, much of places like East Africa would simply grind to a halt.

This is not just a figure of speech. In 1960, when Belgium granted it independence, the Democratic Republic of Congo (then called Zaire) boasted ninety thousand miles of navigable roads. By 1980, independent for two decades and with the highway-maintenance budget having quadrupled, there were only six thousand miles. By 2006, Kemal Saiki, a UN spokesman briefing the media on a passenger plane crash, said that the Democratic Republic of Congo did not even have two thousand miles of roads and that for many people, traveling around the country by aircraft, using small, wildcat aviation outfits, is the only option. Today, with just a few hundred kilometers of road left outside of the capital Kinshasa, people and goods find themselves back where they were in the late 1800s, chugging slowly down overgrown rivers in perilously overloaded barges straight from Conrad's *Lord Jim*.

In Uganda, the most stable, most developed country in the region, there used to be trains. Today, following a disastrous attempt at privatization, the service is suspended indefinitely, tracks now overgrown with weeds and covered with mud, and even having become home to expanding market squares and auto-repair shacks.

Even when you *can* travel by land, you're hostage—often literally—to thieves and bandits. Here, transport companies build in a margin of 33 percent of their goods that they assume will be stolen before the cargo reaches the recipient at the other end. That, of course, means higher prices for the surviving merchandise—both to compensate for these losses and to pay higher insurance premiums. And often that means the produce is priced out of the market. Simply nobody at the other end—in an area in which poverty is legion—can afford to pay a whole third higher than the market price. So they either go without or they steal and buy on the black market. The whole cycle begins again.

American reporter Denis Boyles came out here in the 1980s and interviewed one of the last of the Air America generation, an American bush pilot named George Pappas, tooling his beat-up DC-6 from conflict to conflict, chasing the sweet deal at the end of the rainbow. One of Pappas's clients, a Zairean businessman, told him, "The pilots here are like sharks. They make excuses and wait until we need them very badly, and then they raise their rates. It is very difficult, very expensive." Boyles claims to have been informed by one of these pilots that "ninety percent of the cargo he carries is, one way or another, contraband." The real number, he says, was even higher.

In Africa, whatever you're carrying, you skip a whole lot of trouble, paperwork, and danger—as well as bandits, bribes, police, and military roadblocks—if you take it by air. As one small ad for a reputable Ugandan plane operator in Kampala's local freebie the *Eye* says: "You've a meeting in Arua. It's a 7-hour drive at least [and] you'll get home at night, exhausted. *If* you arrive home. Because 2,334 people died and 12,076 were injured on our roads in 2008. So charter a plane and keep your accountant happy. After all, how much is your life worth?"

Even in Russia itself, according to assassinated FSB whistleblower Aleksander Litvinenko, the secret police favored private-enterprise pilots with military experience for the *really* sensitive jobs, like moving explosives around the country from air base to air base. So prone to theft, prying, and graft were the road and rail networks that the chance of some small-time crooks nicking their consignment from a lay-by, only to stumble across the whole plot, was a chance they were unwilling to take.

But still, to many the idea of a connection between the business of states—wars, insurgencies, government policy—and these chaotic rogue cargo men seemed casual at best. They were hustlers, after all; man-with-van enterprises, nothing more. But suddenly, one afternoon in a luxury hotel in Bangkok, all that seemed to change.

On March 6, 2008, more than two dozen Royal Thai Police, in a sting operation orchestrated by the U.S. Drug Enforcement Administration, swooped down on a conference room on the twenty-seventh floor of a gleaming, steel-and-glass Sofitel hotel in the Thai capital and promptly arrested Viktor Bout, handcuffing him at gunpoint and holding him in one of the suites before taking him off to jail. In its indictment, the DEA charges that during a well-planned sting, Bout incriminated himself in a plot "to sell millions of dollars' worth of weapons [rumored to be Russian SA-model shoulder-mounted surface-to-air missile launchers and attendant ammo] to the Colombian narco-terrorists . . . the Fuerzas Armadas Revolucionarias de Colombia (FARC) to be used to kill Americans in Colombia."

Russian diplomats were livid, calling his detention politically motivated.

The Americans were jubilant. But there would be more twists to come than either could possibly have realized.

The indictment, which charged Vikter Bout with nine offenses including money-laundering conspiracy and wire fraud as well as trafficking, continued: "An international weapons trafficker since the 1990s, has carried out a massive weapons-trafficking business by assembling a fleet of cargo airplanes capable of transporting weapons and military equipment to various parts of the world, including Africa, South America, and the Middle East. The arms that Bout has sold or brokered have fueled conflicts and supported regimes in Afghanistan, Angola, the Democratic Republic of the Congo, Liberia, Rwanda, Sierra Leone, and Sudan."

Perhaps someone had been watching the skies over Latin America quite closely through the 2000s after all.

Then, just three months later, in July of that year, the Africa–Latin America connection was blown wide open, hitting headlines across the world when a Soviet-crewed Antonov seized in Sierra Leone as a result of an American investigation was found to contain a staggering six hundred kilos of cocaine belonging to a Venezuelan *narcotraficante* group using Africa as its distribution hub. At fifty thousand dollars a kilo, there's silly money for anyone with a rusty cargo plane and who knows the value of discretion.

Ironically, it seems the *narcos* know what the world's NGOs, governments, and international peacekeeping organizations have been slow to realize: that if you want a job done professionally and with no conflict of interest, it never pays to squeeze your suppliers. Crewmen seem to have been paid well for such journeys: The captured leader of Venezuela's infamous mob, the Valencia-Arbelaez organization, which was smashed by undercover U.S. DEA agents after it purchased a $2 million plane to run monthly flights between Venezuela and Guinea, claimed he was "paying my pilots $200,000 to $300,000 per trip." He could afford to: The cost of ex-Soviet cargo aircraft for sale and charter had, according to the *Moscow Times*, "plummeted because of the financial crisis." Reporting the bust, the *Moscow Times* discovered that "The [*narcotraficante*] gang hired a Russian crew to move the newly purchased plane from Moldova to Romania, and then to Guinea. Fuel and pilots were paid for through wire transfers, suitcases filled with cash and, in one case, a bag with $356,000 in euros, left at a hotel bar." No wonder men like Mickey can be talked into making a few extracurricular no-questions trips.

Again, the Russian Foreign Ministry thundered that it considered the pilot to have been "kidnapped," not arrested by the United States. Russian Prime Minister Vladimir Putin himself weighed in, telling the U.S. it had "overstepped its mark."

But between the lines, maneuvering of a more subtle kind was taking place. One operation down, one plane impounded. For investigators, prosecutors, and politicians, it must have felt like nailing jelly to a wall. Worse for the growing number of agents and monitors bent on proving and shutting down men like Bout, in their eagerness or frustration, the failures and lapses in their methods that Peter Danssaert had warned about began cropping up again. Ironically, this time it was the aviators who were edgy about shadowy conspiracies.

What Bout's associates, and indeed the Russian government, claim is a politically motivated U.S.-led smear campaign against him has resulted in a bizarre situation in which both sides are crying foul and alleging dirty tricks on the part of the other. In a message from his hideout, where he's taking refuge from CIA interest in him on what he claims is a trumped-up case, Bout's close associate and "brother" in business Richard Chichakli, who oversaw Sharjah's open-door boom time—tells me: "Victor Bout is just a person who may or may not have done wrong. That can be put to a trial in a court of law—and the U.S. will not have, nor will ever provide a ground for, an impartial trial. They have already spent more than $400 million on [hunting him down] and they cannot, just cannot, come up empty-handed. The politics says Victor should go to jail or die, and that will justify the action, make the great American experts look good, and give credibility to the U.S. and its stories. The evidence I have says exactly the opposite, and the U.S. government knows that."

Indeed, Chichakli—who, despite being the subject of many and varied allegations, has yet to be convicted of a single crime, and who points out on his Web site that the presumption in his case appears to be "innocent until ~~proven guilty~~ investigated"—claims the same covert political forces who'd like to see Bout behind bars or dead are playing some very dark games with him. He points to the fact that his apartment was broken into in 2009.

"The attack on my apartment in Moscow was the strangest thing, given that computers and documents were the primary target," he says.

"Who took it and why? Possibly the U.S. intelligence; could be the Russian intelligence, or [maybe] the Easter bunny." Then he drops a hint that there's more to the game than anyone yet knows: "Whoever took the things knew that I have a backup; they just wanted to know what I have available, and who should be worried about getting exposed. The funny thing is that they will never know, because what I have is what is keeping me alive at either side of the equation."

The plot thickened further in 2010 when a public-relations and lobbying company in New York and D.C. called Mercury LLC appeared to have issued a press release linking Bout to trafficking operations from the UAE.

Entitled "Ras Al Khaimah: A Rogue State Within the UAE?," it was seemingly issued on behalf of an exiled sheikh with designs on a victorious return. Yet when I contacted them about the release, they stonewalled. Then one employee denied that the release had anything to do with them (despite having their company letterhead at the bottom). Requests for clarification have so far gone unheeded.

The really curious thing is that Mercury LLC is a key part of the U.S. corporate-lobbying machinery, with access to U.S. Congress and legislators; and if they were also involved in a campaign to destabilize an emirate by "linking" it to lots of bad guys, it would be absolutely perfect if someone were arrested in a blizzard of publicity—someone like Viktor Bout, given Public Enemy Number One status and quickly "linked" to Ras al-Khaimah via a mysterious press campaign.

For their part, Bout's prosecutors, monitors, watchers, and opponents claim that he appears to be in denial, pointing to the masses of arms flights in and out of sub-Saharan Africa and Taliban-held Afghanistan he operated through the 1990s and early 2000s. They point to the charges on which he's been incarcerated and extradited to the U.S., still unproven at this time of writing—an alleged offer by Bout to procure missile launchers and drones for FARC "to kill Americans with." His defenders contend meanwhile that as the source of much of the world's cocaine and seasoned phantom-flight charterers themselves, FARC are just convenient bogeymen in a cynical DEA set-up.

For his part, when I coaxed him on it, Mickey was cynical about both sides. He said: He's a businessman, what do you expect? Just how big the gulf is between what we in the West mean by that word and what Mickey's generation understand by it became clear late one muggy and oddly silent Saturday afternoon in June 2010 at a small, godless garrison town turned municipal dump in Central Africa with one muddy track leading through it. I'd hooked up with Mickey once again en route to another meeting for a quick beer on the understanding that I'd "lend" him fifty dollars in exchange for his time. I soon began to wish I'd left it. We got into quite a heated exchange about it all at a makeshift table (cupboard door, two oilcans, skinny dog in its shade) beside a dust runway stalked by giant, reeking crane birds while we waited for Sergei to finish cajoling, bargaining, and pacing back and forth with the local officials (the "official" uniform round these parts apparently being Manchester United replica shirts and no shoes).

We'd been talking business. Mickey told me the same line I've heard from countless ex-Soviets scarred by the West's robber-capitalist plundering of Russia in the early 1990s. You don't get big in business by being nice—look at the West's magnates. Henry Ford. J. D. Rockefeller. Fritz Thyssen. Robert Maxwell. Take your pick. Hard to argue—and the fact that I'm only naming the dead ones we threw about just goes to show how rough my publishers' lawyers think the live ones can be. Well, I used the Klebnikov defense: Sure, these guys were robber capitalists, but look at what they built! They weren't just bastards, carpetbaggers, exploiters, and wheeler-dealers—they created industries, changed nations, built *empires.*

Mickey pointed out that Bout has done both these things one way or another, and as for empires, he took over swaths of airport land in the South African veldt as his global base.

I pointed out that changing nations could mean a lot of things, but I wasn't sure that illicit arms flights were quite within the spirit of the phrase.

Well, at this point I believe I was sort of shouting, and Mickey was sort of shouting back, if I recall, that he knew exactly what Western businessmen were like, because he and his friends and family had seen their work up close as they stripped Russia bare. It was unbearably hot suddenly, and people were looking, but I do remember him saying *"Biznesman* is *mafiya."* Then that the problem of a lot of people, not just in the West but back home too nowadays, is they just can't stand to see a hardworking Russian make good.

That, in a paragraph, in one overstressed and pissed-off little exchange, is the whole schism, really. And whatever Bout's done or hasn't done, however much in the way of blood diamonds, illicit arms, and black-market cargo he has or hasn't trafficked, smuggled, and brokered, the air-freight industry never, ever had a rock star before. At which point Wayne Rooney (number 10) and David Beckham (number 7) emerged from the hut with rifles and wished us a safe onward journey.

CHAPTER EIGHTEEN

Just Drop the Cash out of the Plane

Uganda, 2009

THE HIGHWAY that runs between Uganda's Entebbe airport and the capital, Kampala, is nicknamed Smoke Street for the acres of semisecret cannabis farm-and-wholesale operations, shielded from passing motorists by simple rows of palms and creepers. The location of these plantations is not a coincidence, as Smoke Street serves both the local and export markets.

Compact, bright, and home to garrisoned African Union troops, UN men, and almost everyone involved in aviation in East Africa, Entebbe town itself is where the exporters and consumers of this exceptionally potent weed—and much else besides—meet and mix in a number of very rough bars with rougher reputations.

The Four Turkeys bar is quasi-legendary among airmen, dealers, and whores, arguably the sleaziest pilot pit in the whole of Entebbe, which certainly puts it in contention for all of Africa; a twenty-four-hour bar-cum-pickup-joint conveniently placed for the air base, just in case any off-duty aircrew fancy loading up before they load up. It's said that this was where the Lake Victoria crash's doomed Il-76 crew was last seen alive, reportedly just an hour before they made their way across the early-morning runway to a plane that would never make it farther than the bed of the lake opposite. A beer before a flight is not considered particularly unusual by many crews like Mickey's, and after one recent crash, one Russian official even told Ernest Mezak, in exasperation: "So they were drunk, so what? The plane does everything by itself. The worst that could happen is the pilot trips over the bulkhead."

It's a hot wet night at the end of another rainy season. Across the way is the heavily patrolled perimeter of the combined military/UN/cargo air base. And in the fuggy night, Mickey is so face-meltingly stoned on a bag full of Smoke Street's finest that he can barely stand. I am here with five very loaded mercs—and all their languages appear to have mystically melded with mine into a series of half-finished gibberish, canny smiles of absolute recognition, and shouted exhortations to drink.

Scanning the dark, narrow room, I spot Ugandan hookers and a handful of tattooed South Africans with terrible teeth. (I read later that SA Special Forces operating in Angola found that local guerrilla scouts could smell the menthol of their toothpaste at fifty paces. They promptly stopped using it for the duration of their deployment—often upward of three months—and have teeth so bad they wear them as a badge of honor.) A team of migrant road diggers from the former Yugoslavia roll in. One character at the door offers to sell us loose Viagra. There's enough pungent skunk-weed aroma sweating through enough pockets to make my eyes sting.

Mickey is letting off some steam, shouting over the televised African football match, downing Club beers with vodka chasers so fast they don't touch the sides, and looking forward to a night on expenses in a collection of huts with towels just down the track. He's heard me on the phone telling someone sadly it was "a hell of a way to live" and keeps repeating the phrase with a proud smile. We've been talking, shouting, and communicating in a mixture of my comically decrepit Russian and his haphazard English—a mixture that regularly leads to chaos for crews like his in Africa, where air-traffic control often speak French as their second language and only have enough English, the international language of air travel, to ask Mickey in a panicked cry, "Are you speaking English?"

We sit and chat, swap tales about Uganda, Afghanistan, Russia, Germany, the DRC, Sudan, and Somalia, about his Soviet air force days and how Kabul is suddenly neck-deep in Chinese prostitutes. And before the booze takes over completely, I try to tell Mickey about the phone call

I got today from someone who clearly doesn't much care for my snooping around things at Entebbe airport and the army/UN base Mickey flies from, but frustratingly, he's not getting what I'm saying at all.

As far as warnings go, it was actually rather good-natured, nothing like the rough stuff that researchers like Brian Johnson-Thomas have endured. The well-spoken, African-accented voice was so disarmingly civil I genuinely thought it was one of the hotel staff at first. As far as I can recollect, because I wasn't writing it down, it went like this.

"Hello, Mr. Potter. How are you? Are you well, Mr. Potter? Because you know, we just want you to know we are concerned with your welfare. We want you to have a pleasant stay, not, you know, having any difficulties."

What kind of difficulties?

"Oh, don't worry, I am sure you will keep out of any dangerous situations. We're concerned for you to have an enjoyable stay in our country. Now, have a wonderful day, Mr. Potter, and we'll see you at Entebbe airport on your departure, but not before then, I'm sure."

Friendly chap, polite, and nobody I knew. Which intrigued me. Someone's interested. And I will find out who it is as soon as I can stand up and straighten out a little. But with the deadly timing of a low-level firebombing run, a bottle of African Nile beer is plonked down hard in front of me by Sergei's filthy, almost nailless hand. I lift it toward parched and buzzing lips. I realize, even as I tip my head back and drink it straight down, that I've switched off as I've relaxed into Mickey's world again; just like him and Sergei, I've stopped thinking too much about cause and effect.

Still, dealing with blue-chip companies and major governments on one side of the equation, and the cargo operators, plane owners, and crews like Mickey's on the other, these agents see the big picture better than most. And it's a big picture that shows just how few degrees of separation really exist between Mickey, out there amid the missiles and warlords, and our own daily lives.

A boyish, muscular, sandy-haired South African, Iain Clark looks more like a tournament tennis coach than an essential cog in the execution of global cargo contracts for a highly respected firm. His smart office is discreetly tucked away beyond a maze of empty corridors and dilapidated, abandoned offices in an unvisited corner of Entebbe airport's main building—so discreetly, in fact, that on the day I visit him, airport security either doesn't know of its existence or isn't telling. But a good twenty minutes after they frisk me and x-ray my bag, he's sitting at his desk, talking me through arrivals of the one São Tomé–registered Il-76 and the three banned white Antonov-12s permanently grounded outside.

As the Africa director of a respected and highly legitimate global air-charter agent, he's the man who calls up the guys with the planes, from Il-76s and Antonovs to Hercules or whatever it takes, when a job comes in from private clients, the military, or anybody else. But he's also got his nose to the ground and sees everything that happens out here and where it goes next.

Clark explains how one flight in spring 2010—arranged by a contact of his, Russian pilot turned Soviet Air Charter owner Evgeny Zakharov—underlines the anytime, anywhere, no-job-too-tough capabilities of outfits like Mickey's for clandestine missions.

"That very aircraft there, that Antonov-12, did a ransom drop recently for some pirates," he smiles, pointing to a photo of a Soviet-era plane with an Air Armenia logo on the side. "It flew from Entebbe, and they flew the money in—it was twenty million dollars—about three months ago. In fact, I don't know who the insurer [who commissioned the plane] was because it was all kept so secret, everybody kept everything separate."

The crew's mission, following orders from the Somali pirates by phone as they flew, is pure James Bond. The arrangements, dictated by the pirates through a chain of gofers, insurers, and cargo middlemen, recall the classic kidnappers' ploy of leading the ransom dropper to a succession of ringing phone boxes at different locations in order to hold off revealing their whereabouts until the last second.

The Russian-speaking crew was briefed on their mission, just like always. Only this time, one thing was different: They weren't to know their destination. Instead they were simply given a set of GPS coordinates—at a glance, they could tell it was somewhere over the waters off the Somali coast—and handed a cheap cell phone.

"They had to fly to certain coordinates given by the pirate ship," says Clark, turning to look out over the runway, his eyes gleaming. "The plan was, once they got those coordinates, they had to come in low at one thousand feet or whatever. At that point, one of the pirates would send them to a text message with new coordinates they had to go to."

The pilot and his crew shrugged. No problem. And if making a dash for it ever crossed their minds up there, flying over the world's biggest radar blind spot with a full load of fuel and twenty million dollars in small denominations in a box, then the thought passed quickly. The plane steered its course toward the GPS coordinates steadily: rising eastward, passing over Kenya and the wild borderlands of Ethiopia, then out over Somalia and low over the pirate-patrolled sea.

As they roared onto their destination coordinates, the phone in the navigator's hand buzzed. The SMS message was blank but for a new set of numbers. The pilot turned his plane in a wide arc and followed this new instruction. Keeping low, the crew's eyes scanned the water for boats, flares, RPG fire, anything. At this point, they could only trust it was not a trap.

The ritual was repeated. Then, at their next set of coordinates, they made visual contact with two small, fast boats in the water below, hundreds of meters apart. The navigator's hand phone rang, and an accented, English-speaking voice said simply: "Don't stop. Just drop the fucking money."

That was the signal the loadmaster had been waiting for. The strongbox and its attached parachute were already positioned, the loading ramp open, affording him a spectacular, dizzying view. He cut the lines and twenty million dollars vanished into the sky; he watched it sail down. The last thing he saw as the pilot turned the plane for home was a surge in the bright blue water as the pirate boats pulled back their throttles with a loud *Vrrrrmmm!*, speeding in to converge on the strongbox.

"And that was it," smiles Clark. "They picked up the cash and off they went."

Because the whole operation was carried out on such a need-to-know basis, nobody—even Clark—sees more of the picture than what takes place in their stretch of the pipeline. But the aircraft's operator, Johannesburg-based Russian aviator and businessman Evgeny Zakharov, tells me the ransom was dropped on behalf of none other than world-famous insurance underwriters Lloyd's of London. "Rather than paying out on the insurance from the lost ship, Lloyd's preferred to give a percentage of the new-for-old cost of that insurance payout direct to the pirates and get the ship back," he explains. "It sounds James Bond, but it's not. For a Russian pilot in Africa, it's normal, just a day's work. You know something? We've done many of these ransom drops for Somali pirates, and for an ex-Soviet air force pilot used to dropping tanks from his plane, believe me, opening the door and pushing a one-hundred-kilogram box of money out is easy."

It's an intriguing counterpoint, and one that highlights the way big Western shipping businesses and former Soviet pilots, legitimate blue-chip multinationals and Somali pirates, coexist, if not happily, then in a way that keeps the wheels of everybody's business oiled and rolling. In my naïveté, I'd always believed that when governments proclaimed, "We never pay ransoms to kidnappers," they actually meant no ransom would be paid to the kidnappers. Instead, they mean that of course a ransom will be paid—but they'll leave it to the private sector. And while a spokesperson for Lloyd's of London told me they could not confirm whether they'd financed that specific drop without more details on the ship and its policy, these ransom drops to Somali pirates are fast becoming routine for the insurance industry.

It's also a fascinating snapshot of the realities of global business, the weird force field of mutually repellent opposites that keeps Mickey flying in the middle. When transactions are regularly called for between perhaps the world's most august, venerable finance institution and AK-47-toting cutthroats in speedboats off the Somali coast, there's only one mutually acceptable, universally adaptable, ready, willing, and able group of middlemen. And it sure as hell isn't UPS.

The shift toward private contractors that has private security outfits like Blackwater and DynCorp playing soldiers in Iraq has given small, unaccountable, and hard-to-trace outfits like Mickey's an increasingly important role in international policing, hostage-release, and peacekeeping efforts, just as they do in humanitarian relief. Between 2005 and 2006, with recruitment targets regularly being missed, the U.S. military began to loosen its rules in an effort to remain viable. Top recruitment bonuses were doubled to forty thousand dollars; the age limit was raised from thirty-five to forty-two; medical standards and rules on past criminal records were loosened; and still they found themselves needing to outsource more "noncore" duties. The delivery of military equipment, cash, construction materials, anything and everything to Afghanistan and Iraq was already up for tender from private companies; now it was spreading like wildfire to anywhere a job needed doing without the risk of what the U.S. State Department termed "entanglement."

Open your eyes to it, and Mickey's world is the one we all inhabit: a world where Blackwater, Halliburton, DynCorp, ArmorGroup, and the other private military companies are making hay in Africa and the Middle East by doing the things national armed forces would normally do. January 2011 saw the news break that Saracen, a private security firm linked to Erik Prince of the private military-contractor outfit formerly known as Blackwater, was training private armies in Somalia. (Saracen International is based in South Africa, with an offshoot headquarters in where else but Uganda; intriguingly, Prince's spokesman denied he had "a financial role" but was, like Mickey, mainly involved in "humanitarian efforts" and fighting pirates off the Somali coast.)

The thing is, for anyone watching the skies, it wasn't breaking news at all. There had been a private air force—or rather, dozens upon dozens of them—out here for some time.

Indeed, it's increasingly difficult for governments anywhere to talk credibly about the "good" or "bad" work that teams like Mickey's do, while the global brands we all love to wear, drink, walk on, talk on, and watch source their labor from developing—read lawless and highly corrupt—economies, and need their own instant transport and logistics infrastructure to match. Of course dirty work is going to need doing by someone so the rest of us can benefit. And any pronouncements about "dodgy" air operators who'll take anyone's shilling begin to sound very hollow indeed.

And it strikes me that this is what all the monitors, the record keepers, the global policemen who watch and wait and report on "shady deals" or allegedly inconsistent paperwork, rogue plane registrations and illicit flights, "merc" crews, and secret ops are missing.

It's not just that some of these hush-hush flights and supply drops in unstable places might in fact be made in the name of completely legitimate causes; but that the very willingness of some outfits to enter into unconventional business dealings, do things that aren't necessarily by the book, and take no-questions-asked mission briefs from unknown clients that the monitors lambaste is precisely what makes them the only game in town when the good guys want a bit of *Mission: Impossible*–style swashbuckling done, too.

As Iain Clark says, "They're easy to deal with, you know? If they can do it, they'll do it. It's not like they're full of shit, basically, like a lot of the Western crews, where it's, "Uh, no, the book says this, so, no, we can't do

that'—sometimes just to be difficult. The Russian crews are quite oblig-
ing, you know? It's like, 'Don't worry about it!'"

Talk to anyone on the ground from Darfur to Dubai, and they'll agree
with Clark—perhaps off the record—that there's a place for small, wildcat
crews like Mickey's too; indeed, the loyalty and admiration they command
is genuinely surprising.

Before I leave Clark's office to navigate the endless abandoned corridors, dead ends, puddles, hanging wires, and shut doors that will finally
open and spill me back out into the daylight, he throws a copy of the
Ugandan news journal the *Independent* across the table to me. "Read that,"
he says. I pick it up. The cover story is a report into the causes of, and alleged government cover-up involving, an Il-76 that exploded and crashed
into Lake Victoria in 2009, reportedly on a secret mission to Mogadishu
for another U.S. contractor. "Jeez, it makes me angry," says Clark. "I
mean, these guys really have their knives out for the Russian guys, the
crews, and the operators."

For the first time, this relaxed, infectiously good-humored man shows
a flash of indignation as we part. "I've always found Evgeny Zakharov—
whose company operated that flight—to be pretty much aboveboard," he
says. "But read that article, and it lays the blame on his planes. Now, I've
never known him to cut corners. A lot of people who operate Russian
planes will go with documents they're given, if you know what I mean—
and if the documents have been falsified, so be it—but I've never had a
problem with him or his aircraft."

By the time I've been searched again and am blinking in the African
afternoon heat on the other side of Entebbe runway's razor wire, Clark's
impassioned defense of the crews I've come to know seems somehow mis-
directed. Because while I was waiting to be frisked and ejected, I read the
report he threw across the desk. And I don't think it has its knives out for
the crew or airline. The real villain of the piece is a very different one. And
like the Mafia itself, it's far more subtle and elusive than any one man.

The demise of the Candid and the men on board was almost crueler for
being so sudden and so complete. Unlike Sharpatov, unlike Starikov and
Barsenov even, the crew never knew what happened. And they never had
a chance to play their one and only ace—their supernatural skill with a
1970s-vintage Ilyushin.

The plane took off from the notoriously slippery tarmac at Entebbe without a hitch, bound for Somalia. It was 5:14 A.M., the March morning still had its bite, and the radar was down again—it had recently had a complete overhaul, but the new, upgraded system had mysteriously stopped working after only four months. The surface of the great lake was smooth, only birds and early-rising local fishermen punctuating the calm through which the huge plane tore upward, still low enough over the water's surface to cause ripples. The men on board were tired but they were professionals, and Mogadishu was a run that always made you concentrate, focused you. Tense, but not too tense. Nothing they couldn't deal with. That one Russian word: *nichevo*.

That's when the universe opened its jaws and swallowed the men and their plane whole.

If there had been radar, the operator in the control tower would have seen the plane abruptly drop from the screen just five and a half miles out over the lake. In fact, there were eyewitnesses—the fishermen, two of whom were nearly killed by pieces of the plane as it exploded, disintegrating in midair. One saw fire coming from the left side of the plane before it exploded. One saw the plane's lights were out a split second before the blast. But it was all so fast, said everyone. In the blink of an eye (and some had the order of impact and breakup differently) the Candid had "split down the middle like an egg," an American salvage technician said later— and plummeted, flaming, into the lake.

It lies there still, buried under twelve meters of silt and mud, itself beneath many meters of water, literally inside the lake bed. X-rays of the earth show the fuselage, sure enough split down the center, and maybe a piece of tailplane sticking up at an angle like a question mark.

The question mark won't go away. And while the newspaper report Iain Clark threw across to me is hardly generous to expat airmen or the charter airline, Evgeny Zakharov's former outfit, Aerolift, it reads to me like the indictment of an ecosystem.

Sure, the piece does point to alleged failures of maintenance on the part of the company, which appears to have been flying a plane twelve years beyond its end-of-service life; more tendentiously, it makes claims about the airmen. First, that navigator Evgeny Korolev had a forged navigator license. "Navigator Licence First Class No. 000316 which you have in your possession was issued on 08 October 1996 in another navigator name," wrote the Ukrainian aviation authority in response to inquiries by the *Independent*. "Please, pay attention to the fact that the photo of Korolev is stuck over the stamp. Therefore the certificate in the name of Korol should be considered illegal." Second, that copilot Alexander Vochenko hadn't flown an Il-76 since his Soviet air force days back in the 1980s and 1990s, and it's never been established whether Captain Viktor Kovalev had ever actually possessed an airline pilot license. And yes, it reports claims that the crew were witnessed drinking in the Four Turkeys at three A.M., then reporting for flight duty at four. But it ends with a cry: "People's lives are worth more than a few extra dollars' profit."

In response, the community is quick to rally to the defense of men, the airline business, and the aircraft itself. Iain Clark's anger at what he called the "knives out" report in the paper is echoed by others I talk to, including Stepanova.

"The Il-76 in Lake Victoria was in very good condition—very good!" she rages.

A friend of the navigator Korolev and an acquaintance of Vochenko and Kovalev, she was with the crew the week before. They were new arrivals, and she helped them open their Ugandan bank accounts and had lunch with them the week before the flight. She says she'd agreed to let them use her home address to open the accounts, and then heartbreakingly, one day in September 2010, a year and a half after the crash, received a bank statement for one of her dead friends through the post.

"I couldn't stop crying," she says. "It was so sad for me. I flew with him everywhere. He even taught me to drive . . ."

Even the facts are less clear-cut than the article suggests. "Evgeny Korolev had his license," she says. "He might have had his revalidation to one of the African countries forged, which I doubt, but if he'd forged it, how would he have got away with flying in South Africa before that? I'd flown with him many times over the Congo, in fact I was sitting with him most of the time, and he was in the cockpit with my friend over DRC the flight the bullets nearly got them."

Perhaps, I venture, and it wouldn't be for the first time, the Ukrainian aviation authorities' records are inaccurate, as well as the Ugandans'. Or it may be that for jobbing airmen, the rush—indeed the need—to get on a crew, get flying, and make a paycheck as soon as possible on arrival in a new country—at the same time as trying to sort out their affairs and get their paperwork in order—means men take to the air before the official t's are crossed, just like the otherwise law-abiding motorist who drives for a few days while his car tax is "in the post." And when it all goes wrong, it looks bad to observers, regulators, and reporters used to getting definite answers.

Even Mickey shies away from some of the stuff that goes on. Ask him to name names, and he'll just say, my guess is as good as his. He mentions the Il-76 at the bottom of the lake. "Who knows what caused that crash? Sabotage? Terrorists? Cargo? The plane? Maybe nobody even knows what was on that plane. The cargo they were paid to take, yes. What else? Probably the crew didn't know really what it was. All of these things. Nobody knows."

But for all the doubts they throw on the validity of the crew's paperwork, and indeed on the condition of the plane, the investigative team at the *Independent* save their real ire for the postcrash cover-up, and for the politics of a system that can allow men like these to fly and die on a secret, quasi-military mission to Somalia in the name of getting their dirty work done cheaply, and then let them—literally—take the fall.

They also point toward a more sinister culprit: an illicit, or at least highly discreet, network of secret dealings between their government, its military, and the warlords, terrorists, and pirates of the Congolese hills that use Mickey, and crews like his, as often unwitting, deniable gofers, mules, and fall guys—with the UN's MONUC base in Entebbe as a fig leaf.

And just as with the Somali ransom drop, the crews' missions into these rebel-patrolled hills tell the secret story behind some of the most high-profile headlines in recent years.

ACCORDING TO THE newspaper's news editor, Patrick Matsiko wa Mucoori, with whom I'm sitting less than an hour after leaving Iain Clark, the frantic rescue mission by locals and airport staff was aggressively hampered by the police and the army who appeared, just like the military and secret service agents throwing a security blackout around the runway in Belgrade back in 1996. Out on the lake, he says, they prevented rescue teams, and even local fishermen, from trying to make their way over to the burning, and rapidly sinking, wreckage.

The more Patrick talks, the more it becomes clear that while the planes, the owners, the crews, the operators are all convenient targets for investigation, their presence is a symptom, not the cause, of a deeper malaise.

Patrick's office at the *Independent* is, it has to be said, pretty grand: darkwood tables, bright, contemporary decor, PCs and polished steel. I tell him so. "It's not my office," he laughs, knocking back the last of his strong tea and cassava. "This is a meeting room. Here we can talk more privately." The privacy (heavy door, no window onto the street, airlock-style reception) is necessary, he explains, because of the constant attentions and office intrusions of government spies at the newspaper offices. "You might have noticed one or two outside the entrance," he smiles. "They just stand there looking like they're waiting for friends, then report on their mobile phone who they see coming and going. They figure they'll spot who's leaking us stories that way.

"They get in, too—you see someone in the office and you assume it's just a new person or a visitor, and it turns out they got in and were looking around." He sighs. "Then after that, we usually get raided and the police take our computers away. Again."

Stocky and smartly dressed with a neatly clipped mustache, Patrick is every inch the image of the urbane city slicker, with a confident, unflappable manner. And since the Il-76 came down, he's needed all the confidence and steel he can muster. Because part of the reason the government is currently so interested in him is his team's investigations—prompted by the Ilyushin's explosion over the lake—into the vast amount of smuggling, profiteering, corruption, trafficking, and mercenary adventuring carried out by the Ugandan authorities themselves.

The Ugandan government and the military, he says, use private operators to do covert work in neighboring Congo, Sudan, and Chad as well as Somalia to the north. Many of these government-chartered flights involve private racketeering and looting by the army's top brass. Given the very visible United Nations presence at Entebbe airport, and its use as a staging post for secret U.S.-led private military missions into Mogadishu, the government is understandably keen to disguise its use of these former Soviet planes.

"I started thinking, why didn't our Civil Aviation Authority guys on the runway check whether these crashed Russian planes were okay to fly before they took off, like they would with any other plane?" Patrick says, though it's worth pointing out that the cause of the crash still remains in doubt, and the aircraft's condition is no more likely to be guilty than anything else. "My CAA source told me, 'These planes are parked at the air force base part of the airport. So they get in these planes, they taxi for takeoff from the military base, then at the last minute come onto the airport runway—where our jurisdiction begins—then off!' As they are actually taking off, you only hear the base commander—that is the commander in charge of the air force base—calling the head of the CAA, saying, 'We have this flight, it's going *now*, please clear it immediately!' So the CAA says no, how can we clear it, we need to inspect it. But when they do, the air base commander calls the minister of defense—he makes a telephone call, and that's it. He just tells them, 'No questions! Just clear these flights from the military base. We take responsibility, but don't ever ask to inspect them, just clear them to take off, understand?' And of course nobody but the crew and soldiers is allowed anywhere near the air force base."

Already alerted by the shroud of secrecy around the lake on the night of the crash, Patrick did some digging. What he and his team found was a huge operation, bigger than anyone had suspected: a regular, top-secret trade corridor involving Ilyushin and Antonov crews being commissioned by the army and government to fly between the lawless, warlord-controlled uplands of the eastern Democratic Republic of Congo and Kampala, carrying priceless natural resources that they could sell for cash to line their own pockets. Clandestinely logged timber, gold, and silver, and even animals and animal furs, are all part of the traffic.

"Eastern DRC, which borders Uganda, is a rebel area, there's no military there, no government—completely lawless," he explains. "It's almost like Somalia; it's in the hands of warlords. You just deal with different warlords and bandits here and here and here. So you deal with them, and of course you buy the goods cheaply, pay them, and come back. Now, the Ugandan army spent about five years in Eastern DRC, claiming that they were pursuing Ugandan AVF rebels that were based in the Congo. So they captured the eastern Congo—it was actually under the control of the Ugandan People's Defense Force—and started transporting minerals and wood and so on using these planes. And the UPDF formed alliances with various rebel groups. Eventually, due to international pressure, the UPDF left, but it maintained its ties with those rebel groups, and now they go in on these Russian planes, buy timber from local militia leaders in Congo—and you can buy *anything*—and just come back."

For insiders, the logistics are breathtakingly simple. You want a local warlord to source the goods for you? Call up an old contact from the conflict, they're all there, and they're all on the same mobile provider as you. You need backup, hired muscle? That's okay—you're the army, just bring a few colleagues or command a few of your men.

Now, the plane. That's easy, you're the army, you've got dozens to choose from, right? Except you want to do it on the cheap because whatever you spend here is coming out of your own sweet pocket, and you certainly don't want to have to ask too many people's permission—less still have the UN contingent camped across the grass ask where the plane is they were going to take on an aid drop today. Bad look. So you hire an independent air operator and a team of mercs—probably one of the Russian, Ukrainian, Bulgarian, or Byelorussian teams—with a giant plane that can fit, say, a platoon of men, a couple of jeeps, and a whole lot of contraband timber. Call it an Ilyushin-76, hypothetically, for the sake of argument. And make sure the guys you're dealing with have that can-do spirit Iain Clark mentioned. If the price they quote is $3,000 an hour, offer to double it on invoice if they'll split the difference. If they'll do it, you pay $6,000 from the army's coffers and collect your $1,500 personal cash-back to share among your men, with maybe a crafty $250 for your commanding officer to look the other way while you're gone. Everybody's happy.

Still, the cheapest planes might not always be the newest or the best maintained. They probably wouldn't pass the CAA's airport runway inspection. No sweat—just use your triple-security, razor-wire, well-guarded, UN-populated air base. And if the CAA boys get uppity on takeoff, that colonel you bunged the hundred-dollar bill to will put them in their place. Hell, cut him in on the proceeds later, why not. With margins this big—and we're talking hundreds in return for every dollar invested—there's plenty to share around.

Patrick continues: "That's how simple it is. First, make contact with your rebel leader. Go armed—contract a local or use your own soldiers—then come with a plane. Your warlord will be armed, and let's say you want timber, he'll just find a road, and say, 'Okay, from here, all this timber, take it.' And your men just roll it and put it on the plane, because these planes are huge."

In fact, it's quicker and easier to make a private mission for black cargo than it is to go by scheduled civilian airlines: no papers, no passport, no visa, no immigration, no customs, and—best of all—no limit on what you carry back, says Patrick. It's all very civilized, too. "You can do it all in a day, or you can stay over—all the warlords have comfortable places where they put our guys up when they come over—and to their contacts they're only ever a mobile phone call away."

Who'd have thought it? In this bright new world of the consumer as king, even the die-hard Congolese guerrillas resisting government forces in the hills and jungles of Central Africa put twenty-four-hour customer service at the very heart of their business plan.

And that's it. Except for customs—and let's even assume you've got some independently wealthy and heroically incorruptible customs guys here for a moment, highly theoretical guys who are immune to bribes. Hmm, could be a problem. Then again, no. Remember, stupid, you're in the army.

"Customs can't go into the military/UN cargo air base," says Patrick. "It's not civilian jurisdiction. It's army and defense ministry property. Soldiers guard it, and if a customs officer goes there, they just arrest him for trespassing. Trespassing! And"—he laughs at the irony of it all— "jeopardizing national security!"

The clock is ticking, Patrick's on deadline, and his editor's getting antsy for this week's news pages to hit the press, so we say good-bye. I decide to walk home and take my chances with the snitches, to see if I'm followed. As I step out into the overcast, red-earth-and-tar patchwork of Kanjokya Street, hobbling between termite mounds and potholes and wondering which of the loiterers in the wet dirt road is the army spy, I'm splashed by a camouflage, open-topped UPDF jeep doing its best to circumvent the foot-deep holes and the Friday rush-hour traffic. In it are four men in tailored suits and jewel-tipped sunglasses carrying antiquated wooden rifles over silk-clad shoulders.

There's no pavement, so I step carefully between road and grass, jeans getting splattered with mud. I turn around at the corner and look back. The guy reading the paper has folded it up and is looking past my shoulder, and there's a man regarding me steadily while he talks away on a mobile phone at the junction. Then again, I'm a wet, muddy *mzungu* on foot in a country where even the hardest-up local trader would rather flag down an illegal *boda-boda* moped ride, so of course *everyone's* looking. Then the rain starts again and I stumble between torrents and traffic, wondering about that anonymous Ugandan voice on the phone who wished me a safe stay. But now there are too many people walking my way to be sure of anything at all.

WHAT ALL THIS means for monitors of illicit activity is something most can't even begin to fight, even though men like Peter Danssaert and Brian Johnson-Thomas have long known it and have seen it again and again, in Belgrade, in Uganda, in Afghanistan.

The problem is this: Mafia activity is by its very nature against the interests of the state. We're used to thinking in terms of "families" and "gangs"—tuxedoed Sicilians making offers we cannot refuse. So when the state itself gets in on the act, as it did in early-1990s Russia, late-1990s Serbia, and in our own time Afghanistan, where President Hamid Karzai's inner circle, including his warlord brother Walid, stand accused of facilitating "Afghaniscam," awarding contracts, and plundering coffers at will, nobody quite knows the difference anymore between organized crime and economic policy. This appears to be true in Uganda.

A UN report entitled "Illegal Exploitation of Natural Resources and Other Forms of Wealth of the Democratic Republic of the Congo," published back in 2002, sums up the reach of this private-enterprise shadow state and its devastating effect.

> The elite network operating out of Uganda is decentralized and loosely hierarchical, unlike the network operating out of Rwanda. The Uganda network consists of a core group of members including certain high-ranking Ugandan People's Defence Force officers, private businessmen and selected rebel leaders/administrators . . . The network continues to conduct activities through front companies . . . Each of these companies may concentrate on one or two commercial niches, though these may change. The role of the companies is to manage their respective niche activities by assembling the personnel, logistics and occasionally the financing for the operations . . . The network generates revenue from the export of primary materials, from controlling the import of

consumables, from theft and tax fraud. The success of the network's activities in the Democratic Republic of the Congo relies on three interconnected features, namely, military intimidation; maintenance of a public sector facade, in the form of a rebel movement administration; and manipulation of the money supply and the banking sector, using counterfeit currency and other related mechanisms.

Everything disappears into the network's ravenous jaws, and then into the holds of the giant cargo planes it charters. Wood from protected plantations; blood diamonds; coltan, a chemical highly prized by African exporters for its value to mobile-phone manufacturers; gold. Local butchers are forced at gunpoint to skin animals and hand over their hides to the network's fatigue-clad soldiers, and even live cattle is rustled, by stealth or force, from herders. And for their complicity, the suppliers, the local warlords, and tribal leaders enjoy the protection of UPDF troops, as well as gasoline, cigarettes, and arms, all exempt from taxation.

Sometimes the logic is so neat that even those most affected can't see it. Later tonight, I'll head to a hotel bar and watch some TV—BBC World, I think, but I can't be sure—and see a documentary on a woman who runs an elephant sanctuary. She's protected by soldiers because of the constant activity of armed poachers in the area and threats to her life, but complains that whenever she leaves her guarded headquarters on the reserve for a trip to town or abroad, "It's as if I'm being followed and spied on by poachers somehow, because they only seem to strike the very moment I go away." She regularly comes back, she will say, only to find that the soldiers she employs have been outfoxed by heavily armed ivory poachers who've raided the reserve, gunned down an elephant using military-grade Kalashnikovs, and disappeared with the ivory, apparently before the soldiers could locate and stop them. The soldiers keep a low profile in the doc, only to scratch their heads and wonder aloud to the woman how the mysterious poachers keep eluding their grasp. "They must be very clever," says one.

And I'll stare, and think, surely it can't just be me? Surely everyone here can see the big, bad question hanging in the air—a figurative elephant in the room? But the woman doesn't see it.

It seems to me like the perfect expression of the failure of agencies,

NGOs, and law enforcement alike to stop traffickers. In the face of the pursuit of profit by any means necessary, anyone thinking in terms of moral right and wrong—anyone looking for criminals—is blind. Like government, like reserve stewards: the unthinkable is happening right under your nose, courtesy of regular Joes earning a buck, and you're out looking high and low for the bogeyman. And the planes just keep coming and going, for the UN, the CAA, the military; for aid organizations and businesses. Wholly respectable and above-reproach operators are forced to compete with those who'll do anything, take anything, work for anyone, and artificially lower their prices because they're carrying secret cargo for cash.

Weeks later, in a rare bust, an unaccompanied shipment of two tons of ivory—317 elephant tusks—and five rhino horns will be seized at Kenya's Nairobi airport, having flown by cargo plane out of Entebbe in huge crates declared as containing fresh avocados. The prime suspect, an employee of the cargo operation, simply vanishes.

THE FUNNY THING is, I've met a few of these pilots, on both sides of the divide, and some who've moved between them, and they aren't bad guys—on the contrary. They're also pretty anxious to do the right thing if they can. So they're doing what everyone's always telling them they need to do to stay out of trouble, just as they had to back in the air force, and just as we all have to. They're keeping their heads down, working hard, and doing exactly what the authorities ask of them. If those authorities, if the state itself, is doing something wrong, they rightly ask, should somebody important not be doing something about that?

A week on. I'm standing on the wet perimeter track of Entebbe airport, looking out along the runway from which all flights—including, it is said, countless "merc" flights—depart and on which they land. To my left, the civilian airport. To my right, the military air base, with its containers stacked and ready for loading by soldiers onto flights to eastern Congo and, cuddled up next to them, its rows and rows of stenciled UN tents. Welcome to the world of advanced globalization. Welcome to the world where a mafia is not a mafia but is reborn as the state itself. Welcome to a place where even what is illegal is not illegal, if the network is doing it. The UN-Ugandan military base is for their use only; but the going rate for bribing your way to use it for a commercial flight is a mere $300 from the pilot.

Then again, if the network doesn't want it done—poking around like Patrick over at the *Independent,* or me here—it'll send someone to put a stop to it right away, legal or not. And right on cue, here's the drab green jeep, purring round the perimeter to check my ID, make a call, escort me away.

The neat rows of UN tents, huts, and offices are so close I could pick up a handful of gravel and break the windows, but uncannily, despite the howling noise of the engines, the unloading of loot in front of them, the soldiers and airmen scattering through the gates, the daily coverage of the smuggling ring in opposition newspapers, nobody in the UN camp seems to notice a thing. The network is, after all, the government. And these people are its guests. So like everyone in every mafia economy, they make nice. Play the game. Make their pacts and deal with their devils. Focus on the always-worthwhile bigger picture. And meanwhile here come the goons with guns and wraparound shades, and here, as we talk, comes another planeload of goodies from the DRC.

There are no absolutes, and everything is allowed if the right person says it is allowed. Out here, away from the tiny, exclusive gated community that is the first world, out here in the sweltering dusk of the developing world, big rights and abstract wrongs are outweighed by cash on the barrelhead.

CHAPTER NINETEEN

Getting Your Kicks on Route Il-76

Central Asia and the Caucasus, 2009

MICKEY DOES PLENTY of what he calls "pizza delivery" runs, too—a common feature of the routes over former Soviet territory from Afghanistan through the dusty wastes and old Red Army bases of the Central Asian 'stans and the Caucasus, as well as Africa—in which some cargo planes still take hitchhikers and drop off casual packages in lieu of there being any serviceable roads or functioning infrastructure. These are impromptu or short-notice landings and diversions, sometimes for fuel, sometimes for pickups and dropoffs, sometimes just for social visits. We'll remain on the ground just long enough for Mickey to run over to the terminal, hut, or patch of earth and point, and for the one, two, or three uniformed or squinting, shirt-sleeved men to shout and point and drive their flashing, bleeping truck up to the plane and rummage about and disappear again, waving.

These runs don't appear on anyone's flight plans, so wherever we land, pizza-delivery stop-offs are often a surprise for the conning tower, air traffic control, and even the runway cleaners and sleeping technicians (whose first indication that they're about to be landed on is when they see an Il-76 bearing down on them over the perimeter fence). They'd be just as big a surprise to Mickey's clients, bosses, shippers, and business partners if they knew.

Mickey's not alone. One European security contractor who's flown with these outfits on business for coalition support illustrates just how ad hoc many of the missions undertaken by pilots like Mickey are. "I was in an Il-76 en route to Afghanistan from an airport in Germany, or at least I thought we were en route to Afghanistan. But halfway there we just banked and landed with no warning on some godforsaken barren runway. The pilot himself leaped out and disappeared into the Nissen hut. He was back five minutes later, which was when I found out he'd just stopped as we entered this particular country's airspace and paid for over-flight permission using his own credit card! It was just like buying some petrol for the car."

Reporter Doug McKinlay, meanwhile, recalls an incident from one aid flight to northern Afghanistan during the first freezing post-invasion winter of 2002. "I'd traveled out there in an Il-76, stretched out on top of a pallet of tomatoes someone was sending as aid," he says. Once airborne, he found he wasn't the only noncrewmember on board. As McKinlay stretched out, he found himself greeted by "this creepy American pastor" who was along for the ride. The pastor explained he was heading out there doing a tour of the refugee camps and an aid flight was the only way to get him and his camera crew there from Dubai. There were warning signs in the way the man seemed preoccupied with his appearance, and kept bawling out his long-suffering personal assistant. But nothing prepared McKinlay for the bizarre spectacle of the pastor's attempt to engage with the locals he was there to help. "The whole thing was a circus," recalls the Canadian. "He was standing on stages in front of these starving people freezing their asses off and holding up boxes of food, telling them through the mic that whoever said they wanted to know about Jesus could have some food. The Afghans were just bewildered and he kept on asking for shows of hands for Jesus, then shouting that wasn't good enough, and the security goons kept beating on anyone who got too close to the food truck."

To add to the surreal scene, the pastor's assistant was "all hair spray, too much makeup, and high heels right in the middle of the refugee camp," recalls McKinlay. "Just in case the evangelical address to the camp was shown on local TV back home."

It was on the home leg, heading back toward Sharjah, that these unlikely Samaritans got their own first taste of just how flexible a crew used
to pizza runs can be. "So over Uzbekistan you could see this assistant
started looking a little weird," laughs McKinlay. "She tottered up to the
pilot and said she needed to use the bathroom. Now this is an old plane,
they've ripped almost everything out, so the toilet was a bucket. Plus she's
gonna do it around a bunch of journalists, the reverend, and eight
Byelorussian airmen. So she went back and pleaded with the pilot, and he
just said, 'Okay,' and banked this gigantic Ilyushin, found an airfield he
used to know from Soviet days right out on the plains, and landed it on a
dime." The grizzled airmen, the pastor and his entourage and one veteran
Canadian reporter all found themselves looking everywhere but out the
right-hand side of the plane as the assistant clattered down the steps in her
heels, then hobbling to a concrete shelter in the distance that the loadmaster had pointed her toward. "Two minutes later she emerges," laughs
McKinlay, "stumbles across the dirt trying to be ladylike, climbs back up
the ramp, and we're gone. That plane was on the ground for ten minutes,
max. But with the amount of fuel it takes to get that thing off the ground,
it had to be the most expensive piss in history."

The speed and agility of our load-offs, stopovers, and informal super-
market sweeps encapsulates everything that makes crews like Mickey's so
fundamentally perfect as business partners to organizations of all stripes.
Often, deals are done and loading handled so quickly to maximize turnaround and minimize red tape that the first time Sergei will audit or ad-
just the cargo—if he goes to it at all—is at cruising altitude.

Like any long-distance truck driver, Mickey's come to know the best
places to make convenient refueling stops, too. Indeed, he'll often divert
from his route specifically to refuel at what first appear to be little more
than glorified filling stations; places like Baku, the oil-rich former Soviet
republic of Azerbaijan's capital.

Fly with them and you'll notice this booming, freewheeling oil town
holds a special place in the hearts of many of these *Afghantsy* cargo dogs
and their business partners. There's something of the Here-Be-Monsters
about it for Mickey; the last bit of Caucasus before you enter Central
Asia. And with thousands of square kilometers of metronomic oil pumps
pushing black stuff out of the ground so manically, the suburbs are often
knee-deep in cheap fuel. On our final approach, I saw ragged men dip-

ping buckets into shiny back puddles in the bare earth by the roadsides to light their lamps and fire their tractors.

Low avgas prices, even by Russian crews' standards, make it the cheap-as-chips place to refuel a twenty-five-year-old superplane—especially when you're on a European aid run from Germany, the UK, or Scandinavia down into Afghanistan, Iraq, Dubai, Sharjah, Pakistan, or China. Receipts are plentiful and generously prepared. But one thing Mickey is far more circumspect about, and what puts the chills on just about everyone here you mention it to, is the illegal market in the other black stuff.

Baku, on the shores of the Caspian Sea, an inland sea covering more than 1.4 million square miles, is part of a watery trade crossroads linking Iran, Russia, Caucasian Azerbaijan, and the first of the Central Asian 'stans—Kazakhstan and Turkmenistan. Fed by Russia's Volga and Ural rivers, and home to the world's largest concentration of sturgeon—the fish whose caviar commands prices of up to sixteen thousand dollars for a single kilo—it is also a smugglers' playground with a long and dark history.

The city's organized-crime cartels were legendary even in pre-Soviet export-boom times, when one of its most feared enforcers was a young upwardly mobile *biznesman*, bank robber, kidnapper, trafficker, counterfeiter, and killer by the name of one Ioseb Besarionis dze Jughashvili—later known to the world as Josef Stalin. Today its growth as a freewheeling buffer zone between Iranian, Russian, and Turkish spheres of influence has, according to Russian diplomats, turned it into a thrilling, terrifying arms traffickers' paradise. But it is also home to one of the most powerful former-Soviet *mafiyas* on the planet: the caviar mafia. Though supposedly protected, the gourmet black eggs are increasingly in demand among the new rich of China, the Arab world, and Europe. According to the Convention on International Trade in Endangered Species (CITES), more than $25 million worth of illegal caviar is airlifted from these shores into the Arab Emirates every year, where it is bought and sold by Dubai's all-powerful organized-crime networks, with whom Baku's own institutionalized mob can do good, good business. The caviar, says CITES, is then shipped onward to hubs in Asia, North America, and Europe, where it is sold as being of lawful origin. From dirty to clean, as laundered as a Sharjah sheet.

Normally, of course, airport security would notice. But airport security just might not be Baku's high point. On one journey back out of Kabul, the guards' state-of-the-art bleeper detects some old ammo I picked up in Bamiyan, northern Afghanistan, and have hidden about my person as a souvenir. I'm stopped. We talk. They take one of the bullets away, wave me on through to the plane with the rest.

So the caviar heads somehow, and very quickly, to the UAE, global hub for planes, businesses, and Mickey. From where I'm crouching in the glass belly as we take off again and climb over the Caspian, the aerial view is spectacular: oil tankers and glittering blue water, and all the business connections laid out before us. We circle round, above the city center, and over Baku's upscale shopping district, where row upon row of empty upscale boutiques provide the perfect wash for all that money coming back; then past the swankiest hotels in town, the Baku and Absheron, where Chechen warlords were flown by Soviet-made cargo planes via Turkish Cyprus for rest and recuperation during the wars with Russia. There, says Russia's NATO representative Dmitry Rogozin, they received "Azerbaijani passports on which they could travel to Turkey or Russia on criminal business, while those who did not fancy long-distance trips could stay and earn money on the side through racketeering and drug trade, as Azerbaijan became a transit point for weapons supplies from Turkey."

Then up, into cloud, and toward the Gulf.

Rogozin talks of an illicit "air corridor" that was opened up between Cyprus and Chechnya via Azerbaijan and Georgia in 1995, a wormhole through which guns, troops, and cash could be teleported. But if the route and destination sounds familiar, then so do the men: rootless, international business types haunting the air-conditioned, high-class-escort-lined, luxury-branded malls and corridors of Dubai's hotels and palaces, rubbing shoulders with old armed forces, GRU, and JAJ pals; crews and captains of Sharjah-based planes, and captains of import-export industry from the former Soviet Union, Serbia, Britain, the USA, Europe, China, Japan, Australia. Indeed, stories of Il-76 and Antonov-operating cargo businessmen with checkered pasts in this "caviar mafia" are legion.

CITES says that these Dubai-based mafia groups coordinate the caviar smuggling by "forging documents and making false declarations to customs officials to obtain re-export certificates from local authorities." With a huge, speedy pipeline in hidden cargo capacity using Baku as a staging post on its way to and from whiter-than-white aid drop-offs and

Sharjah, Dubai, and Western Europe, not to mention Central Asian forg-
ers selling diplomatic IDs and Russian driving licenses at roadside markets, the risks are phenomenally low. But the rewards—a kilo that costs
twenty dollars to buy from a Caspian poacher retails for four thousand
dollars in New York—are sky-high.

So it's no surprise that feuds, murders, and double-crossings are common. Since the 1990s, guards and policemen who've attempted to stop
the trade have been assassinated, with the most deadly attack killing
sixty-seven people—twenty-one of them children—when a nine-story
apartment building for border guards in Kaspiysk was bombed. A few
years ago, a hundred-man mob raided a coast guard station on the Caspian and liberated confiscated caviar boats in what officials described as
part of "an ongoing war with the caviar mafia."

Unsurprisingly, some claim the link between the caviar *mafiya* and the
planes goes deeper than client-courier. One clearly bitter man claiming to
be an *avialegioner* wrote a letter to an African newspaper recently denouncing a Russian business associate as having very strong links with the
"black caviar mafia" at home in the former USSR. The mafia had, claimed
the man, lent him money to purchase the cargo aircraft he started out
with. "But because they have been in jail for some years [the operator] has
never repaid his investors' money. The problem is, now they are out of jail
and searching for him in order to get it back." But again, there were some
strange points in the letter that cast doubt not only on its credibility but
its origin. For one thing, the writer claimed in his letter that his former
associate had relocated to Africa as a way to remain out of reach of his
creditors in the mafia and "keep a low profile"—although if that's true,
then his base, the most GRU-haunted, Russian-speaking enclave in sub-
Saharan Africa would seem an odd choice of bolt-hole. The African telephone numbers supplied by the correspondent are disconnected (mobile)
or ring until they cut off (landline), while the e-mail seems to be dormant.
No wonder the newspaper to which it was apparently sent refused to
publish.

Indeed, one pilot on a Russian forum calls the writer "a very-informed
person with a good imagination and a bad upbringing." Of course, embittered former employees and business associates will say much, and even if
the letter did originate from the name given at the foot of the page, there's
no evidence that this is more than an attempt to smear a former business

partner—perhaps even to tar him with the same brush, fairly or otherwise, as Viktor Bout. I asked the subject of these accusations for comment,
but though he said he would respond, and though I chased him, I never
did hear back either way. And I can't honestly say I blame him.

In any case, a low profile is always good even for those on the legitimate side of the cargo business too—which is the vast majority of hardworking airmen and businessmen from ex-Soviet backgrounds.

Still, sometimes, unavoidably, Mickey's profile sinks lower than even
he would like. Downtime is the part he and the crew all dread, with a
Soviet-bred fear of famine. Nevertheless, it's a reality nobody, whatever
their connections, prices, or networking skills, can avoid completely. It
lasts as long as it lasts, too—for unlucky crewmen, there can be months
of trying to exist on the last paycheck, eking out an existence in some far-
flung corner of the developing world or a flat in Ulyanovsk until another
job comes up. Little wonder the pressure to take on jobs that look dodgy
or downright dangerous starts to tell.

Which is where Mickey and Sergei's entrepreneurial touch—their
shuttle traders' instinct for business within a business—pays off. When
something breaks, when a deal falls through, when there's simply no work
on and we're kicking our heels, their time is filled with "shopping"—
though not of the air-conditioned-mall variety. In late-2000s Kampala
and Jinja, we brokered deals together for ten-kilo sacks of this, cases of
that, paid in cash, got it into a rusty old Mercedes with a flatbed trailer,
and drove to the plane, lugged on and pushed down and covered over. The
next morning, he took me shopping at an open-air market in Kampala,
stacked high with bald car tires and bolts as big as your forearm, "for
spares."

Wreathed in the barbecue smoke, the tumbledown avionics marketplace straddles the muddy disused railway line by the side of the highway.
Festooned with garish, hand-painted ads and hoardings featuring lurid
approximations of Nokia phones, medical symptoms, pop stars, and
Heineken cans, these pile-it-all-on-the-dirt-floor markets are as close as it
gets to repair centers for the lower-end Antonov and Ilyushin jockeys
passing through. Gigantic, bald tires lie in heaps; dials and panels are
stacked and swept into table corners; wing and tailplane flaps weigh down
the canvas roof coverings in the African breeze; more bolts, screws, and
washers, nuts and clips, glisten among assorted tat (the front half of a VW

camper van, sawed off; dozens of "found" car registration plates from South Africa, Nigeria, Kenya; seats torn from an airliner).

"Everything's very cheap," says Mickey, "but only if you don't tell them how much you need it."

The stallholder says he had a flight recorder here once. I am surprised. "Who wants them?" I laugh, without thinking.

"Maybe somebody just wants theirs back," deadpans the merchant.

Only later, when I read about the cloud of uncertainty around so many crashes here, and the semi-illicit nature of some of the flights that have come down, do I realize he's not joking at all. If I was behind at least a couple of the flights that have come to grief somehow in Africa over the years, and about which the rumors of sabotage and weapons running refuse to die—and when clients include warlords, corrupt military, big business, and government interests from Somalia to the Congo—there's plenty of scope for pissing off the wrong people and racking up scores that need settling, as well as the paranoia and suspicion that lingers around any unexplained incidents. I'd want to get my flight recorder back from whichever fisherman found it, and pretty badly.

The make-do-and-mend attitude to using whatever you've got on hand spills over into other areas too. If we're short on time, we eat whatever's on board, and some of us—but never Mickey, and never Dmitry the navigator—take our bottles of beer, Coca-Cola, or spirits with us to finish during the flight. Once the flight's over, it's fair game for everyone, but on the wing, it's only Sergei who really unwinds—sometimes unravels—with the airborne partying, knocking back anything he can find among the cargo and from time to time hitting the aviation spirits.

For loadmasters, the job's pressures come in quicker bursts than most. They are the ones who must cajole, wisecrack, and charm everyone from local herders to militiamen and customs officials to airport baggage handlers into helping get everything in. They are the ones who need to remember what's where and who knows it. And if that means Sergei self-medicating to the brink of psychosis with whatever's handy, so be it. I've seen him sleep on the runway, in the shadow of the plane, joint in hand, and I've seen him drink to celebrate takeoff. On one flight he gashed his head so badly falling off the pile of crates where he'd been dozing that the skin on his temple opened like a hatch, and the hot, greasy floor began to stink like an abattoir with his congealed blood. He'd been drinking neat spirit and African *waragi*, or "war gin"—a potent, home-distilled alcohol made from yam or banana plants that regularly kills whole villages in East Africa. Even while we cursed, bandaged him, and poured water into his mouth, Sergei only woke up enough to mutter and turn over. I next spoke to him shortly after landing, where he appeared bright as a pin, though as pale, skinny, and bloody as a Times Square down-and-out. He coyly ruffled his bandaged wound as if I'd complimented him on a new haircut, and seemed quite baffled by my concern that he get to a doctor. After a while the others were pretty much leaving him to it. "Sergei is Sergei," shrugged Mickey when I told him.

Just how close Sergei came to death that day doesn't dawn on me until a few months later, when three Russian aviation technicians on the Indonesian island of Sulawesi die, having been found staggering, vomiting, and complaining of breathing difficulties. Toxicology tests will later confirm they were killed by drinking methanol—a highly toxic form of alcohol used for aircraft maintenance. In fact, Sergei falling off the crates midclimb because he was dizzy may have saved his life. In the Islamic hinterlands of Indonesia, Sudan, and Somalia, where drinking alcohol is illegal, potentially lethal local moonshine or, failing that, aviation spirit is the scourge of expat aviation guys.

One high-ranking Russian diplomat and Afghan war veteran speaking to me on condition of anonymity recalls garrisoned Soviet pilots out on "the spirit" in Kabul. In a curious twist, it was noticed by Soviet commanders that the pilots and crew who drank their aviation spirit, though they were often unreliable and occasionally died, never came down with hepatitis or parasites because they drank it instead of water, which was often unsanitary. It became an article of faith among veteran crews that methanol drinkers enjoy a net gain in lifespan. Still, through accidents, liver disease, or OD, it was a winter-warmer habit that would kill thousands.

And so Sergei drinks. And try as I might, I can't understand the continued allure of the life for men in their mid-fifties, or the need Mickey and the rest of them, one way or another, have for taking risks. Their very continued existence feels like an airborne contradiction to me, a Self-Preservation Society for kamikazes, an ultimate survival course for men who don't seem to fear death at all. Which concerns me greatly, because I'm a dedicated chickenshit with a healthy aversion to any kind of danger.

Sometimes the combined promise of the big payday and this unshakable faith in their own continued existence leads Mickey and the crew to take on the world's Premier League death trips. One day Mickey asks me, just casually, if I'd like to stow away, for a small consideration, on a flight to Mogadishu the next time he flies there. "See-It-and-Definitely-Die Mogadishu," as one expat pilot cracked to me, is officially the most corrupt, lawless, and dangerous place on earth, patrolled by pirates, stalked by the Islamist guerrillas of al-Shabab, and a graveyard for shot-down Candids. Even Soviet Air Transport's Evgeny Zakharov calls it the most dangerous of them all. "For operations in very dangerous places, like Somalia," he says, "people know what they're doing. We pay big, big money for people to fly there."

The Indian Ocean is regularly awash with cash, the strongboxes and parachute pods used for drops bursting on impact with the ocean occasionally. But if you believe Mickey, there's another side to it all, beyond the money, that makes Mogadishu both genuinely scary and weirdly exciting to fly into. We don't get it together this time. The UN's got it sewn up officially, and the crew have nothing on with them this week, though the Candids flying U.S. military contractors on Somali black ops are an open secret, as are the regular "rogue" flights carrying arms for al-Shabab, and it's anyone's guess as to who else is coming and going. But Mickey tells me not to miss it if I get the chance. "It is," he assures me with the weird half smile of the connoisseur, "something very special."

But then so, it turns out, is his specially formulated approach method, which is even more taxing than the crazy downward lurch into trigger-happy Kabul. Or more suicidal. On missions to Somalia, with pirates rattling off machine-gun rounds from their boats and the local al-Shabab militia firing antiaircraft rockets from the ground, Mickey's gang have learned to barnstorm in, wave-hopping low over the water, dropping to "well under" a thousand feet, skipping the spray straight onto the salty tarmac at Mogadishu's beachfront airport.

This is a navigator's favorite nightmare—Dmitry hunkered down there in the glass blister hanging beneath the cockpit for one long panning shot across the bright blue ocean as shoals of fish, ground-to-air missiles, and more shoals of fish zip past below. Weird, he says, how the presence of pirates has done wonders for the local sea life; now the *Moonraker*-style Japanese supertrawlers have got kidnap fear and are staying away like everyone else. All very beautiful, "like Eden." The navigator distracts himself by thinking about such things because, well, what else should he think about? In fact, the whole crew knows Mickey must get his approach absolutely right again—and that they have to be lucky.

If Mickey needed anything to focus his attention on the takeoff and landing in Mogadishu itself, it came in the form of two Il-76s piloted by friends shot down within days of each other amid the Battle of Mogadishu.

On March 9, 2007, the crew of a Byelorussian Il-76 were flying into Somalia from Entebbe carrying a top-secret African Union cargo—described as aid. The plane was on its final landing approach, just under three kilometers from the runway at Mogadishu International Airport, when a rocket fired from a small boat a few hundred meters out to sea blew a hole in the left of the fuselage, damaging the landing gear. The rocket should have exploded, sending shrapnel through the plane, and yet mysteriously, neither crew nor passengers received a scratch. Unverified reports suggest this is because it hit the armor plating of an unlisted piece of secret cargo, unknown even to the Ugandan troops on board—a tank hidden in among the cargo in the hold. As it was, the plane caught fire but the pilot managed to wrestle it to the ground safely. While the fire spread, the crew and passengers—Ugandan soldiers—smashed through the escape hatches. Their speed saved their lives: Mogadishu airport's only fire engine took more than an hour to reach them because of a fuel shortage. An airport employee had to run and fetch a can of petrol and fill it up first.

The stricken eighteen-year-old Candid sat charred and smashed on the runway for two weeks. But just as with the plane whose crew were wiped out by malaria, there were forces at work that would see the plane fly again, even fatally damaged. Or at least pieces of it, for there was too much money in its parts for it to be written off completely. Its four Soloviev engines alone would fetch hundreds of thousands of dollars if they could be rescued. So on March 23, 2007, just two weeks after the downing of the first Candid, another Il-76 and crew was dispatched by the owner, bringing equipment and engineers who would cannibalize the dead plane.

The second Il-76 crew, all Byelorussians, some from Mickey's old base in Vitebsk, flew in and dropped the repair team without incident. But someone had been watching them closely. Shortly after takeoff, at a height of just three thousand meters, the pilot reported "a problem" with engine number two. As he turned to return to the airport, the second and third of three surface-to-air missiles slammed into the plane. The wing exploded, falling into the ocean, while the plane, now a ball of fire, continued along the beach line, smashing into a farm. Witnesses saw crushed farm animals, human corpses, and wreckage spread over a four-acre radius. Ten of the eleven-man crew died instantly, while the eleventh was found staggering around the crash site and died later that day. Reports suggest that missiles were fired from a farmhouse near the airport and from a small boat, suggesting that the attack was coordinated. Somali troops quickly cordoned off the area—not to trap the pirates who'd shot the plane down, but to "clean up" the scene. Within hours, they'd stripped the wreckage and issued a statement claiming no missiles had been fired after all, and they didn't know what had happened to the Il-76.

Back in Byelorussia, mourners lined the streets to welcome the airmen's corpses home. Talking about it, Mickey himself is obviously affected by the fact that the Byelorussian airmen were Vitebsk alumni, and some were returned to his old billet town for burial. I was pretty shocked myself—I'd done a humanitarian run from Denmark to Baku on the plane with its Byelorussian crew a couple of years before. But guerrillas' rockets and pirates with RPGs have long been a fact of life on Somali flights. In a curious twist of fate, May 6, 2010, saw a Spetsnaz commando raid to free a Russian supertanker's crew from pirates (who were threatening to blow up the $93 million ship) launched from a Russian destroyer called *Marshal Shaposhnikov*.

Information is everything to Mickey's crew: who's shooting, who's paying, who else has been, who's made it back. These guys are info addicts, and that makes them incurable gossips. They'd make great reporters, I tell them: They'll shoot the shit with anyone—bag ladies, cops, soldiers, crims—if it'll give them a lead, if someone'll let slip a phone number, if it'll help them get a fix on the weather, the fighting, or some guy who's in the market for a couple of crates of Courvoisier they just happened by over the border. Where there's reception, they talk on phones in short snatches or while we're waiting for takeoff, then switch to radio to finish the conversation. We live point to point, not day to day, and measure out our lives in stacks and crates—the toppling, strapped-down bar chart of the independent trader.

The crew get supremely antsy whenever they're on the ground for longer than it takes to pick up or drop off. Because while everyone in the aid game keeps telling you it's a race against the clock, everyone in business will tell you just as straight that time is money. In any case, as far as the guys shipping the goods are concerned, they are indistinguishable—same game, different logo.

In some ways, it's infuriating to chat with Mickey and have the most casual questions batted back at you. It took me ages to find out where he was from, simply because his gut response to everything is to shrug, mutter something vague like "the USSR," or fob me off with a half-truth. Conversations about destinations, cargoes, or friends and family connections are nonstarters. In a moment of exasperation, I once told him the only reason I asked so many questions in the first place was because he didn't tell me anything to start with. Mickey just shrugged and offered me a cigarette, then called to Dmitry and started talking to him.

But looking back, I can't really work out why that surprised me so much.

On December 12, 2009, apparently working on a tip-off, Bangkok police raided and grounded an Il-76 on the tarmac at the city's international airport. The plane was refueling on a bizarre, twenty-four thousand–mile planned route from arms-embargoed North Korea that zigzagged over most of the earth, taking in the Ukraine, Iran, and Thailand.

This time, the mysterious tip-off was spot-on. As they ripped the plane apart, they found case after case of what were listed as "machine parts for the oil industry," but was in fact thirty-two tons of RPGs, bombs, ground-to-air missiles, and other military hardware, guns, and ammo. This was big: a sanctions-busting run carrying an illicit arms consignment from North Korea. The crewmen were taken away, the plane impounded, the cargo confiscated. For the Thai police, the raid was a total success.

That's where the jubilation ended, and the bafflement and frustration began. Because this was where investigators looking for answers encountered the same blurriness that drives me to distraction with Mickey and the boys.

The man whose crew was manning the Il-76—a Kazakh from Shymkent called Alexander Zykov whose cargo aviation company, East Wing, may or may not have been operating the flight, instantly washed his hands of the shipment. Zykov and his wife—who, it turned out, was registered as the Il-76's legal owner via her Sharjah-based company—denied all knowledge of the flight and its business. They claimed to know nothing of any arms, and reportedly told journalists that, although the men worked for him, they were all currently on holiday, having rather mysteriously taken unpaid leave together a few weeks before. Indeed, when reporters from the Associated Press called Zykov by telephone prior to paying a visit to the compound where the men had stayed, he's reported to have told them he'd no idea how to find out who'd even booked the flight, or on whose behalf, slamming the phone down after suggesting they "Go find them" themselves.

Yet when the detained crew's close friends and families were tracked down, they reacted with indignation, intimating not just their belief that the crew (who'd all worked for East Wing for long enough to be known locally as the *Zykovtsy*, or "Zykovites," and even had their own bedsits in a military-style company compound for downtime between jobs) had been very much on East Wing business at the time of the Bangkok bust, but that this obfuscation was pretty much par for the course, along with faked papers and sketchy jobs. The crew themselves protested they'd assumed the cargo was what it said on the manifest: components for oil equipment. Beyond that, it was "don't ask, don't tell."

Then things began to turn *really* weird.

The more investigators tried to find out who was behind the flight, or who'd placed the order, the more they felt they were wandering in a labyrinth of mirrors. Airmen, charter agents, customs officials, monitors all weighed in, coming up with company after company whose name appeared on different forms and certificates. Yet every single one turned into a dead end. Contacts explained they'd never heard of the plane, flight, or owner. Telephone numbers turned out to be dead. E-mails bounced back. People named on the documents denied any responsibility for the contraband. The plane had been leased and chartered onward, through shell company after shell company, and finally to a firm created just one month before the flight in Spain whose listed owner appeared, after much research, to be fictitious. Then, in a further blow, the North Korean company who appeared as having fulfilled the order for the weapons turned out not to exist either.

Days later, the crew were quietly released from their Bangkok jail and sent home without charge. After all, there was no evidence at all suggesting that they had any knowledge of the nature of their cargo. Even seasoned trackers like Brian Johnson-Thomas shake their heads looking back on it. "It smelled of a setup," he says. "There's something fishy about it, all the way from the tip-off to the fact that the guy behind it all now seems not to exist. Is it a failed sting, something bigger? We have to wait and see."

While the bust and intercontinental goose-chase gained brief news value for its perfect storm of sketchiness, there's so much about this case that's actually pretty typical—almost textbook—for gray ops. If you take all the statements at face value, neither crew nor owner knew of the cargo; nobody was responsible for the plane; the crew were employed by the airline, but not flying on the airline's business or behalf; and clients existed on paper only.

"The phase we're in," says Moisés Naím. "is about certain activities becoming tightly interwoven with other very legitimate operations, so much so that it's hard to detect them, and even harder to legislate against them." In other words, there's sufficient room, here and on many such flights, for doubt, deniability—and for a lot of clients, that's just fine. Nobody wants to put their stick into the anthill for fear of what they'll stir up. Right now, the shippers get their flights, the pilots get their business on the side, the airports make money, everyone's happy. Like Brian Johnson-Thomas's pilot friend, who came across as highly public-spirited by offering the NGOs his services for free on some routes, Mickey's generous terms are a gift horse to aid agencies. Understandably, with rates as cheap as his, many are reluctant to dig deeper into his motivations.

Still, the Dunkirk-spirit nature of the cargo business—not just humanitarian flights to emergency zones, but just-in-time commercial and military logistics deliveries too, along with a breakneck schedule of too many flights in too short a time frame so familiar to small-time man-with-van operations everywhere—means turnaround is often alarmingly quick and scrutiny often comically low.

Even the most brazen stowaways and bizarre cargo consignments get carried through. After the 2004 tsunami sent waves over thirty meters high into coastal communities from Indonesia, Thailand, and Malaysia to Sri Lanka and countries across the Indian Ocean, destroying cities and killing more than 230,000 people, the veteran Eastern bloc A-Teams with their cavernous superplanes and anything-anywhere attitude were the first on the scene with relief and reconstruction supplies in what, at the time, was close to hell on earth.

When the Sri Lankan Tamil Tigers mounted their first air attack in March 2007, the *Times* (London) reported that the Tigers' attack aircraft had been smuggled into the country in kit form after the tsunami of 2004, exploiting lax security amid the aid effort.

There was time to pick up plenty extra to smuggle home, too. John MacDonald remembers having the wits scared out of him by one vodka-drinking stowaway while flight managing for the hordes of swarming Ilyushin and Antonov crews that turned the skies black over the disaster zone.

"During that period in Southeast Asia, there were these Il-76s and these two Antonov-12s; they were taken out there to be based in Kuala Lumpur and to fly aid and supplies all around the region," he says. "I was running around these aircraft, just running around like crazy, finding out whose they were, just to make sure they were okay and safe—it all went well. So I walked into one plane, and the crew compartment's not that big in those things, and I could hear this unearthly shrieking. I walked through the cargo door, and walked up, and this horrible screaming was getting louder. I looked up, and from the floor to the ceiling, there was a huge, four-foot-six, maybe five-foot-high cage there in the darkness, and in the cage was this huge tropical bird with half its feathers fallen out, just flapping and squawking. These guys had been based in west-coast Africa, and the pilot had bought it on the black market over there the week before the tsunami thinking he was going home the next week to the Ukraine and would give it to his little girl. But then when the emergency came, there was too much work to turn down getting relief jobs in. They traveled halfway round the world, and all the while there was this man-size bird, they'd been feeding it vodka and bread, and its feathers are falling out, and it's just squawking away with this unearthly sound in there. You could hear it for miles around."

He laughs as he counts off all the checks and landings they'd have had to make with their shrieking passenger on the way.

"Just look at the map and the range of the plane—they'd made all these flights to get from West Africa to Malaysia, it took them ages, from

Pointe-Noire to Nairobi, then Addis Ababa, then the UAE—maybe Sharjah—then somewhere in India, then one more stop somewhere else, then over to Kuala Lumpur. All with this giant bird squawking and flapping. Nobody saw a thing. Not only that, but bear in mind the crew have been sleeping, eating, *everything* on the plane: It's a madhouse. Anyone who's been in these planes at the best of times knows the smell is like the back of a Moscow taxi, all body odor and grease and whatever else, and on top of that you've got a giant bald alcoholic bird."

In fact, animal life is a frequent stowaway with some crews, and a nice little earner if you can keep it alive long enough to deliver it. But these extra cargoes have unintended consequences, too. Within a year, black-cargo flights in and out of Africa were being identified by TRAFFIC, the wildlife trade monitoring network, as the real culprits for several outbreaks of bird flu in previously "clean and contained" countries.

"The official line that it was migratory birds was rubbish," says TRAFFIC's Richard Thomas. "It's no coincidence that in Nigeria, where they banned the import of chickens because of bird flu, a supposedly sealed-off and certified farm right next to the airport was the site of their outbreak. They'd banned imports, but of course diseased birds then began being smuggled in on these masses of unmarked planes."

Their laissez-faire take on import-export "piggybacks" when flying aid to tsunamis or peacekeeping runs for the UN has made them legends, even among UN staff themselves. "I can't help but miss them," sighs one aviator who flew supplies during the Angolan war in the early 1990s. "Back in Luanda my colleague was flying for the UN," he recalls. "He wanted to buy an African gray parrot for the pilot house, so he promptly went over to the Il-76 crew, who were also flying for the UN, to ask for a favor—he wanted to ask them to buy an African gray parrot in the northeast of Angola on their next trip, during the week. Well, they invited him in and offered him a vodka or two—and this was *at ten* A.M. My friend declined the vodka and showed them his walkie-talkie; he said he was on standby and asked them to get him a gray parrot on their next trip. The conversation got involved and more vodka flowed, then all of a sudden the drinking stopped and the Il-76 crew got up and walked out. My friend asked if this was an inconvenient time and apologized for interrupting their socializing time in UN camp. The captain turned around and said,

'No problem—we fly now and fetch the bird!' And so they did. By six P.M. there was an African gray parrot in the house!"

The stories are legion—birds, tanks, pigs, helicopters, statues of pop stars, pianos, whole wine cellars, people, fake watches, arms, drugs, there's nothing that hasn't at some point become a bit of piggybacked "cash cargo" on a fully legitimate humanitarian run paid for by someone who has no idea what's coming in and going out with their lifesaving goods.

But beyond the hijinks, there are clues that this casual approach—and the black-hole status of airports in places like Afghanistan and sub-Saharan Africa—prevail at least partly because of the reluctance of the people we'd normally think of as the "good guys" to clean them up.

Because sometimes, even humanitarian-aid flights in Mickey's Il-76 become a cover not just for illicit extra cargo the crew themselves might want to carry, but for top-secret, Bond-style "black ops" missions by governments like our own.

Just as the bad guys are all looking for a little legitimacy from the cover a UN contract or humanitarian mission provides, so do the people we'd normally think of as the good guys.

Which means someone very powerful indeed has an interest in providing the best smokescreen possible for whatever Mickey's crew is doing—and some of the "illicit" cargoes we're all trying to track are in fact carried as part of a highly complex, well-planned web of operations on behalf of our own governments. There have long been reports of unlisted passengers arriving and being spirited out of crisis areas by easygoing crews or game-playing operators. Diplomats and UN officials are known to fly undercover, inside specially comfort-fitted Il-76s, when they have to fly en masse. The photos are on the UN Web site after the fact; but for security reasons, the details are kept vague until they've landed. Indeed, I've been unlisted on most of my flights, albeit under less salubrious conditions, dealing directly with the crew alone and paying them for the inconvenience rather than go through official channels, airlines, or lessors themselves; it's simpler that way. But it's now clear that the odd cash flight, and the occasional scandal over "extraordinary renditions" of suspected Taliban combatants, is just the tip of the iceberg when it comes to governments turning to ex-Soviet black-cargo planes themselves when there's a shady job they need doing. According to Igor Salinger, Damnjanovic and Djordjevic's doomed arms shipment from Belgrade under the watchful eye of the Milošević regime was far from the only black-ops waltz the former Yugoslavia's cargo charter men danced with world governments. "They made a number of flights out of Bosnia on behalf of U.S. arms trading companies," he smiles. "And we both know that in Bosnia you can't pee your pants without Langley CIA being informed."

In 2007, a UN panel of experts report circulated to the UN Security Council even found that the Sudanese government in Khartoum had chartered Antonov-26s, painted them in white United Nations livery, and used them to ferry secret stashes of arms to the Janjaweed militia with which to terrorize villages in Darfur.

On occasion, these heavily disguised cargo giants themselves had, it was revealed, been used as bombers in a secret bombardment of civilian populations by President Omar al-Bashir's Sudanese regime. "The most astonishing revelation," reported the *Times*, "was the use by the Sudanese armed forces of [these] white-painted military aircraft in Darfur." On March 7 [2007] a photograph was taken of an Antonov An-26 aircraft on the military apron of Al-Fasher airport, the Darfuri regional capital. Guarded by soldiers and with bombs piled alongside, the plane was painted white and has the initials "UN" stenciled on its upper left wing. Another Sudanese military aircraft was disguised in the same manner. The report said that white Antonovs were used to bombard Darfur villages on at least three occasions in January.

Like Damnjanovic's doomed arms shipment from Belgrade on behalf of the Milošević regime, like the masses of spontaneously combusting, flapping, vaporizing-in-midair flights over the Congo and Angola, these apparently harmless humanitarian-aid flights have a strange habit of blowing up—almost as if there were high-explosive cargoes on board instead of the tires, sanitation equipment, foodstuffs, and tents that appear on the manifests.

And whenever these flights *do* come down, it feels like Surcin all over again. I do some more digging into the fate of Katya Stepanova's navigator friend. And the more I discover, the more it looks like talk of incorrect paperwork, faked licenses, alcohol intake, and so forth is (intentionally or not) a very convenient smokescreen. Increasingly, it seems that nothing the crew did or did not do would have saved them. And equally, perhaps Stepanova is right when she says the Candid was in tip-top condition.

Because the simple, inescapable fact is, the Ilyushin-76 blew up midair, shortly after takeoff from Entebbe, just after five A.M. on March 9, 2009, disintegrating with such force that an engine shot off, missilelike, and sank a local fisherman's boat on Lake Victoria. That looks like an explosion. And if the plane was sound, and the crew didn't ever know what hit them, then just what exploded up there?

This is something the investigators seem unusually keen to gloss over, preferring to ask questions about the navigator's paperwork and the pilot's CV to questions about the nature of the cargo. Indeed, early claims coming from Ugandan authorities and the owner were that it had been carrying water-purification equipment and tents for the African mission to Somalia. And then the wreckage, physical and metaphorical, began to float up to the surface. And something else emerged with it: claims that the plane was carrying Burundian soldiers on a peacekeeping mission, and men from the Pentagon's new breed of corporate mercenaries, a U.S. "private military contractor" called DynCorp, then at the center of controversy about its conduct carrying out contracts for the Pentagon in Iraq.

If there was a secret military cargo on board—perhaps one so clandestine that even the flight's operator, Evgeny Zakharov, perhaps even the pilot, didn't know what it was—could it have caused the crash?

It's a conclusion that has plenty of support among aviation communities in the area. Some—and Stepanova and the operator of the flight, Zakharov's former company Aerolift, appear to agree on this—go further, believing the flight was sabotaged by Somali militants opposed to Uganda's assistance in the UN peacekeeping effort there. They point to the fact that peacekeeping operations have been sabotaged at Entebbe many times before; that organized attacks on peacekeeping operations in the region are frequent and the subsequent bombing, in July 2010, of venues showing World Cup games live in Kampala, were carried out by Somali Islamists al-Shabab.

One thing's certain: Whenever a cargo flight explodes, focusing on the crew and raising the possibility of human error is convenient for everybody but the dead men. From insurance claims to official secrecy, everything gets easier if the crew caused the crash, not the plane or the cargo. And ironically, the pressure the Ugandan army put on the CAA to clear flights as they take off not only means their cargo can't be inspected; it also denies ground staff the chance of finding any other irregularities. An al-Shabab bomb, for example.

There are too many questions to leave it alone. So I decide to return to the crash site myself, in the company of one of the first men on the scene.

The sky is black and bruised over the northern shore of the world's second-largest freshwater lake. On this overcast June afternoon, the breezes in the grass ringing the gunmetal waters have the look of the rural East Anglian coastline, albeit with eerily calm sea and thinner cattle grazing on the adjoining fields. On the far shores, invisible on the distant, watery horizon, are Kenya and Tanzania.

One year on from the crash, boats still comb the endless waters close to the shore, known as Magombe, where the parts of the Candid's fuselage and engines fell. "Magombe actually means 'death,'" says Entebbe-based investigative reporter for the national *Daily Monitor* newspaper Martin Ssebuyira, pointing out to the spot, a couple of miles out, where the Candid's remains lie, split and smashed, under eighty feet of water and a further forty feet of impenetrably thick mud. "It's had the name for centuries—I think nothing good happens there. Fishing boats sometimes don't come back from that patch, so most of them avoid it. And now it's death again."

A wiry, soft-voiced Ugandan in his early twenties, Ssebuyira looks nothing like the kind of hard-bitten gumshoe who'd pose as a member of the secret police to get on the hastily scrambled boats and see the crash site close up, but that's what he did. The Entebbe reporter was chased away from the crash scene the night the UPDF boats and their searchlights went out on the lake. But unlike the other reporters, he came back, hid a camera beneath his jacket to resemble the bulge of a plainclothes officer's shoulder holster, bluffed his way onto one of the boats, and was one of the first to the point of entry.

"We kept finding body parts," he says. "A lot of things. And it was clear from the floating wreckage that this plane did not simply crash . . . But that was the story that kept coming out! One of the fishermen said he saw fire on the plane in the air. Then he was taken away by the authorities. Then boats came to patrol the shore of the lake. All the local people on the lakeshore were prevented from fishing."

Ssebuyira filed his reports. More witnesses appeared, more evidence surfaced. Slowly, the official story changed. In addition to the crew, seven "others" had been killed in the crash. They were later claimed to be fighting men, service personnel on a low-profile flight to join a Burundi peacekeeping mission. Then the DynCorp connection came to light.

The reasons for the crash, though, are shrouded in mystery; not because there are too few of them but, unusually, too many—certainly more than enough to lead Ssebuyira and others, like the expat Russian airmen and their families, to suspect smokescreening. "It was announced that the crew were drunk," says Ssebuyira. "They were seen drinking at the Four Turkeys at three A.M., before reporting for flight duty at four A.M.," he says. "And there were claims the captain thought an hour's sleep was enough to sober up. But they also claimed that the plane was past its service life—it had expired, but they were still flying it. Then they found that the crew might not have been the expert fliers they thought. There were a great many things that should have been fixed, but they weren't."

So who was behind the smokescreen, if indeed there was one? In addition to the Ukrainian aviation authority casting doubt on the navigator's qualifications, over at the opposition paper the *Independent*, news editor Patrick Matsiko wa Mucoori's sources also told him that the CAA of the Russian Federation had drawn a blank in tracing the pilot's papers, too. Their report concluded simply: "Maybe Kovalev did not have a pilot licence." But despite the accusations regarding the crew's fitness to fly, the plane's state of repair, and the rebel activity in the area, another story slowly began to emerge.

The huge explosion onboard that "cracked the fuselage down the center like an egg," in the words of U.S. divers who attempted to raise it, was, according to this version of events, not caused by any water-pumping or purifying equipment or other innocuous aid; and the DynCorp "peacekeeping contractors" bound for Mogadishu weren't just hitching a lift. The water burned so fiercely and long that even the military stayed clear. Something down there was worrying them, and with the high-explosive nature of the event, it didn't take too long to figure out what it was.

"They weren't carrying aid equipment," snorts one pilot who claims to have known the men. "They were carrying a payload to Somalia for the Pentagon's private army. Then the plane blew up before it hit the water. That was a big fucking bang. And now they're arresting anyone who goes near it or saw the flash in the sky. It doesn't take a genius to spot a cover-up."

Without evidence, without transparent investigation—and U.S. navy divers subsequently being called in to conduct the salvage operation inside a cordon sanitaire didn't help calm the conspiracy theories one bit— these are the theories that spread. And now, with the plane buried under forty feet of mud at the bottom of one of the great African lakes, it's likely we'll never know the exact cause.

Still, Mucoori continues to hope something good will come out of it, for the sake of the crews if nothing else. "Hopefully," he wrote in his report, "this will mean that aid agencies and large logistics companies will start using legitimate operators rather than just using the cheapest option and feeding the cowboys. People's lives are worth more than a few extra dollars."

But with even blue-chip Pentagon partners willing to use shadow planes and lie about the cargo—not to mention using "humanitarian aid" as a fig leaf for whatever military payload they are really transporting in beat-up Soviet charter planes with crews like Mickey's—suddenly every cop is a criminal. Indeed, those who've known Viktor Bout for many years claim his gunrunning was as much for the major governments and their cronies as for anybody they disapproved of, and that's why he was allowed to continue for so long, with so many investigative task forces being pulled off the case and resources constantly being diverted from the departments monitoring his activities.

Typically, investigations are halfhearted or too quickly concluded. Causes are covered up. E-mails—mine and others'—to investigative teams, to governments, to aviation authorities, go unanswered, calls unreturned. The UN's Congo operation lists a phone number in Kinshasa, but I rang it every day for six months and never once got picked up. Even the UN secretary general's office becomes evasive with me when I ask how come the UN base in Entebbe is so unaware of the extra cargo on flights in and out, saying they can't tell me "when we'll have an answer for you, or if we'll have one at all." Africa is chaotic, say all parties, and a soft, universally beneficial vagueness descends again—one from which Mickey and his men may be small winners, but from which there are those who stand to gain far, far more. And while everyone has an interest in leaving room for doubt about their use of this secret superpipeline, men like Patrick Mucoori continue to push for transparency, men like pilot Viktor Koralev and navigator Evgeny Korolev continue to die, and the Soviet-made steel keeps roaring overhead.

PART VI

The Journey Home: East Africa and Russia

CHAPTER TWENTY

The Ghost Factory

Russia, 2008

FALSE NAMES AND BORROWED IDS are part of the plan for me just as much as for the aircrews themselves while I follow Mickey around. At times I feel like I'm wandering the world in a strange dream in which people, like planes, keep switching faces, names, lives. There are whispers of more airmen's bodies being recovered from crash sites than there were airmen in the planes. Of planes that crash, only for investigators to discover they'd already been completely destroyed in another crash years before. The whole thing begins to feel like some gothic tale from Kipling.

There are, of course, more worldly explanations. At most checkpoints in Africa, a flashed dollar bill is as close as I get to telling anyone my name or showing anyone a passport, and a piece of borrowed ID (in which I transform into a hulking middle-aged Russian) settles the rest.

As filmmaker Hubert Sauper wrote when he trailed these crews' progress round the African lakes in a Candid, "In order to fly with cargo planes we had to disguise ourselves as pilots and loadmasters and carry fake identities. In villages we were mistaken as missionaries, and in fish factories managers feared we might be EU hygiene inspectors. We had to become Australian businessmen in the fancy hotel bars, or just harmless backpackers in the African bush, 'taking pictures.'" His submersion was so effective he even found himself making news headlines across the world as having been kidnapped, simply because of the American Embassy's confusion as to his whereabouts.

Even to those who know him, Mickey's cultivated protean quality makes him time-consuming, and often impossible, to trace. In the years between our meetings, while preparing for trips to Russia, Africa, and elsewhere to chase Mickey, I find hooking up with him impossibly difficult because his telephone SIM cards are changed wherever he goes, and in any case seldom last the month, and because clients, charter agents, and bosses rarely seem to have any more of a clue than I do where to find him. Even when I know the hotel he's in, reception haven't a clue if he's there or not because he uses different names and IDs to check in.

But if Mickey is vague and elusive out of habit and necessity, many operators higher up the food chain turn it into an art. One of the most mysterious cases on the intelligence agencies' files is a woman. Intelligence officials know her simply as Tatyana, and professionally, they are as spooked by her as anybody ever was by Keyser Söze.

She is believed to be one of the closest aides not just to Viktor Bout, but to other international traffickers operating in the triangle of Moscow, the United Arab Emirates, and sub-Saharan Africa. She first appeared on the radar back in those first heady Wild East days in Milošević's Belgrade. Since then, she's displayed an uncanny nose for imminent war and a tendency for turning up wherever the second horseman rides into town, including a tour of West Africa that kicked off in Monrovia, Liberia, in 1999, just as the shooting began.

"Tatyana" is a curious, semimythical creature even to those who make paper-trailing their business. Sightings of her are often reported but she has never been successfully tracked, and although Tatyana is always her first name, her last name is different on almost every signature she leaves behind.

She is known to turn up wherever a number of traffickers of arms and "gray" cargo, including Bout, are setting up new business operations and to be a lawyer, or at least legal advisor, for Bout. Her birthday always appears as the same date, though on each piece of ID a different year is given according to intelligence officials quoted in a second 2010 intelligence report commissioned by the deposed ruler of Ras al-Khaimah, written by a former member of the U.S. air force's special forces, and issued by Mercury LLC suggesting the emirate and its Sharjah neighbor may be a "rogue state" possessing terror links with Iran.

Tatyana's role, according to Farah and Braun, was—perhaps still remains, his physical imprisonment notwithstanding—to scope out new business territories for Viktor Bout's organizations, going on ahead of him to do all the legal and financial research—dot the i's, cross the t's, and gather paperwork—before flying back to her office in Moscow. And while some sources say she is in her late twenties, a woman matching her description has served Bout's companies, and those of other known traffickers, for a decade or more.

"She was first identified by European intelligence officers," says the Ras al-Khaimah report, "[who were] monitoring the activities of the Bout operation in Europe and Africa," and has appeared for contractual meetings just before the arms shipments arrived in Belgrade, Liberia, Dubai, Sierra Leone, South Africa, Thailand, the Congo, Belgium, and the tiny emirate of Ras al-Khaimah itself. If Tatyana really is now in her late twenties, her appearance in Belgrade would have made her a sixteen-year-old legal expert.

Everyone who sees her, deals with her, looks at her, or knows people who know her agree they're talking about the same woman, only each time she's different somehow. According to the anonymous author,

> the ability of [these traffickers] to use nimble corporate branding to hide their activities appears to be the work of [Tatyana]. Tatiana . . . —it is unclear if this is her original name—manages [another cargo baron] Egli's business operations. A woman matching [Tatyana's] description has frequently appeared in both Egli and [Viktor] Bout's operations over the past decade or so. "Her first name is always Tatiana but the last name is always different, but usually a Russian variation on the same theme," says the source. "There's always this woman around. Same birthday, same month, always a different year. My theory is that she is an administrative secretary for Egli and maybe even Bout. She has been found working with both men in Dubai, RAK, Ostend, Monrovia, Freetown, South Africa, Bangkok, and Kinshasa, if you follow me . . . She is the expert in all sorts of paperwork and incorporation rules.

Or this even more intriguing twist: Her full identity has, according to research by Farah and Braun, proved unusually difficult for intelligence agencies and investigators to definitively establish. So difficult, in fact, that the only plausible explanation from the officials monitoring Tatyana's activity is that "she" is in fact a composite of two or more different people—apparently almost identical in appearance and with the same level of expertise, sent from the same office, under the same name, passport, ID, and job title, to different places at either the same or different times. Thus Tatyana can then disappear at will, only to pop up thousands of impossible miles away in another conflict zone, seconds later; or put the clock back, so to speak—younger today than when she was while clearing the last-minute legals in mid-nineties Belgrade or early-2000s Liberia.

Brian Johnson-Thomas has an even more tantalizing lead on this shape-shifting woman—one that hints at just how powerful this blurring of roles may be. "Tatyana, so far as I know, is the daughter of a major-general in the old KGB and the sister of one of Putin's 'advisors,'" he says. "All of which, of course, adds credence to Viktor Bout's claim to me, over a beer in Kisangani, that he himself was also responsible to higher authority, as it were."

Again, for all the rumor and allegations, there appears to be no hard evidence of any wrongdoing; just frustration at what seems to be the ever-deepening mystery of the woman's identity. For a Westerner, it seems incredible. Can it really be so easy, even today, to pull identity tricks like this? To cultivate blurriness to the point that it fools the CIA, Interpol, and MI5? There's only one way to find out. And for me that means going back to Russia, where it all started.

Ekaterinburg is the home of Russia's military-industrial complex, where the stockpiles of weapons, APCs, and ammunition Mickey flies around the world were—and still are—made, stored, diverted, sold off. Its parts factories and workshops keep the clouds of Candids and Antonovs flying beyond the life spans even their makers imagined. It was also, as it happened, ground zero of Russia's 1990s *mafiya* apocalypse.

This is the former Soviet Union's own arms-trafficking Bermuda Triangle. But it's also Mickey's hometown, or as close to it as you can get and still be somewhere.

Ekaterinburg is the spot where Vladimir Starikov's doomed Il-76 crew slipped their moorings one last time, bound for Belgrade. Near here in 2000 following the ski-masked FSB bust back in Moscow, fugitive East Line crewmen abandoned their contraband-laden Il-76 and melted away, leaving only their modern-day *Mary Celeste* aircraft on the runway.

It's a place where airmen go to slip off the earth. Gary Powers's U2 spy plane was downed here in unexplained circumstances in 1960—even now, fifty-one years later and more than two decades after the end of the Cold War, the CIA and National Security Agency judge the flight transcripts to be so sensitive they refuse to declassify them.

To this day, it remains a place known for its citizens' habit of vanishing—becoming fugitives, outlaws, *disparus*, or corpses. And in the summer of 2007, it's here that my acquaintance with Mickey flickers briefly into life again.

I've driven all the way from Moscow via Tatarstan and Bashkortostan, piggybacking a work assignment on the sly to see him, and the Urals' eastern slopes are dark already. A planned meeting with one of Mickey's old cargo comrades in Kazan has already been a bust, partly because I'm on a shadow mission myself, attempting to fit these illicit meetings around another journalistic schedule that, as it turned out, put me several hundred clicks from where I needed to be, but I still have high hopes of catching up with Mickey after a couple of years' peace. Ahead and behind as I loop down the slopes, the low red sun turns the trans-Ural highway into a river of fire. Ahead is Ekaterinburg, formerly Sverdlovsk, and before that, Ekaterinburg—and at various points in between, a carefully edited blank patch on Soviet-published maps. The Urals' reputation as the Soviet Union's own gigantic Area 51 is chiefly owed to a wall of secrecy that for decades swallowed up entire towns, cities, mountains and forests, secret bases, and "disappeared," dead, or deformed populations. The region was off-limits to all foreigners and many Russians until 1992, and many sudden blank areas on the local maps remain that way.

Throughout the Cold War, it was the heart of the Soviet "nuclear archipelago" (alongside neighboring Chelyabinsk—known here as Tankograd—whose main employer in 1991 was a secret chemical weapons facility):

a place of so-called ghost factories, weapons facilities, and secret arms bases disguised as car-manufacturing plants, foundries, and farms.

But these ghost factories also produced their own ghosts, a city of people whose true work had to be concealed from families, friends, and even colleagues. Cover-ups are what Ekaterinburg has always done like no place else, and on an industrial scale. When Moscow came under threat from the German advance in 1941, most state facilities, from weapons production to secret government bunkers and chemical facilities and even the St. Petersburg Hermitage museum's art collection, were relocated here, behind the towering border of the Urals. After the war, the industries remained. When the world's worst nuclear accident before Chernobyl happened here in 1957, a total media shutdown and army-enforced quarantine ensured that no one beyond the affected valleys, towns, and forests knew about it until decades later—even today, the Lonely Planet guide warns would-be picnickers that leaked radiation around Lake Karachay and the Techa River will kill a man within an hour.

When in 1979 a bioweapons plant disguised as a factory in a southern residential suburb leaked weapons-grade anthrax into the neighborhood, again the Men in Black appeared, the cordons went up around what was now being described by the Soviet authorities as "the abattoir which was the source of the food poisoning outbreak," and for the next few days the city was simply erased from news, radio, and public discussion. As with the 2002 Moscow theater-hostage crisis, even the emergency services were kept in the dark by the KGB's cleanup squads. To this day, most locals believe it was the result of contaminated meat, not an accident at a lab where antibiotic-resistant bubonic plague bacilli were stored next to silos of anthrax and superstrains of smallpox big enough to wipe out nations.

Even the town house in which the Bolsheviks shot the Romanovs was "erased"—bulldozed by order of an aspiring local politician named Boris Yeltsin, specialist in the disappearance of state funds, who as president of Russia and friend to Commander in Chief Evgeny Shaposhnikov would oversee Mickey's transition to a freelance career.

Threatened by a 1991 coup attempt, President Yeltsin would nominate this his plan-B capital—a secret bunker for his cabinet to disappear into if threatened. But the reputation of the city today rests on the early 1990s explosion of criminal, mafia, and semilegal economic activity that continues even now to make its mark on countries, economies, wars, and politics around the globe. Even for Muscovites, it's the Wild East. This is the edge of the steppe, where for centuries fugitives, Il-76 pilots fleeing mysterious FSB busts, mafiosi, and careless travelers alike have simply melted away, into the grasslands or under the roads. Here, the *mafiya* have their own clubs, neighborhoods, sports teams, even cemeteries.

From these mob-controlled factories, Ilyushin and Antonov engines were spirited to Africa, Central Asia, and the Caucasus to service the wandering airmen there. Local chemical and nuclear weapons, liberated in the cataclysm of economic collapse, attracted potential buyers from Iran, Pakistan, and Central Europe. Businessmen put two and two together and founded air ops, scouting around for talent from local garrisons.

It's been a long drive from Moscow and I really don't want the sun to set before I reach my hotel in town. The plan is to keep going, with the needle hovering just far enough inside the speed limit to deter bribe-hungry cops. But as I snake down the valley side, something happens that illustrates just how tenuous identity becomes here, even in Russia, just miles from where Mickey grew up.

Beside the narrow highway that winds down through the first half of the Urals and into the grasslands is a mirage of bustling roadside activity: thin, whining dogs on rope tethers, buyers and sellers, brightly colored stalls, the spiced gray smoke of kebabs grilling on an open breeze-block fire. Except it's not a mirage. Here are Oriental faces, Uzbek-registered cars coated in primer and hitched to wagons; sick chickens and luminous plastic footballs, toys, bootleg goods, jarred honey and battered tanks full of petrol. My traveling companions and I stop at the informal Central Asian bazaar in need of a stretch and hungry, but hungrier still for human interaction, for the sound and sight and smell of someone other than ourselves; for a bit of up-close and a break from distance and uncertainty.

Suddenly, and without knowing how, I'm talking bad Russian to Zayna—for reasons that will become clear, she asks me not to use her real name—a girl from Uzbekistan who travels as part of this impromptu caravanserai through the empty heart of Russia in summer, and for whom we are items of outlandish, absurd exotica. She ushers me to the shaded back of the tent and opens a drawer. It is full of replica and blank-templated Russian driver's licenses, along with laminate and a small camera. She looks up from the samples pegged along the top: one for fugitive oligarch Boris Berezovsky, "Godfather of the Kremlin," now living in London; one for President Putin himself; one for Osama bin Laden (patronymic middle name: Terroristovich). One for Lenin, too, now apparently a resident of Moscow and with no points accumulated. ID costs five dollars. I return to the Russian rental car with five new, utterly different Russian driving licenses and ID cards: just like Bout and Minin.

I decide to back myself up in case they're found, adding a couple of cheeky celebrity names so I've got dumb-tourist-with-a-novelty-souvenir room to maneuver with the cops if it comes to it—I'm O. bin Laden on one of them, a Moscow resident. I flash one to the receptionist at my crummy hotel that night when she asks for it. To my astonishment, it passes. Not a flicker. Though to this day I'm unsure if she was fooled or saw through it but genuinely couldn't give less of a fuck who I was. The number gets noted down, entered into the guest registration system, and I can't help but think of Iain Clark's defense of Russian operators in Africa: "They'll go with what documents they're given, and if they're fake, so be it."

This is just a five-dollar cheapie; if it was part of my business plan, I'd invest much, much more time and money in getting the best. Besides, your ID is only ever as good as the willingness of the person checking it to accept it. For Tatyana, just like Mickey, with only the paperwork and underpaid officials in third world countries to negotiate, slipping through that door is a daily thing. The rules say someone's name has to go here, here, and here? Of course I've got a name—why not take two or three?

Charter agent John MacDonald laughs when we talk about Mickey's can-do approach to paperwork. "Get him to tell you about the invoices!" he hoots. "If you want phantom paperwork, that'll put the wind up you!"

I finally catch up with Mickey over an early vodka breakfast in the center of town, where he's back with some stuff for his mother and sister. The canteen is cheerless, Formica benches and fast-food chairs ill-suited for his golem frame, but he knows it and thought even I might find it. He's a little grayer in the face than I remember but in fine fettle, relaxed and even talkative. I show him my new Russian driver's licenses, and we talk about why they're no good, and why in most parts of the world, in most situations, nothing has to be any good anyway. Then, ordering another drink, he explains his invoicing practice.

"You want me to bring you ten thousand dollars of cargo. We talk and agree a price of twenty thousand dollars. I will invoice you for twenty thousand. Your company receives the invoice and pays. You and I stand on the runway, or we sit on a chair under a tree or in a hut, have a beer and a cigarette. We relax, chat about business, and then I give you five thousand and put the other five thousand cash into my own pocket. Then we drink to success."

You need to spread it around a little, naturally, he says—you need to keep your colleagues sweet—and so everybody wins except the official buyer you work for. But then, that might be an oil-type company, the UN, some government or aid organization, at any rate someone with big, deep pockets who's got so used to being ripped off and paying over the going rate that they actually think it *is* the going rate. The names on the invoices can change, of course, says Mickey. They might be paying the outfit he flies for, or any one of several companies owned by either him or that parent company. Depends what it is, who it's for, and who needs to know.

We talk about Ekaterinburg, the nightlife, his mother's illness; about the ghost factories and how it was back then when it seemed everybody worked for a different highly classified military facility. With a slow, rheumatic roll of the shoulders as he twists his lanky frame around on the fixed plastic chair, he tells me that just like the jobs he flies now, the whole secrecy thing is overdone. "It was normal," he shrugs, "like London or anywhere, people who work for the military would tell you something different if you asked what they do in their job. Secrets were part of life. But still, you know what they do. People talk."

Before we part, he wants to take me round town, but I've got more leads to chase up and I tell him I'll see him on the road, thinking Kazakhstan, his next stop. As it turns out, it'll be another three years, hundreds of fruitless phone calls, and thousands of miles farther south, but that's how it is with people like Mickey. Mark Galeotti believes this identity-hopping quality, this ability to slip seamlessly off the radar and into different roles and identities, goes deeper for Mickey, Tatyana, even Bout, than a calculated wish to deceive.

"It's not actually a situational thing," he says. "It's a reflex. You've got to remember that this is one of the glories of the old Soviet system. On paper it was hierarchical, ordered, rational, and everything had its place.

In practice, it was everything but. And if Russians have a genius, it's to screw over those people who try to rule them, and at every occasion.

"So for a lot of people, it did become second nature—a habit, where you automatically do it. You know that you don't trust the system, and you are constantly looking at ways of screwing the system—not because you're a rebel, but because that's the only way you get anything. Everyone plays the black market. Everyone looks for how they can get away with minor infractions. It doesn't matter if you're a Communist Party official or whoever you are, everyone operates *na levo*—on the left. And after a certain point, certain instincts get ingrained. Now add to that the professional instincts of people who operate in a very gray area.

"You don't trust the powers that be—it doesn't matter who they are or what they are, that's just the instinct that you've got. And therefore you will automatically do everything that you can to be as amorphous, as invisible, as possible. From a legal point of view it means that when push comes to shove, no one can ever really prove you're anywhere. You can always claim there's ambiguity."

Their ghost selves accompany these men through their lives, but often they are only exposed when they crash and suddenly things get binary: definitive identification, established causes, and insurance assessments and payouts that want black or white, alive or dead, name, date of birth, dental records. But sometimes it seems the men have disappeared and the ghosts are all that's left. I find myself thinking of another crew, friends of Katya's killed when their Antonov-12 crashed in Uganda in 2005. Even the black-box flight recorder was empty, its layer of magnetic tape having faded to nothing.

CHAPTER TWENTY-ONE

Death and Taxes

Entebbe to Ekaterinburg, 2010

THE BREEZE IS PICKING UP, carrying whirls of sand and grass husks on its warm jets. And on the foggy, overgrown hook end of this disused up-country air base deep in the West African bush, among rusting helicopters and a cement-mixer graveyard, the 250-square-meter iron bird is popping and blinking as it cools down. Night sounds drift in through the plane's iron skin: motorbikes, wire-mesh gates being clanked, a rifle firing, dogs. Somewhere farther off, a televised football match and the unsettling human-voice-in-distress cries of the night birds wander in and out with the direction of the wind. A fuel truck backs up in the distance, and once or twice another plane crosses the sky.

Inside, the pungent smell of dope is everywhere. Everywhere is full so it's piss in a tin, crap outside with the little red malaria-carrying mosquitoes sucking you dry, or don't do either. And there aren't any showers, but that's immaterial because I haven't changed clothing or even taken my shoes off for at least twenty-four hours, and now I'm not sure I want to. No one else has either, as far as I know, with the exception of the late-substitution loadmaster I haven't met before, a young, even slightly hip, shaven-headed Ukrainian with an iPod, named Alex, defiantly slipping into Jesus creepers whenever he comes "indoors"—something Sergei always used to do. He's added a dressing gown over his tracksuit bottoms and jumper and looks like a mental patient, grunting and swearing at bulging, tumbling cargo and struggling with canvas straps. Here he is now, bug-eyed, pale, and sweating, on his way past with a bundle of rags, his unplugged headphones dangling loose from his ears.

He points at the towering mass of loose cartons. "I think we can do it." Then he licks his lips. "Yes. We can do it." Seeing my frown, he sticks out his hand. "A hundred dollars?" But neither of us has a hundred dollars.

They say nothing's certain in life but death and taxes. And with his cash business, at least, Mickey's got tax pretty well licked. But the older he gets, the more I fear for him. The planes are aging, the loads creeping up and up past even the physics-defying abilities of men like him. Still, spectacular escapes and close shaves always stick in the mind longer than the bodies by the road, and like all of them, Mickey is convinced he's lucky. Perhaps a part of him has started to believe the myth, I think. That larger-than-life creation, the schizoid comic-book caricature that jumps from the pages of the trafficking reports and the mouths of other bush-jockey pilots is so dazzling—a sort of Bond villain/Scarlet Pimpernel combo—it's pretty much all that I saw at first, back in Belgrade and wherever else I looked. Until I met Mickey. Then, when the layers come away, you're left with a bunch of blue-collar guys and the muggy, canvas-packed shadows inside an Ilyushin-76 at night, and things look different. Less glamorous.

Back in London I get a call from my anonymous pilot-informer who's haunted the hangars of Sharjah with these men and seen them push the make-do-and-mend cult as far as it'll go—and further. "I've been in crews where we didn't have any contracts for technical support in most places, but still we had no problem," he shrugs. "When there's a new wheel change, there's always a local guy who can change a wheel, and a number of crews have that knack and like sorting their own problems. It's not for everybody, but if you're driving a '61 Ford Escort to work every day and you get a technical problem? Well, you know your way under the hood—you know its workings inside out. After a couple of years, and it's the same for these airplanes.

"With modern aircraft, with all the electronics it's a lot harder. But the Il-76 and the An-12 are very rugged—they can take a lot of punishment. There's still scope to use high-speed tape, like duct tape, and they won't be taking any real risks where they see they're putting their lives in danger. With these old Russian aircraft, it's mostly mechanical, and something you can fix if you have a flexible mind. It's like the pioneering early years of aviation, you know, the de Havilland flying into the Arctic and something happens, and they have to fix up a propeller by hand. It's not pretty but it will get you home. It's the same with these guys—they still have the pioneering spirit of the early days of aviation. You make temporary repairs and you get home the best way you can."

After I put the phone down, for the first time in weeks I think back to Starikov and Barsenov, talked into taking off for the final leg of their journey to Malta with a pay bonus and faulty electrics. Then to Mickey's words that day we first talked: "The lifestyle kills as many of us as the planes."

No wonder Evgeny Zakharov bemoans the shortage of veteran pilots to train the younger generation out there: They're the least publicized of all Africa's endangered species. Another pilot puts it on a community forum, half jokingly: "I'm always surprised when another one of these planes crashes. Surprised that there are any still left to crash, that is."

There's something unutterably sad about it all, as if in some way the risks are part of some divine plan for these men; as if the business they're in and their demise—the death and the taxes—all amount to the same thing, the same shadow following them and snapping at their tails until they run out of luck, stamina, or speed tape. Or until, one clear morning on a shelled runway somewhere, they look at their leaking fuel tank and flashing warning light and just decide that, flashing lights notwithstanding, they finally want to go home.

For the first time, I realize how tiring it must get to be torn between the thrilling, often lucrative independence of their own businesses and their paper status as expendable cheap labor with a life expectancy measured in flying hours. It's a curious double life: both master of their own destiny and servant of others' demands. The two businesses can coexist quite comfortably and for many years: Mickey Inc., independent shuttle trader, shares a two-hundred-ton airborne office with Mickey the employee. On the one hand, they're just the messengers, the gofers; on the other, the kings whose fifteen tons or more they make every flight are their own import-export business and nobody else's. Since I've known him, albeit intermittently, I've often caught myself on the verge of asking him whether he ever wishes he'd chosen the other path; a different, more stable life; settled down and become a . . .

But to my shame (or maybe it should be my pride), every time they pop into my head the words sound oafish and stupid and I duck the chance. Does he ever wish he'd become a what . . . an accountant? A doctor? An advertising copywriter? Had he ever thought about insurance? Jesus. I know what I saw in 1992, and it wasn't a nation full of people taking the time to ponder the stability of future career choices. How fucking crass. If I were Mickey and someone like me asked about the wisdom of my professional path, I'd throw him out of my plane over the Arabian Peninsula without a parachute.

You see, for me that's the funny thing about the whole business, about Bout, Minin, all of them. We want answers. Is Viktor clean or dirty? Is he the Merchant of Death or, as he contends, "the ideal modern businessman"? Entrepreneur, criminal, misunderstood visionary, or puppet? Innocent, cunning, or in denial? Or maybe something altogether truer, if less certain: maybe something in between. Something right there in the wide gray expanse between black and white, just like the arms business he followed.

Viktor Anatolyevich Bout, born in 1967, now a bony shadow of the flash, somewhat corpulent young mover and shaker who was arrested in that Thai hotel room in 2008, languishes in a U.S. jail awaiting trial. He wears a boilersuit, endures solitary confinement, and listens to Voice of Russia to hear "a familiar voice." The vegetarian suffers, he says, from a lack of fruit and vegetables and tea—only warm water is available in prison. He looks old and worried and shaggy and stooping in his prison chains, which has started to give him a demeanor and posture not unlike Mickey's. Away from the political grandstanding, some who met him, even those on the "other side," have their doubts whether he was ever more than a schmuck, someone else's chess piece. "Viktor Bout was not the great Merchant of Death, as the government and the reports and the Americans claim," says investigator Brian Johnson-Thomas. "Though admittedly he may be *a* merchant of *some* death, of course. But to call him that, to label him the Merchant of Death as Peter Hain did, is absurd."

Another insider who, during an off-the-record phone conversation, echoes Bout's own statements and those of the Russian government, says, simply: "The CIA, Interpol, MI5—they've spent that much time investigating him, and this is the best they can do?"

Even as the trial approaches, the man seems somehow smaller than the monstrous Merchant of Death glowering from the UN reports, articles, and indictments. Indeed, there are even moments of dark comedy, as the Mr. Big image built up over the years meets with altogether more mundane realities. Bout watcher and blogger Alexander Harrowell recently wondered whether the plane that disappeared en route to the plinth in Smolensk might finally have turned up. His research had led him to a particularly battered old Candid, grounded where else but in the Arabian desert. A photograph on his Web site is captioned: "TL-ACN, serial no. 53403072; ex-Centrafrican Airlines, now rotting in Umm Alquwain." In the tiny, sparsely inhabited Emirate, the plane has become a sand-spattered ad for the Palma Beach Hotel—its fuselage now exhorting passers-by to call 06-766-7090, should they wish to sample what the hotel calls its "classy facilities and amenities that give pleasure."

Bout himself has turned his Web site into an archive of documents that he claims prove his innocence, clips of his accusers, and UN reports in which he either appears or is, he contends, tellingly absent, to back up his claims of a frame-up. At the time of writing it's still active, although he appears to have caught the post-Wikileaks zeitgeist with claims the U.S. government has "ordered Google to take it down"—and indeed, it's interesting to wonder whether, as Bout goes to trial having entered a plea of not guilty in the U.S., his testimony will become another test of how transparent the U.S. government and others *really* want their statecraft to be. If he gets to tell it, Bout's story may yet turn out to be more of a Pandora's box than the controlled release of incriminating evidence his accusers are hoping for.

Meanwhile, Bout's wife, Alla, languishes in Russia, championing her husband's cause and experiencing, it seems, a distinctly Cold War welcome from America when she attempts to visit him in jail. Elsewhere, the underground chatter grows. Will there be a deal? A swap—perhaps at Vienna airport, both sides' preferred venue for the last exchange of spies? Or will Viktor Bout stand up and attempt his biggest trick yet—to remain fuzzy and insubstantial in front of prosecutors and TV cameras?

Whatever the result of his trial, there are questions about his degree of influence that remain. And about those "huge forces," too. Like Ilya Neretin said, if Viktor Bout is a prince, let's ask who the kings are.

Bout's business partner, Richard Chichakli, remains in hiding as I write this, probably still in Russia, posting occasional video diary pieces on the Internet about his predicament, his innocence, and mysterious break-ins to his apartment. Like Bout, he has a Web site on which he energetically protests not just his innocence but his insignificance. "Victor is just a person, and I am pretty much a nobody," he tells me in summer 2010 while awaiting the result of the extradition hearing that saw Bout sent to America for trial. I get the feeling he'd like to disentangle himself from Bout, the legal process in which he finds himself, the whole situation. He's clearly a shaken, frightened man who no longer trusts anybody; first claiming Viktor Bout's guilt or innocence will be "determined at trial," then that no trial he will receive at the hands of the U.S. can possibly be fair. He's just written a letter to Barack Obama protesting his treatment and lamenting what he sees as a continuation of the persecution he received at the hands of the Bush-Cheney administration. His assets have been frozen, and a new U.S. Government indictment has just been issued against him, this time for alleged violation of a sanction placed upon him in 2005. Yet despite the endless investigations, charges, and accusations ranged against him, this former accountant, real-estate man, U.S. soldier, and airport manager whose life was "dismantled and destroyed" by the armed, masked government agents who leaped from black armored trucks and surrounded his suburban home in Richardson, Texas, just after breakfast on the morning of April 26, 2005, has not been convicted of any crime. No wonder he's cautious.

My approach to him for an interview elicited written answers on an e-mail—and an attached PDF file containing those same answers as a sealed record, should I try to edit or misrepresent the e-mail's in-line content. He ends with the sigh of what seems like a disillusioned man—or at least one who has realized late in the game that he and Bout are not kings, perhaps not even princes, but tradable pawns. "Politics is always politics, and today's fugitives could be tomorrow's heroes and the opposite is true," he says. I remember Peter Danssaert's sardonic laugh when he told me about traffickers "being hired by the same governments to do the same thing legally that they're doing illegally."

As Chichakli signs off, there's another tantalizing hint that things are more than they seem. "As we speak," he finishes cryptically, "there is a horse trading going on in connection with this matter, and we just have to wait to see which horse was made to go." And with that, he's gone. I mail him again, but the silence has descended.

I've seen guilty men wriggling on hooks, and innocent ones too. And for the first time, I find myself thinking how much worse it would be to wriggle on a hook when you're neither black nor white but gray, eternally convinced that the man they're describing might have your name and life story but really isn't the true you at all. It sounds like purgatory, and perhaps for Bout and Chichakli it is.

For his part, party-hungry Leonid Minin no longer looks quite as impressive, or as much like the Lord of War on whom Nicolas Cage partly based his character Mickey Orlov in the 2005 film of that name. Released after serving two years on relatively minor offenses, he was acquitted of charges relating to arms trafficking because, of all things, the Italian courts felt they lacked the appropriate jurisdiction. Like Bout in jail in Thailand, he looked smaller and thinner and was rumored to be embarrassed by the coverage of his arrest. In 2006, he tried unsuccessfully to appeal against the freezing of his funds as a person associated with the now former Liberian president Charles Taylor. Delivering its judgment in 2007, the Court of First Instance of the European Communities noted the applicant's name, date of birth, and nationality:

> Leonid Minin (alias (a) Blavstein, (b) Blyuvshtein, (c) Blyafshtein, (d) Bluvshtein, (e) Blyufshtein, (f) Vladimir Abramovich Kerler, (g) Vladimir Abramovich Popiloveski, (h) Vladimir Abramovich Popela, (i) Vladimir Abramovich Popelo, (j) Wulf Breslan, (k) Igor Osols). Date of birth: (a) 14 December 1947, (b) 18 October 1946, (c) unknown[)]. Nationality: Ukrainian. German Passports (name: Minin): (a) 5280007248D, (b) 18106739D. Israeli Passports: (a) 6019832 (6/11/94–5/11/99), (b) 9001689 (23/1/97–22/1/02), (c) 90109052 (26/11/97). Russian Passport: KI0861177; Bolivian Passport: 65118; Greek Passport: no details. Owner of Exotic Tropical Timber Enterprises.

Then the court rejected his appeal and ordered him to bear his own costs and that of the Commission, and I can't help but read his statement, brief though it is, and feel a little sad on his behalf. "The applicant adds that all his funds and economic resources in the Community were frozen following the adoption of Regulation No 1149/2004, so that he was not even able to look after his son or pursue his activities as manager of a timber import-export company." Perhaps the pathos was intended; perhaps he got off lightly with two years in jail and the quiet life of a small citizen in Israel. Still, it's not the life he once enjoyed in Odessa, Ukraine, or Milan or Africa or any of those other countries. As a man, like Bout he's clearly highly intelligent, talented, and, well, he knew how to enjoy his old life. He's disappeared now—some claim he was strangled in Kiev, the death hushed up; others claim that he's alive and well. But if anyone ever pondered wasted career choices, the forks in the road that led him to this, I wonder if it might be him.

Tomislav Damnjanovic seems to have disappeared even more completely than Minin since the *New York Times* kicked up a stink about his work for the Pentagon back in 2007. Hugh Griffiths's guess is that he's still "sharking about somewhere"; Peter Danssaert reckons he simply became too hot for anyone to touch him, at least for a while. As I write this in spring 2011, a picture looking very much like him still haunts a MySpace page in his name that lists him as "Male, 56, Serbia," but the page is dormant, and his only friend is the social network's customer-support avatar. Milos Vasic, talking to me fifteen years after the Belgrade crash investigation he still calls his "greatest moment," even finds it hard to recall much about the man in the piece he calls "the broker."

Igor Salinger tries for a while to get me in touch through a go-between, but the go-between either can't trace him, or he doesn't want to be traced. A former employee of Damnjanovic's tells Salinger he could pop up in Sharjah any minute. After all, he's a businessman, one who may have become involved in things most of us would try to avoid, but who is just as innocent of any crime as you or I.

I want to find him again; he seemed happy to chat openly with the guy from the *New York Times* back then, in those pre–Viktor Bout bust times, despite a few memory lapses and his feeling that it was all official, all a matter of record, so why the fuss? I chase shadows for months, but it's as if he's just faded away. I tell Danssaert, who just says with a grim laugh, "Of course. He's a small, small fish."

Even Milos Vasic, whose article named him in the wake of the Surcin crash, pauses. "I'm sorry, I can't . . . this name, it doesn't play any music to me," he sighs, finally. Then he too is gone, and I'm overcome with the creepiest feeling that I've gone crazy and the man I call Tomislav Damn-janovic is no more substantial than the words I'm now writing on this flickering screen.

Somehow, something about all these men, and I can't be sure what it is yet, is making me uneasy. For one thing, as Moisés Naím told me, "Just imagine! If we'd only found a way, back when it mattered, to offer strategists like them worthwhile leadership or business roles on the legitimate side!" Arthur Kent, a veteran Canadian TV newsman who reported the first Gulf War, flew into Afghanistan with the cinemas during the Soviet-Afghan conflict, and now reports on the Afghan heroin connection for his own independent news agency Sky Reporter, puts it another way: "The irony is if you put people like [Bout or] your friend Mickey in charge and told them, 'The objective is actually total success and peace with the Afghans, plus you'll make a lot of money on the side,' they'd do a lot better than Karzai, NATO, the UN, and Obama anytime. Because those guys fool themselves into thinking that they are decent and God-fearing and honest, but it's their inability to monitor and audit properly that has the bad guys making money hand over fist but not really getting an opportunity themselves to contribute!

"All the decent buccaneers that *I* know would love to see things get better for the ordinary people. They don't want to make money on other people's backs *entirely*; they want to make *more* than other people, sure, but many buccaneers I know—smugglers and black marketeers—they are still critical, even while they are flourishing in the black market. They still point the finger at your politicians and say, 'Man, they're so full of shit, the stuff that's going on.'"

Maybe he's right. Maybe right now we need more pragmatists. In these times of extremism and idealism, just maybe Mickey's guys, with their can-do attitudes and their realism, are the closest thing we have to hope of reconstruction, despite—or perhaps because of—the things they carry.

But there's more to it, and it's making me itch badly now. Somehow, men like Bout, Minin, even Mickey make me feel, whether they are guilty or innocent or all shades in between, like we're all missing something very, very big. Only I don't know what it is yet.

Maybe, just as with Mickey, it's the nagging sense that Bout, Minin, and the rest of these Lords of War are just links in a bigger chain; that their champagne lifestyles and poster-boy statuses are somehow partly constructs, the very thing we need to believe cogs in the illicit arms trade should look like; just as we need to believe that fundamentalism looks like Osama bin Laden, or Mickey looks like Han Solo. Maybe Bout and Minin are just like Mickey, men trying to handle the lethal pressures someone makes it worth their while to handle.

And as one comment on a pilots' chat room said the day after the Entebbe crash that killed Evgeny Korolev: "If that plane was overloaded, I hope that the commercial guy is unable to sleep for a long, long, long time."

MICKEY TELLS ME he has never crashed (crash-landing doesn't count, nor does clipping a telegraph pole, having things fall off the plane, or turning round and landing immediately after takeoff with an engine problem). But the life's left visible scars on him nonetheless. Even the younger ones like Dmitry and rookie part-timers like Pavel, an African-trained copilot I only ever meet once, who must have been at elementary school while Mickey was undergoing his baptism of antiaircraft fire over Soviet-occupied Afghanistan, look permanently drained; pallid even through their tan in the heat of Africa and the Middle East.

They smoke way too much, just like they drink, just like Sergei loved his government-issue East African reefer—to unwind, to find common ground with strangers and with each other after twenty years of flying a sitting-duck target. Talk radio jabbers through the night, and all those off-the-leash nights in Entebbe and Sharjah start to make sense. The trashing of the same restaurants week after week and the wads of cash good-naturedly handed over; the "local wife"; the drinking; the drugs; the hijinks in six-to-a-room company doss-houses all cover a gaping absence of real family.

It's a gap otherwise filled only by Mickey's crumpled, cardboard-framed picture of his two daughters and his worries about his elderly mother back in western Siberia; regular barbs about Dmitry's Ukrainian ex-wife; and a mischievous look from Sergei when I ask if Lev's Ugandan "wife" was really his wife.

Sergei told me once with a weary smile that of course they all have families, but they became used to being away; life in the armed forces wasn't great for partners, what with all the deployment, and "coming back from something like the Afghan war is worse." Not everyone's di-

vorced, he says. But like oil-rig workers, they're forced to base even enduring relationships on absence and paychecks.

"It's a different life," he nods. "If you are stationed somewhere for a
period of months, they sometimes move over. But then they're all alone,
with no job or families around them, and for the kids, well . . ." He
shakes his head and winces. Mickey agrees—this is no life for kids.

The crew sleeps like this, on the plane, "sometimes, maybe too much,"
whenever they're away and there's an option to keep the money they're
given for accommodation; when they're in the arse end of nowhere, when
they fall behind and the whole damn airfield is shut, locked, and dark by
the time they arrive, when it's too dangerous, too expensive, or just too
much hassle to find a room; or when whoever they're flying for doesn't
lay anything else on.

"We get expenses for every payload," says Alex the Ukrainian. "Seventy-
five or a hundred dollars for a hotel, some extra for food. But it's better to
have the money."

Fuck 'em, snarls Lev: For more or less anyone but the pilot and navigator of the hour, it's "perfectly possible" to sleep on the wing through RPG
fire and storms too, once you get used to it. Besides, stocking up on the
hours like that means the loadmaster and a couple of other crewmen get
more time out and about at destination turnaround, which in this case
they use "looking for more business," he laughs, "or on ladies missions."

Brian Johnson-Thomas's eyes light up with admiration as he remembers one crew who, even when paid to sleep in a nice hotel in the Emirates, preferred to spend it on something more worthwhile and see the
dawn in shopping instead. Flight managing an International Red Cross
relief run from Sharjah into Mogadishu back in 1993, he'd just paid one
recently privatized Candid crew their money plus the seventy-five dollars
per diem. "We were in Sharjah, having returned from a relief cargo run
into Mogadishu, and I'd paid them their five days' subsistence each on
landing in Sharjah. So we parted and I went off to my hotel for a shower. I
was lying in my bed draped in a towel, enjoying the air-con and thinking
of home, when the concierge called. She said, 'Shall I put the lorry on your
room bill, sir?'

"I said, 'Lorry? What the hell? What lorry?' So I got dressed and came
down on the double, and it turned out that instead of checking into a
hotel, relaxing, sleeping, having a meal, or freshening up, the crew had

immediately gone down to the duty-free shops and spent all their per diems—their hotel expenses, subsistence money, *everything*—on washing machines, TVs, microwaves, and luxury consumer kit they thought they could sell on somewhere else at a profit. They'd had to hire a truck to get it all to the plane and started stuffing it into the belly—charging the truck to me, of course. Then they were going to sleep on the plane. I mean, there was this whole convoy of brand-new goods in there.

"I said, 'How the hell are you going to get all that into that plane as well as the cargo?' It's only a small belly space on the Il-76, and it just wasn't going to fit. It was impossible! So I just laughed, y'know, 'Good luck with that.' But sure enough, two of the loadies went down there in the very early hours of the morning, and by takeoff time the whole lot had miraculously vanished as usual."

Even Mickey laughs at that one: a short, wheezing shake, then a lick of the cigarette paper. I look at him from the corner of my eye while we smoke. The great first generation of ex-Soviet airmen are nearing retirement age, but as Evgeny Zakharov says, there are few enough left who can train the next generation on these Antonovs and Ilyushins. Pilots like Mickey can still make good money instructing, if they want to—better and better as their numbers dwindle. But the numbers are dwindling fast, and the worry is that there'll be a shortage of apprentices for sorcerers like him. Of course, the old Soviet-Afghan warplanes may be falling apart, but the Ilyushin factory has just announced a new model. Even so, I can't shake the idea that I'm looking at something passing, and that we'll never see men like this again.

The plastic around a cardboard tray of Heineken is torn open. Cigarettes, horrible oversugared Ugandan cake, and rolling papers are thrown around, but nobody says much, and after a quick walk round the plane with Mickey in a futile attempt to get him into conversation while he distractedly checks the look of nothing in particular and kicks some grass, we head back "indoors." There's a radio somewhere, playing an Arabic-language talk-radio station.

"It helps with sleep," says Dmitry with a disarming half smile. It is the first time I've seen his face do anything but glower. "We always just hear work talk and each other. Not so interesting." One of the other guys he used to fly with would put the TV on in his hotel all night. That drove them all crazy.

The radio chatters to itself until someone turns it down, but not off. It's unexpectedly touching to see them flattening out their mattresses and unrolling pajamas. I haven't brought any of that, so I just shift my bag under my head and stare at the insides of our giant tin can. My thoughts are going at a thousand miles per hour and there's nothing I can do to slow them down. It's said that Sudan is the latest country, even down here, to join Angola, Iran, and much of Europe in banning these old planes, the Antonovs and Ilyushins that have worked their skies for two decades. Rumor on the *avialegionery* grapevine says Sharjah, the very bosom on which the business was suckled, will be next.

I put my arm over my face and turn, trying to stop the galloping sense of it all closing in, and suddenly I understand how lonely it can feel to wander the skies, even with comrades, and why they drink, and why, in the face of all that, they carry on. Out of the blue—perhaps just to hear the comforting, familiar sound of my own suburban voice out here—I tell Mickey in English that they remind me of cosmonauts on a space station. "We cover more kilometers," he says, smiling back. In the stark yellowish light, he looks every one of his years.

I'm tired too—too tired to keep trying to communicate in our awkward mix of pidgin languages, their halting Hollywood English against my feeble, rusting Russian. As I try to settle back down, home seems like a very long way away indeed, and deep in my chest I start to get a small inkling of why Starikov, Matveenko, Sharpatov, and all those other airmen took one last leap into the sky. After a while, the other reasons you're flying fade, and there's only one thing left. And like them, I really, really want to go back home.

CHAPTER TWENTY-TWO

The Gathering Darkness

Russia, 2010

A PIECE OF FILM SURFACED on the Internet in 2009. Taken from behind the glass of the conning tower, it shows what looks like a heavily over-loaded Il-76 rolling onto the grass verge at the edge of the runway in a bid to get as long a run-up as possible. On the film, you can hear the voices of the Australian observers becoming more and more concerned that the plane won't make it. When it does finally lift off—having left the runway and begin to touch grass with its tires—the cameraman is heard to lament the fact that "I'm running out of film—gee, I hope I've got enough to film the crash." In another clip taken by planespotters, one voice remarks that "it's only the curvature of the earth that got that one off the ground!"

But while it looks to outsiders like a miracle every time a plane like this gets airborne, in fact there's a specific trick to getting a suicidally overloaded ex-Soviet warhorse like this off the ground in time. And, says Mickey without a hint of humor, "It usually works."

I've spent whole flights tensed and petrified, hunched in a full-body rictus in the absolute certainty of my impending fiery demise. I've wad-dled across asphalt afterward like a seasick sailor and waved my arms up-ward inside the cabin as we cleared a fuel bowser with inches to spare. But

I'm still here, so maybe he's as good as everyone says. And what he says is it's just like swimming instead of running: Everything takes a little bit longer, is all, which is where experience pays off. You get to know what's coming up and start avoiding it a good ten minutes before you see it. That way you can do whatever you like—10, maybe even 20 percent overweight. Except he's wearing a half smile as he says it, though, and in a split second of dreadful clarity I know he's wondering whether 21 percent might be feasible. Under certain conditions, of course.

In any case, it explains why knowing the Afghan, Central Asian, and Caucasian terrain served him so well; and why Evgeny Zakharov is so keen for his pilots to have their ten thousand hours in Angola or wherever else specifically. When you're pushing your plane to the limit and beyond, there's no substitute for knowing what you're flying into.

It also explains Mickey's habitual full and free use not just of the runway, or the perimeter track, but of the grass, bare earth, warehouse courtyards, and any other flat surface around the air base he can access to get as big a run-up as possible for takeoff. As one air traffic guy in Entebbe told me, hooting with laughter: "You hear about all these fences and telegraph poles being clipped by wings on takeoff, streetlamps ripped out of the ground—there was another one recently. What you don't hear is that half the time they were only *backing the damn plane up* when it happened!"

We're all right, though. Like Mickey says, "First thing. Know your plane." And after three decades, he's more or less married to the Candid and knows exactly what he can get away with.

Still, something's been bothering me. Listen to Mickey and he'll tell you it's his bird; he decides what goes on or doesn't. But I'm increasingly aware that Mickey's founding myth about "liberating" an Il-76 and flying it down to Kazakhstan and setting up in business, while undoubtedly true, is some way from being the whole truth. You get used to that, of course— though when even the infamous, exhaustively investigated Viktor Bout himself can answer the question by simply spreading his arms and declaring mysteriously that as a twentysomething air force man, although "I never had a single investor . . . finding the money was never a problem," this something that isn't adding up starts looking like something very, very big indeed. And I'm naturally curious. So after my last try at broaching the subject last night it was made clear to me that there was no way

I could realistically push the issue without blowing our comfy-but-tenuous relationship and landing up on the concrete with one bag and no ride, I decided to do some digging.

"Looking at it from a commercial aspect, it's impossible to survive as an airline without a network of commercial contracts," says one cargo pilot who's followed Viktor Bout's loose network of planes and crews around the world for over a decade, and knows the hangars of Sharjah and their planes and crews well. "The crew often see themselves as independent because—it's quite common—one aircraft will have a full crew with lots of people, plenty of pilots, more loadmasters than you have fingers on your hand. And they work, fly, and stay together with the aircraft, so it *is* their plane—they go everywhere in it. They live on their own plane, they live from their own contracts. But they're all part of a bigger thing somehow."

"It's more complicated than everybody realizes," laughs Peter Danssaert. "Okay, you'd think, it clearly belongs to *somebody*—but to give you an example from another actual Il-76 crew, the fuselage belongs to one person, but the engines belong to somebody else. So they 'rent' the engines from the other party to actually fly this Il-76!"

"Not only do your crew not own their planes," says Johnson-Thomas, "but nor do their partners, or their employers, or people above them. Almost every single Il-76 in the world is ultimately controlled by one of three people, and they are all very, very high up in countries of the former Soviet Union. And they are powerful men whose names you will never hear."

This view is echoed by another source who goes further, suggesting that these three men ultimately correspond to three countries—Ukraine, Russia, and Byelorussia—and that they are more or less the same level of men who would have controlled them before the breakup. It seems fantastical until I remember Russia's wholly state-owned commercial arms business, Rosvooruzhenie, now called Rosoboronexport, in which none other than Marshal Evgeny Shaposhnikov took an advisory role in later life; and how one of the biggest Il-76 operators on UN preferred supplier lists is Byelorussian outfit TransaviaExport (based, ironically, on Zakharov Street in Minsk); state-owned but out there in the cutthroat African, Asian, and Middle Eastern marketplaces with the rest. It was their pair of Il-76s that got shot down over Mogadishu.

Indeed, the extent to which these state operations compete or cooperate with the smaller fish—and, for example, their relationship to men like Mickey or even heavily tracked celebrities like Viktor Bout—is unclear, even to relative insiders. Russian mafia expert Mark Galeotti has tried to follow the paper trail, too. And it's led him to some very grand, heavily guarded, and firmly shut doors indeed.

"I've come across a pattern where, for a bigger business concern, it's handy to have a 'tame' independent out there," he says, "so when somebody comes in and for business or political reasons their cargo is not something you really ought to be carrying yourself, you also don't want to say no to the customer. So having these tame associate 'independent' operators means you can say, 'Well, we can't touch it—but we know someone who can.' And therefore there's a deal. It may be that they own it, or sometimes there's just a relationship there, and the big boys will pass on their business to a small stable of semi-independent operators.

"The most malign ownership pattern, though, is where these so-called independents' metaphorical mortgages are owned by organized crime. Most of the time they'll ply very ordinary trade, but then sometimes the cell phone rings and it's, "We've got someone we want to fly out of somewhere very quickly," or, "There's a consignment we want to make sure reaches Tashkent.""

Galeotti pauses, mulling something over as a New York siren wails in through his apartment window. "And then, like I say, a lot of these crews are, frankly, deniable arms of military intelligence."

He stops. I whistle down the line, stunned at the list of potential silent partners in Mickey's business. The usual suspects indeed: oligarchs, the *mafiya*, high-ranking commanders in any one of the new armies that rose from the ashes of the Soviet military; the former KGB and now the Russian, Ukrainian, Byelorussian secret service. Quite a networking event for any small-time entrepreneur.

So which one did Mickey choose? Or, to put it another way, who chose him?

THINKING TOO MUCH about that kind of question can give a man a dose of fear wherever he is. I'd advise against it in the strongest terms when in the cannabis-filled cabin of an ancient, jam-packed Il-76 of indeterminate

ownership with a long record of home repairs and close shaves. It's especially not the sort of thing to focus on with a head full of last night's alcohol and a printout of the Aviation Safety Network's Il-76 crash-report
database in your pocket, as the plane takes off nothing like steeply enough,
juddering and swaying all over the sky.

Clearing truck height is one thing, but the hot air rising from the road
creates an updraft that, at this altitude, feels like someone's grabbed both
wings in his giant fists and is shaking us to see what happens. Mickey told
me always to look forward, through the same glass he sees. But against
my will, I do look down. And when I do, something unexpected happens.

As we climb through billowing clouds and level off in the evening sun
at twenty-two thousand feet, I get a flash of something else. Call it Mickey's aerial view—it's either that or everything I've experienced in the past
few years flashing before me, and I know which one I'd prefer. Call it
what you want; it's okay with me. Because the noise of the engines in my
ears has stopped and suddenly everything's gone very, very calm.

Here's what I see down there, scattered among the clouds and rivers
and deserts and smeared Perspex.

There's Andrei Soldatov, over there in Moscow, looking into who's
"protecting" crews like Mickey's on their flights in and out of Afghanistan
and the Caucasus, and wondering aloud whether the government might
not secretly want some of that heroin to get through; with him is former
Duma minister Anatoly Chubais, trapped in his own small purgatory,
forever explaining to anyone who'll listen that he had no choice: It was
either a criminal transition to the free market or no transition at all.

Over here on the left, just above London, is Brian Johnson-Thomas,
sharing a beer with Viktor Bout, making father-in-law jokes and talking
about how "all the Candids in the world are ultimately owned by three
men who are so high up, you and I will never know their names."

I can see Mark Galeotti, too, way over there in New York. He's explaining the way the mafia and the state work together, and off each other,
and how one or another of them is usually fronting the cash for the pilots.
There's Leonid Minin—acquitted of arms trafficking by an Italian court
despite admitting his involvement—complaining to the courts about how
much his business has suffered, before he too falls silent.

There's the UN man in Uganda, watching as the plunder comes and
goes. Richard Chichakli is somewhere just out of view, drawing the blinds

and talking to his webcam about how he's being persecuted by huge, shadowy forces. And here's his old stomping ground below: Sharjah airport, glittering with money and promise, just as it always used to. And like stars spread out below, I can make out the constellations of Baku, Dubai, Kabul, and Rangoon; Tripoli, Mogadishu, Entebbe, Kinshasa shining brightly.

And that's when it hits me. And it's not just beautiful: It's *perfect*.

The Il-76 is packed like a flying skip and it's handling like one. Gravity toys with us like a killer whale with a seal in its jaws; it comes and goes, then suddenly grips us and sucks us down before tossing us back up, and I swear the wings are shaking so hard they're flapping. The whole plane's wobbling about like a seasick sailor, everyone's gone tense and quiet until we get through this, and even Sergei's hanging on to his canvas strap. It's always the same. We all feel it. Maybe this time it'll be our turn to make crash-report headlines.

But not me, not this flight. I've got a strange opiumlike chill rising over the skin. The hairs on my arms are standing on end, the stupidest grin is building up inside me, and I know from the palms of my hands to the soles of my boots that we'll be fine. Like Mickey would say, *zhizn harasho*.

Because I know the secret now, the last secret, the trick behind the greatest, most ambitious, most devilishly simple and brilliantly effective illusion that anyone's ever pulled off.

Me. Out of all the millions who've witnessed it, who fell for it, who became its stooges, its victims, its assistants, its marks, its technicians, its master illusionists, all over the world. I know what they did, and I know how they did it. And if we're *not* fine, and our number's being called, then you'll hear no complaints from me. Because now that I've seen it, I can fall through six miles of sky and die happy.

How close the mafia, big business, and military intelligence got in the white heat of an imploding Soviet Union surprised everybody—even, at first, the mafiosi, the FSB agents, and the oligarchs themselves. All except, of course, the blue-collar types who did their dirty work.

They came from the returning military—the *Afghantsy*, of course, but also the hundred-thousand-plus soldiers who found, upon returning from their stations across Eastern Europe, that they were now homeless as well as penniless, around a million of them without pensions.

But they also came from the ranks of the workers; the factory floors that howled and hammered through the night, a corridor of yellow light, iron, concrete, and chemical smoke that lit up the giant, smog-clad industrial suburbs of Ekaterinburg and Tankograd. These were the men who made the machines: Mickey's classmates, his land-bound counterparts, without the wings to fly or his aerial view. They too were desperate. And like him, they had had just about enough.

Today, two unusually well-kept graveyards, one on either side of Ekaterinburg, tell the story. In the roaring official silence, they are all that now testifies to the cataclysmic levels of gang-related violence, murder, intimidation, opportunism, and sheer commercial flair the 1990s brought to Mickey's hometown. Russia's former mob-crime capital boasts not one but two dedicated *mafiya* cemeteries—lovingly tended by relatives and surviving buddies, popular with tourists seeking a little of the city's badass thrill at a safe historical distance.

At Vedensky Hills and Vagan'kovo, row upon row of polished marble tombstones depict, in huge, lovingly detailed tattoo-art-style engravings, the Bermuda-shirted, bomber-jacketed *bratki*—mafia "little brothers"—slain in the privatization gang wars of the 1990s. One is clutching a Mercedes key ring; another's hand is thrust deep into the pocket of his leather bomber jacket in the classic stickup pose. Brand clothing and luxury goods are prominently depicted. It's the classic language of capitalism's dispossessed, from L.A. to London: no education, no prospects, no home of their own, but dripping with designer logos, status symbols, and gold.

In the 1990s, in the same convulsing agonies of a broke, faltering state that set Mickey free, these men saw their chance too.

The heavy industry and arms production for which the area was so infamous—though it had been cloaked in secrecy by the government—was on its knees, and organized crime moved in. One such industrial giant, Uralmash, was the Ekaterinburg region's major employer. An arms, military-transport, chemical, mining-equipment, and heavy-machinery behemoth, it was responsible for a veritable greatest hits of game-changing Soviet weaponry—from the Howitzer M-30 to the T-34 tank—and in modern times, long-range-rocket and aviation manufacturing. Its ties to Russia's military and its secret service went deeper than supplier-client; it was, effectively, the Red Army's own weapons-manufacturing arm. Its employees were revered for their skill and importance.

And increasingly, they were feared too. Even before the Union's breakup, Uralmash factory workers had their own criminal gang, the Uralmash Boys, whose meager and increasingly sporadic wage packets were, in the 1980s and 1990s, first supplemented, then eventually dwarfed, by the money they made from black marketeering, protection rackets, pimping, fraud, and extortion. And when, in 1991, the company found it couldn't make the payroll, the Uralmash Boys offered *it* a loan to tide it over. So, was it an offer the board could not refuse? And if it was, what strings were attached?

This was their route to semilegal status, and it quickly set the pattern across the former Soviet Union. This was a world in which mafia hard men not only influenced, but swiftly took over, chaired, and owned the biggest businesses in the country—including thousands supposedly owned by the state.

"The economic aspects of Uralmash's activities on their own suggest that the Uralmash Boys were the first to find a productive way to use violence and force to protect investments and guarantee property rights," wrote Vadim Volkov, associate professor at the Department of Political Sciences and Sociology, the European University in St. Petersburg. "According to police data, the Uralmash Boys were behind around two hundred companies and twelve banks, and partially controlled ninety additional companies, from petroleum processing to cellular networks, car dealerships, and breweries."

By the mid-1990s, the Russian Center for Social and Economic Policy Analysis published its first figures on organized-crime activity in Russia. They made shocking reading: Criminal gangs either controlled or owned outright forty thousand firms, including two thousand supposedly state-owned companies. German and Czech police had made at least half a dozen stings in which Russian organized-crime groups like the Uralmash Boys, with access to the weapons stockpile, began exporting nuclear weapons components to the West.

For their part, the authorities could—or would—do nothing, partly because they were now stakeholders in the mob's own business. High-ranking KGB then FSB officers refrained from interfering with the mob's activities in return for a piece of any state-run business they carved up; intelligence officers failed to turn up for work because they were at their "other" office, wearing a newly purchased Armani suit and negotiating the purchase of a new plane to ferry their merchandise in without fear of hijacks, holdups, or their uniformed colleagues' roadblocks.

In 1999, in a tantalizing glimpse of the mind-set inside Russian intelligence at the time, former FSB man Aleksander Litvinenko, later assassinated in London when a fellow agent exposed him to radioactive polonium over sushi, wrote: "Our secret services are now at that stage of decay when it becomes hard to deal with direct obligations on account of business commitments." In other words, they had gone the same way as Uralmash: bought out by vested interests, profitable sidelines, and political paymasters, they were too busy doing business *with* the bad guys to do their jobs stopping them. In 1994, the Urals Transport and Machinery Works factory built eighty-four self-propelled minesweepers and received funding for the Russian government to finish them, even though there was not a single buyer on the books. Somehow, these arms would find their way out there, even if it wasn't through official channels. Perhaps even to customers the official channels were banned from dealing with. Somehow they would vanish, and reappear in the third world's savage frontiers. But how?

For anyone with a few connections in the Russian Bermuda Triangle, now wholly owned by the Uralmash Boys Inc. and their shareholders in the FSB, finding the answer to that question meant lots of money. And that meant blood. As the gang factions fought for control, the violence exploded along with cars, homes, and mail parcels. Ski-masked men concluded buy-outs with Kalashnikovs; ambitious executives suddenly and inexplicably fell from high tower blocks, leaving the way clear for what one jewelry trader called "a state-mafioso economy like Nigeria's, when state institutions merge with criminal structures."

These graves, their polished marble and buffed black granite glinting in the morning sun, are all that's left of the unlucky ones—the ones who got as close to the big payday as owning that Mercedes, or buying those Gucci loafers, before being gunned down. But for the lucky ones, busy moving into legit commerce, rebranding themselves *biznesmeny*, opening subsidiaries in sunny places with easygoing officials, the paydays were about to get much, much bigger. All they needed to go global, really, was a logistics division. Planes. Big planes. And crack crews, too, men who could fly anywhere and needed work. Now where would they find such a division?

And the union steward, the secret policeman, and the banker paused and looked at each other.

The cabin is lit up by the sun now, and the cinema screen shows nothing but a tunnel of gold and blue heaven ahead. And as well as I can, I'll explain to you how it plays out.

Back in the early 1990s, that seismic rupture in the fabric of the Soviet Union looked like chaos to the West, and believe me, it looked a whole lot more like chaos when you were there.

"It's maybe difficult for you to grasp the whole scale of what happened," Dmitry Rogozin, Russia's ambassador to NATO, says over tea at the heavily fortified Embassy building in Brussels. I take another sip from my china cup, holding the saucer carefully as an extra insurance against spilling any on the plush carpet that covers the marble-floored anteroom to his office. Grandly framed portraits of epaulette-festooned Russian generals glare down at us—the ambassador, his deputy, me, and our pale, skinny, and clearly very nervous young interpreter. Though I speak a little Russian, and Rogozin speaks some English, this is clearly considered too important to risk misunderstandings.

Rogozin himself is a huge, disarmingly baby-faced bear of a man— clearly confident, proudly controversial, funny, and instantly likable, he's got "rising star" written all over him; a self-professed nationalist who cut his teeth under General Lebed in the early 1990s, he tells me with a smile he comes from an aviation background, while his brother-in-law is one of the directors of none other than the Ilyushin aircraft-manufacture bureau and plant head office in Moscow. He also counts himself a friend, he says, of Sharpatov, the pilot of the Il-76 captured by the Taliban back in 1995. He tells me how he observed the collapse of the Soviet air force close to the eye of the storm. "It happened twice—in 1917 and in 1991. One after the other, the armies these men belonged to no longer existed. They didn't know to do anything else. Sure, theoretically, they could go to civil aviation—but that was shrinking too. So they tried to find a role in a state that had split apart. And even if a very few took the criminal way with their activities, I'd rather not call it criminal but 'gray business.'"

The world's biggest standing army had been split apart, denied funding, and more or less evaporated. But the men needed something. Nobody could figure out just how it had got this bad, this quickly. Their families were living in tents. Near-starvation brought Mickey and his returning comrades to the brink of civil disobedience; there was almost no air force left. Some planes were mothballed; plenty of pilots, engineers, radio operators, loadmasters, navigators, were all desperate for work.

Then came the order, the understanding, from broad-shouldered, much-loved Evgeny Shaposhnikov, commander in chief of the armed forces, soon-to-be representative of the president of the Russian Federation of the state arms-export operation Rosvooruzhenie, and a few years later, chairman of Aeroflot. They were available for work all right, starting immediately, travel no problem. Here came the "liberation" and overnight respray jobs of all those hundreds of aircraft by men, free and enterprising. The best and the brightest sons of Russian, Ukrainian, and Byelorussian air academies and regiments, spiritual sons of Gagarin and of Shaposhnikov's fighter-ace heroes, took to the sky again, apparently free agents. They were out of the armed forces, out of uniform. They could take jobs or leave them at market rate, and hunt for whatever else they came across.

So, sure, it looked like chaos—disorganized crime, the free market gone wild, as Mickey and the boys ran goods all over the world, busting sanctions, trafficking those conveniently sold-off arms stockpiles in conveniently sold-off planes, arming rebels and governments, and making big, big money. The law of the jungle.

Take the aerial view, though, and you can trace a certain spooky symmetry.

Viktor Bout's secret flights armed first the Afghan Northern Alliance, then reportedly the Taliban too—almost as if these freelance delivery men could achieve something with commerce that the Red Army hadn't managed, and arm all mujahideen factions so well they'd annihilate each other! And all the time bringing money in for all those old weapons to a bankrupted treasury, too. It really could not have been planned better if the FSB itself had been involved. It's tempting to see the masked commando raid on his house in South Africa—so reminiscent of the secret agents who shook down East Line —as a warning to toe the line. And the "mysterious forces" he spoke of who'd plug him if he spoke—who were they? It's always tempting to speculate. But we know that this was just Viktor Bout, a lone operator, playing fast and loose with the Northern Alliance and then making a deal to get his plane back from the Taliban, not part of a greater plan or anything. So he came by the money from the planes mysteriously. So what.

That was business in Russia.

Then, of course, there were the African wars. Sierra Leone, Angola, Liberia, Rwanda, the Congo, DRC, Sudan, Somalia, Uganda, Tanzania, all full of presidents and rebels more than willing to trade diamonds, gold, coltan, timber, and other precious resources to import-export hustlers—including owner of Exotic Tropical Timber Enterprises Leonid Minin, and taxi driver Viktor Bout—for some of the now-redundant stockpiled weapons these freelance, wildcat operators kept bringing. To the uninitiated, it might seem as if the empty exchequers of the former Soviet Union had found a way to replenish themselves with under-the-counter deals in a way that no state could legally have attempted. But of course we know this was every man for himself. We're told there was no greater plan. It was business.

Serbia: That was business, all right; these same planes, belonging to the same "network" of aviation outfits, so diffuse and so different but with an odd habit of sharing jobs, people, and methods. Those flights from Ekaterinburg via Belgrade, selling arms to Libya (did they pick up in Belgrade, or were they already full and just making a tech stop there?) weren't something a government or anybody connected with the establishment could be seen doing, not with UN and U.S. economic sanctions in place and Qaddafi a global pariah for protecting the Pan Am bombers. But they would be very lucrative, undoubtedly; and who knew what private businessmen with shady connections and some cronies in government got up to? These were lawless times, that was all. A series of unfortunate coincidences.

Then came the coalition occupation of Afghanistan and Iraq, and the flood tide of drug money leaving Afghanistan on these privately owned planes—ten million dollars every single day through Kabul alone in 2009—all of it heading to places like ex–Soviet Central Asia, Sharjah and Dubai, home to dozens of crews, networks, and business associates like Mickey's, where Farah and Braun reported 1,186 bank accounts had been opened by hundreds of different Russians in just one branch alone, suggesting "money laundering on a huge scale." One wonders who these people were and how much of it worked its way back home every day. In 2004, a diamond smuggler for the *mafiya* was executed in Dubai along with his entire family. Members of two rival smuggling militias were involved in a massive shoot-out inside one of the emirate's main tourist hotels in broad daylight. Both incidents bore the hallmarks of professional training. And though these are hugely complex, large-scale operations, again we are led to believe the men are simply rogues, criminals, and lawless deviants.

Now there are arms-for-drugs bazaars down by the old Soviet air bases on the Tajik border, and the steady tide of heroin entering Russia itself. "All of a sudden we hear a lot of declarations about how the threat [from Afghan heroin] is dire, and growing, and something has to be done," says Soldatov. "It looks like convenient political theater. Someone is clearly giving these flights some protection."

All those planes, all those crews and their individual sleeping partners, all swarming around the same places—it's enough to remind you of the good old days, the Air Transport Regiment operations.

I can feel walls dissolving my head. As I shut my eyes, the abrupt end to my exchange with Mickey's old commander in chief Marshal Evgeny Shaposhnikov crackles back to life:

> "Marshal Shaposhnikov, in the mid-1990s, did you know about
> flights in Il-76 aircraft to supply the mujahideen of Afghanistan
> with weapons? Or rather, did these flights ever have official (or
> unofficial) government approval?"
> "No comment."

It's as if, to misquote W. B. Yeats, each of these falcons could indeed, somehow, still hear the commands of a distant falconer. Perhaps that falconer was no longer a commanding officer; perhaps he'd successfully made the transition to the market economy all by himself, as their boss. Could it be that those three men—former high-ranking Soviets from Byelorussia, Ukraine, and Russia, men whose names we never hear yet who ultimately own every Il-76 in the sky—had suddenly woken up the day the Union was dissolved to discover that, miraculously, they now owned a controlling interest in a fleet of forty Antonov-12s?

Just as Grigory Omelchenko, the former chief of Ukrainian counterintelligence, told Peter Landesman of the *New York Times*, "Traffickers like Bout are either protected or killed. There's total state control."

Those huge forces. The East Line bust came eight years in, but it came courtesy of the FSB—or was it the shadowy Reconciliation and Accord Foundation, shutting down crews, operators, and planes who threat-ened their monopoly and who, even all these years later, never were identified? Were the secret state and private business one and the same, as Litvinenko said before he, too, got shut down? The FSB, the govern-ment, wanting to make money the same way private businesses did. Con-tacts everywhere. A lot of muscle. All the men and machines. None of the competition. No structure, no comebacks, no contracts, and don't come to us if your embargo gets broken. Almost too perfect.

At our meeting I broach the subject with Rogozin. He talks, cagily, about the virtues of the men, then about how his recently published mem-oir, *The Hawks of Peace*, contains "plenty of bombs" for those who read it in the West. He asks me to read the just-finished English translation. Maybe I can pass it to any interested publishers. And suddenly, time is up. Rogozin stands, envelops my hand in his colossal right paw, and bids me good luck even as I despair at not having got more from him on the nature of this global shadow network. Then, as we part, he looks at me and winks. And smiles as he says to me, in English: "Every Russian has good connec-tions."

My mind's racing now. Reagan, Thatcher, Kohl, then Bush, then ev-erybody in the West, got to feel they'd seen off an Evil Empire; "won" a Cold War. But the Soviet air force didn't break; it bent, reshaped, and re-formed. They are still out there, flying whatever needs to be flown. Just the terms of their contracts have changed. Same company, new logo. All those superplanes, pumped out by a Soviet military-industrial com-plex as fit for military or commercial use, dual-registered, ready for any-thing, anytime, anywhere with just a change of insignia. Mickey talking to me for the first time back on that runway: "We just rebranded, though that's not what we called it at the time."

And with that simple coat of paint, that change of name, the largest, most elaborate illusion ever staged was finally pulled off. After that, it was all easy. Once you'd turned a whole armed force into a thousand SME businesses and congratulated NATO on winning a game well played, no one was watching anymore. And after that, getting the world's greatest stockpile of decommissioned weapons to magically change places with billions of dollars in African blood diamonds would be child's play. Outfits like Mickey's can do things no state could ever do in its own name—even one as powerful as Russia or as strategic as Ukraine. A black op, an arms run, drug couriers, clandestine human cargo, extraordinary renditions, mercenary drops would be unthinkable for the military. Who commanded it? Who signed the orders? Who authorized the plane? They would be ordered to stop. But for shadowy, maverick SME businesses within businesses, well, who knows what they're doing?

This was a secret state running its business on the al-Qaeda model: loose affiliations, no pyramids, independent operators reporting to no one. The old way had foot soldiers and lieutenants. The new way just has enterprising solo operators: Mickey.

I remember what Mark Galeotti said the day we talked about the rise of the Ekaterinburg mafia. "Any of the individual players is often going to be very ramshackle and doing things very ad hoc. They might be wily and have street smarts, but they're not intellectuals. They don't have business plans or mission statements. However, the organism as a whole and the economy that it represents is often surprisingly sophisticated. It reacts very rapidly. The role of the umbrella 'gang'? Simply to set the turf rules, to mediate disputes because shoot-outs are bad for business—to maintain security, and a brand name people will respect."

Then I think of the Il-76 grounded in Bangkok with arms from North Korea. The bust, the uproar, then nothing. The crew were freed to return home to Kazakhstan and Belarus with no suggestion of charges being brought. The owner of the company who chartered the plane down in Shymkent claimed they'd taken holiday and were working *na levo*. The cargo's paper trail led the CIA through a trail of shell companies and finally to a man who, it appeared, had never existed, except on paper. You had to love that.

There are huge forces, just like Viktor said, and they'll bring you in from wherever you get caught out—Kandahar, Bangkok, Darfur.

Outsourcing, it turns out, was the way forward in the East as well as the West. Whole armies of crack aviators, no job too tough or too hush-hush; almost untraceable, and paid by the hour. And maybe, while you're using them, you can even pick up some info about what they're carrying for the competition. Soviet Air Transport's Evgeny Zakharov now: "These ex–air force crews *thought* like military crews—the order comes, they'll carry it out."

In the end, of course, as in the beginning, this is a story about money. It's what works the magic, blinds the audience, produces rabbits from hats and valuable contraband from seemingly empty cargo holds. It's what democratizes Soviet regimes, and it democratizes weapons, power, drugs, too.

So a standing air force became a private air force, doing the same job but free of the ideology—pilots "resigning" from one permanent contract, going freelance or taking unpaid leave, and flying off to Angola in the same planes for the same people; people who now bore no responsibility for them. They were now able to break the embargo, run the guns, collect the cash in a way that they could never have managed in government livery. Factory trade unionists, soldiers, generals, ministers, and secret policemen—even Marshal Evgeny Shaposhnikov, commander in chief of the CIS forces, the Soviet Union's last minister of defense, soldier of distinction—became slick, designer-suited advisors, consultants, CEOs, corporate decision makers at global aviation companies, government-funded export firms, charities, think tanks. There was money coming in, and nothing else mattered anymore. Behind the smoke and mirrors, the invisible networks, the armies turned SME businesses and the regiments now man-with-van outfits: the misdirection, the plotting, and the double-dealing, that's the simple, banal, everyday beauty of it all.

The Soviet Union didn't implode because it changed its mind but because it ran out of cash. The truth behind the secret is that there are no sides; there is no right, no wrong, no left or right. There never has been, really. There is just money. And like money, Mickey and the boys will simply flow with the gradient of supply and demand. To talk to them about sanctions is to talk to the wind about treetops, or the waves about drowning men. They are no more essentially good or evil, left or right, moral or immoral, than investment, insurance, advertising, business, politics, journalism, flying, or money itself.

The devil's greatest trick was making mankind believe he didn't exist. No wonder the monitors, cops, and spooks have a hard time tracking these men—they've been forced to look for plans, for chains of command, for paper trails, for Mr. Big figures. Yet these men have found a way of carrying on without any of that. They don't have a plan, chain of command, a governing body, a modus operandi, a belief system, allegiances, or a set of rules. Except one: When enough people want them, and when the time and place demands, they will appear. Look at them down there. Mickey, Tatyana, Viktor Bout, and their friends and crewmen and business partners aren't the horsemen of the apocalypse; they're just chasing the money like the rest of us. The Soviet Union is gone. Long live the new Union: the one without a name or an anthem, a currency or even a border.

Silently, invisibly, this has become the Union we all live in. Theirs is the invisible empire, mighty in its weakness, invincible in its ethereal nature, hidden in plain view out on the open spaces and empty runways of the world. And if you think you can see them coming, or know what they'll do next or who they'll be tomorrow, good luck.

Then I feel a jolt and another shudder, a blast of bright, holy sunshine through cloud and smeared cockpit glass, and we're clear.

OLD SMUGGLERS DON'T die; they just pull one last disappearing trick.

It sometimes seems to me that Mickey's whole life had been a series of quiet departures: home and family in the hills, his garrison, Afghanistan, the air force, the Soviet Union, and any place that seemed like it was getting too regulated, too real. And as I think of him, a moment comes back to me with lightning clarity and makes me laugh.

It's 2007, and I'm standing beside Mickey's plane on a July morning so hot the secure airstrip perimeter and the minefields beyond are quaking in the haze. While we kick the ground and wait for our friends with the paperwork to show up and take their boxes of cigarettes, whiskey, and whatever else, I can feel the skin on the back of my neck blistering in the sun. Mickey and the boys have hats on, towels round their shoulders, long-sleeved jackets, whatever it takes to keep the sun off; and if it makes them look like bag ladies, *not* having them is starting to make me look like a burn victim.

We've just landed, but the waiting's killing me. For some reason, we've got to meet someone else out here on the perimeter track. Mickey—that ill-fitting captain's jacket now splitting at the elbow and so worn and shiny it's starting to glint like it's wet—looks across the tarmac with that disappointed half smile of his. McKinlay the Canuck is shuffling over; I can hear him grumbling. But the crew seem oddly fidgety, and no one's making a move to get the fuck out of the heat. There's not much talk.

McKinlay and I offer to stick around, but Mickey's not having it. He sends us on our way. We're heading off, arms full of bags and boxes, across the shelled, cracked runway, picking our way between the tussocks of grass. As we head for the dirt verge to make our shortcut, Mickey shouts to us above the din.

"Hey! Remember . . ."

We stop, turn back to him, looking very small across the shimmering asphalt. He stops waving.

"Don't step off the tarmac."

And with that, he's gone again.

Mickey's a master at disappearing acts, just like so many rogue aviators of the Union. Having pulled off the greatest collective illusion in history, these days these unlikely outlaws are more modest; some vanish in a puff of smoke into the sides of mountains. Others disappear into the African Great Lakes, or tropical seas, and the waters and the forty-foot-thick silt beds and stones close over them leaving not a ripple to show they or their plane had ever passed this way. They fly into thick fog, low cloud, dark forests, never to be seen again.

Some take off one day and are swallowed by the air itself, man and two-hundred-ton ship finally escaping the dull pull of the earth, the demands of the paperwork, the cops, the yee-hawing Chechen crazies with their RPG launchers, the business hassles, the border officials, the clients and bosses, the radar and the mujahideen, the FBI, the CIA, the mafia, the fixers, and the congressmen.

Others just want to go home.

After I turned down the offer of a ride to Mogadishu, I never saw Mickey again. For a while he had his other SIM cards. Then his number rang again for a couple of days, but he never answered. Then the tone was gone again and I just heard dead air in the speaker. Those he flew with or for, at least the few I had anything like a lead on, said he'd not been around. Maybe he'd left the business, said one, but I didn't buy that for a minute. Mickey only really ever felt happy flying; the ground was where it all got dirty. Like he told me once, take the aerial view or go mad and die drunk. So I started to worry. Not all the time, of course—I mean, really I hardly knew the guy—just a nagging sensation partly, I suppose, from feeling I was off the ride. I got into checking out the rumor networks, kept tabs on the air-crash sites. Pretty soon I began to feel like a naturalist on the TV whose tagged elk hasn't come home with the thaw.

The elk never did show. Like their lives, their deaths are rumors, trails leading off into the fog. Then, about a month before I began collecting together all the notes that eventually became this book, I finally heard Mickey had touched down for good: nothing to do with flying, just a plain old heart attack, back in Russia. And that was it, the way I heard it; no drama, no plane crash, no Viagra, no mafia, no Nubian princesses or bar brawls, no mountainsides or lakes, no flaming engines or Stinger rockets, Janjaweed abductors or Taliban warlords; just what I like to think he always called the Life. Bullets in the air, vodka on the ground. One way or another, they'll get you in the end.

By last summer Sergei, liveliest of them all, had also bought the farm. The sky took him (of all people; the general feeling is that it beat the bottle by about a week) while he was freelancing on another plane with another crew. Unlucky is what they say, but even the greatest sleight of hand can only hold off gravity for so long. I tend to think of him when I drink too much and regret it, and also on the rare occasions I skip stones, their kinetic energy and lift slowly giving out until they fall. I'm sure he'd laugh if he knew.

Word is that Lev just disappeared one day—he just didn't turn up for a shift, a perennial favorite of crewmembers chasing bigger bucks. Posted missing, presumed got out in time. The last anyone heard from him, he was muttering about moving to Thailand, flying with smaller planes and setting up in the bar business, but it doesn't look like he ever got it started—it's all been way too quiet out there.

Eternally pissed-off Dmitry and whatever friends or strangers made up the numbers flight by flight could still be out there, flying for whoever has the work. I actually spoke to Dmitry on the phone, once, after I left Africa. After all his prickly attitude, he turned out to be the one who told me to keep in touch, and I lucked into him on a call home. He said times had been pretty tough; they're all banning Antonovs and Ilyushins for being too noisy, too old, too unregistered; plus everyone else was starting to get in on the act.

As it happened, Evgeny Zakharov was saying the same thing at the same time: "You know who kicked us out of the Somalia contract? White South Africans. We were a bargain, but now they're the bargain fliers in Africa." The airline owner's got a weariness about him today, but I can't help thinking he sounds almost relieved as he says, before we bid good-bye: "Russian pilots are not as attractive as they used to be."

The phone call with Dmitry was shorter than I'd hoped. He seemed different, younger, more relaxed somehow away from the plane. He said he had been marooned in Asia without a flight out of there for weeks, and he'd realized it couldn't carry on that way for too long anymore, not financially. He said maybe it's time he put in some hours as a trainer. Then a woman's voice was shouting in the background, and he had to go. Now the piece of paper's gone, but it doesn't matter. So is my connection to his world. Like the man Wittgenstein said: Even if a lion could speak, you wouldn't understand what it wanted to tell you.

And the others? Well, if you hear anything, tell me. They've melted away, two or three removes too distant for an armchair stalker like me to hope to keep tabs on them. Maybe the bullet in the night got them too, maybe not. I'd like to think maybe they made it through, cheated the most dangerous, nobody-gives-a-damn business on this flyblown planet, and came in for their final landing okay. It's a phrase a lot of these Eastern flyboys use when they want to say retire, and now I can see why. Say "retire" and you tempt fate, invite smoking engines and moving mountaintops. *Retiring* is a laughable ambition; *landing* is something they know they can pull off.

So happy landings, whoever's left. I like to think you catch a drink together sometimes, by a poolside in Dubai or some back porch in Tatarstan, Thailand, or God knows where, but maybe that's just me. Are you alive or dead? I guess you get to be both until I track you down and find out. And you know as well as I do, that will never happen. So for now, I just keep looking at the sky.

One day, somebody will write a real book about these men and the dangers they face; the kind of book that makes politicians sit up and listen. And then the whole damn circus will stop; there'll be no more junk planes, no more deathtraps, no more exploding cargoes, no more cash deals, no more bribes, no more four-day, nonstop operations, and no more of the kind of lives that push men like Mickey to the edge and over. The last of the independents will be unionized, grounded, regulated, the skies made safe, the business brought into line, the men protected. Like the rest of us, they'll live their lives on CCTV, pay their taxes, get mortgages, join what passes for regular society. One day it'll happen.

Meanwhile, the clouds keep moving, the rivers flow; the dust blows forward and back; the last free men on earth fly across those great, dark spaces between the radar; and the planes, money, and cargo keep on flowing across the lines we've drawn on a few bits of paper.

It's getting cold. Back home, February's already here with an easterly wind that chills the bones. Time to go inside, where there's light. It's only when I reach the pool of yellow light by the door of my home and look back that I realize how quickly the night can fall here in the Northern Hemisphere. Now there's just a small point of light crawling high above, making its way across the sky to the northeast. And it cheers me to think that up there, high above the black earth, someone is looking through a cockpit window and thinking about home.

Mickey, if you're up there somewhere, I'll see you for that cold Baltika on the other side sometime.

And Sergei, you were right. I worry far too much.

Author's Note

While Mickey's world is one that bears a striking resemblance to the world we live in, it is a world that straddles not only the ambiguities in national and international law but also lines of loyalty and conduct in personal, command, legal, and business relationships. It has been made very clear to me several times in the course of researching and writing this book that the disclosure of the identities of many of the men herein would potentially lead not only to serious implications (for them and their continuing employability), lawsuits (from them), or unwelcome attention and even criminal charges (against them), but to exposure to serious harm.

For these reasons, and in many cases the trust placed in me by these men and women, the names and characters, not only of the man, men, and combination thereof whom I have elected to call Mickey and his crew, have been changed, scrambled, and composited, along with enough physical, business, geographical, and biographical details to make them wholly unidentifiable—and although Mickey and Sergei are now dead, it is out of respect to them and their associates, as well as regard for the small world in which they operated, that I adhere to this policy there, too. For the same reason, and because flight plans are filed and kept, I have changed dates and locations for the action around flights and destinations in almost all cases. (To be clear: None of the men who could be this pilot was named Mikhail, Misha, Mickey or anything like; they were not from Siberia or Vitebsk, and the real Mickey's features have been altered to render him unidentifiable. So if you think you recognize him, Sergei, or any of the others from the physical description, name, personal history, flight paths, airplane details, or by patching together flight times and places, you are mistaken, and any resemblance to real persons, living or dead, is a coincidence.

Otherwise, throughout the text I have changed or withheld other names only when expressly asked either for a pseudonym or to be quoted off the record for that contribution or part of his or her overall contribution. In some instances I have changed and/or withheld names gained in conversations and interviews long ago for other projects, simply because I believe that not to do so would have been to compromise the individual and betray his or her trust.

For all of these reasons and more, and with apologies to the aviation-hardware buffs out there: Even though I make no suggestion that their employers, colleagues, or other contacts are involved in or even necessarily aware of any of these activities on a corporate level, I have also elected not to specify the precise models of the planes on which I was privileged to have been invited, nor their businesses, numbers, or distinguishing features by which they can be identified, and enough locations and dates have been altered to render them securely anonymous—and such inconsistencies as that entails are acknowledged. For legal reasons, I have in many cases withheld identifiers.

It is worth noting that the term *Russian* is used by many—especially in Africa, Arabia, and the Far East—including by Russians themselves (Evgeny Zakharov calls the Tajik and Ukrainian planes Russian here), as a cover-all for people from largely Russian-speaking Slavic countries of the former USSR. While this blurring is deplorable (ask any Welshman, Scotsman or, heaven forbid, Irishman who's been called English abroad), it is understandable, and as the strange cases of Viktor Bout and Leonid Minin show, such blurring is often positively encouraged by the men themselves.

My policy has been to correct infelicities of language in my interviewees, cutting out stumbles over words and repetition—this has simply been done for clearer reading, and not to change the sense. For instance, Richard Chichakli refers to "the Eastern Bunny" in his original letter to me, and in person, many of the airmen's conversation is almost as littered with pauses, vocab questions, and malapropisms as my Russian.

Finally, the men who form the core of this narrative are also what used to be called Soviets, simply because they were the ones in the eye of this particular hurricane, and they are the ones whose lives I glimpsed. They are men—no better or worse than any others—and indeed they could be, and just as often are, Americans, British, Germans, Ugandans, Moroccans, South Africans, Chinese, Dutch, French, Mexicans, Italians, Congolese, Brazilians, you, me.

Acknowledgments

My thanks to the many friends, aviators, monitors, fellow travelers, and experts who gave their time, and sometimes more, even at risk to their personal safety, generously. And most of all, my friendship and gratitude to the crews, and to Mickey's crew—Mickey and Sergei especially, wherever they are.

Special thanks: First and foremost, my thanks to the crewmen with whom I flew, drank, and talked.

Thanks to: Marshal Evgeny Shaposhnikov, Nikolay Viktorovich Korchunov, Brian Johnson-Thomas, Milos Vasic, Igor Salinger, Nigel Tallantire, Katya Stepanova, Ambassador Dmitry Rogozin, Peter and Ira, Evgeny Zakharov, Martin Ssebuyira, Ilya Neretin, Iain Clark, John MacDonald (and his Secret Friend), Moisés Naím, Ernest Mezak at the Komi Memorial Commission of Human Rights, Linda Polman, Andrei Soldatov, Mira Markovic, Aaron Hewit, Arthur Kent, Andrei Lovtsov, Sharren (Shazz) Glencross, Terry Bonner, Dr. Mark Galeotti, Richard Chichakli, Dominic Medley, Ahmed Rashid, Dmitry Tarasevich, Tatyana Parkhalina, TRAFFIC, Andrey Formin, Patrick Matsiko wa Mucoori, Peacock at *Red Pepper*, Kigongo at *New Vision*, Sarah Robson, Kevin O'Flynn and Oksana Smirnova at the *Moscow Times*, Branislav, Planecrazi, Dr. Christopher M. Davidson, the Embassy of the Republic of Byelorussia in Great Britain, Alexey Zaytsev, Haroun, Tricia O'Rourke, Jock, Andrew Hirsch, Dean Fitzpatrick, Savita Singh, Rachel Butters, Boris, Zayna, Jamie, Gordana and Natalya, Ian Belcher, "The Antonov Man," Hugh Griffiths at SIPRI, Damian Clarke at Olympus, "A" at Ilyushin, the nice guys at the MONUC compound (you know who you are), the amazing, elusive *Vreme* writers who worked with Milos Vasic on that story, Jovan Dulovic, Ilija Vukelic (Belgrade) Branko Stosic (Moscow) and Sergei Kuznetsov (Ekaterinburg), who worked with Milos Vasic at Vreme and whose investigative brilliance, along with Vasic's, formed the basis for my account of the Surcin crash, and the countless crews, ground staff, witnesses, researchers, and businesspeople who have given their time freely and gone to greater or lesser lengths to contribute, and have trusted me to use their input responsibly. I hope I have not let you down.

Without whom this book would not have been possible: Peter Danssaert of the International Peace Information Service (IPIS) generously put his time, assistance and expertise at my service at several crucial moments over the course of this book's gestation, and I am endlessly grateful. Jane Mulkerrins, Doug McKinlay, Humfrey Hunter at Hunter Profiles, Clare Conville, Jake Smith-Bosanquet, Susan Armstrong and Henna Silvennoinen at Conville & Walsh. Ben Adams, Michelle Blankenship, Nathaniel Knaebel, Patti Ratchford and, copy editor Will Georgantas at Bloomsbury USA. Ingrid Connell, Bruno Vincent and Ali Blackburn at Pan MacMillan, Juergen Diessl at Ullstein, Alan J Kaufman, David and Linda Potter, Richard Hamilton, Laura Cope, Alisdair Donaldson, Jeremy Points, Jacqui Grice, Ron Piper and the mysterious Mr E. You know who you are. Most of all, very special thanks to my wife Lila, whose help with the countless interviews conducted for this book has been invaluable, and whose patience and belief made it possible.

THE FAMILIES OF THE CREWMEN WHO DIED IN MOGADISHU

A charitable fund has been set up by the company who employed the crew of Candid EW-78849, shot down over Mogadishu in 2007, to help support the families of the slain Byelorussian crewmen. For information on how to contribute, visit www.transaviaexport.com.

Bibliography

Further reading, and books to which, to a greater or lesser extent, I am indebted:

PRIMARY BOOK SOURCES

Although my focus and conclusions differ from the authors', I am deeply indebted to the research carried out by Douglas Farah and Stephen Braun in *Merchant of Death*.

For their expertise on the planes and their history and specifications, as well as stories of the exploits and mishaps seen by the planes and their crews, I am similarly indebted to the excellent series of guides by Dmitri Kommisarov and Yefim Gordon, the most essential of which (to me) are mentioned below.

My account of the Belgrade crash owes much to the work of the newspaper *Vreme*—not just the reporters mentioned above, but the entire organization.

Alexeivich, Svetlana. *Zinky Boys: Soviet Voices from a Forgotten War.* London: Chatto & Windus, 1992.

Armstrong, Stephen. *War PLC: The Rise of the New Corporate Mercenary.* London: Faber & Faber, 2009.

Barrand, Jude, and Dominic Medley. *Kabul: The Bradt Mini Guide.* Chalfont St. Peter, UK: Bradt, 2004.

Bowden, Mark. *Killing Pablo*. London: Atlantic Books, 2001.

Boyles, Denis. *African Lives: White Lies, Tropical Truth, Darkest Gossip, and Rumblings of Rumor—from Chinese Gordon to Beryl Markham, and Beyond*. New York: Ballantine, 1989.

Bulgakov, Mikhail. *The Master and Margarita*. London: Picador, 1989.

Collin, Matthew. *This Is Serbia Calling*. London: Serpent's Tail, 2001.

Conrad, Joseph. *Heart of Darkness*. London: Penguin Classics edition, 2007.

Davidson, Christopher M. *Dubai: The Vulnerability of Success*. London: C. Hurst & Co., 2009.

Farah, Douglas, and Stephen Braun. *Merchant of Death*. New York: Wiley, 2007.

Feifer, Gregory. *The Great Gamble: The Soviet War in Afghanistan*. London: Harper Perennial, 2010.

Gilby, Nicholas. *The Arms Trade*. Oxford: New Internationalist, 2009.

Glenny, Misha. *McMafia: Seriously Organized* Crime. London: Vintage, 2008.

Goldman, Marshall. *Oilopoly: Putin, Power & the Rise of the New Russia*. Oxford: Oneworld, 2010.

Hatfield, James. *Fortunate Son: George W. Bush & the Making of an American President*. London: Vision, 2002.

Hobsbawm, Eric. *Bandits*. London: Abacus, 2001.

Hoffman, David E. *The Dead Hand: The Untold Story of the Cold War Arms Race and Its Dangerous Legacy*. New York: Anchor/Random House, 2010.

Holdsworth, Nick. *Moscow: The Beautiful and the Damned*. London: Andrew Deutsch, 2003.

Klebnikov, Paul. *Godfather of the Kremlin: The Decline of Russia in the Age of Gangster Capitalism*. New York: Harcourt, 2000.

Klein, Joe. *The Natural: The Misunderstood Presidency of Bill Clinton*. New York: *Doubleday*, 2002.

Kommisarov, Dmitri, and Yefim Gordon. *Antonov An-12: The Soviet Hercules*. Hinkley, UK: Midland Publishing, 2007.

———, *Ilyushin 76: Russia's Versatile Airlifter*. Hinkley, UK: Midland Publishing, 2001.

Lanning, Michael Lee. *Mercenaries*. New York: Presidio Press, 2005.

LeBor, Adam. *Milošević*. London: Bloomsbury, 2003.

Litvinenko, Alexander (with Yuri Felshtinsky). *Blowing Up Russia*. London: Gibson Square Books, 2007.

Meyer, Karl E. *The Dust of Empire: The Race for Mastery in the Asian Heartland*. New York: Public Affairs, 2004.

Naím, Moisés. *Illicit: How Smugglers, Traffickers and Copycats Are Hijacking the Global Economy*. London: Arrow, 2007.

Parsons, Anthony. *From Cold War to Hot Peace: UN Interventions, 1947-94.* London: Penguin, 1995.

Polman, Linda. *War Games: The Story of Aid and War in Modern Times.* London: Viking, 2010.

Rashid, Ahmed. *Taliban.* London: IB Tauris & Co., 2000.

Robbins, Christopher, *Kazakhstan: The Land that Disappeared.* London: Profile, 2008.

——— *Air America.* London: Corgi, 1988.

Rogozin, Dmitry. *The Hawks of Peace.* Unpublished manuscript, 2010.

Schroeder, Matthew, Dan Smith, and Rachel Stohl. *The Small Arms Trade.* 2007.

Soldatov Andrei, and Irina Borogan. *The New Nobility: The Restoration of Russia's Security State and the Enduring Legacy of the KGB.* London: Public Affairs, 2010.

Stiglitz, Joseph. *Globalization and Its Discontents.* London: Penguin, 2003.

Stockholm International Peace Research Institute. *Armaments, Disarmament and International Security: SIPRI Yearbook, 2009.* Stockholm: SIPRI, 2009.

Taylor, Brian D. *Politics and the Russian Army: Civil-Military Relations 1689–2000.* Cambridge: Cambridge University Press, 2003.

Transparency International. *Preventing Corruption in Humanitarian Operations: A Handbook.* Berlin: Transparency International, 2010.

Vaisman, Alexey, and Pavel Fomenko. *Siberia's Black Gold: Harvest and Trade in Amur River Sturgeons in the Russian Federation.* Cambridge: TRAFFIC Europe, 2006.

SELECTED REPORTS

Amnesty International. *Democratic Republic of Congo: Arming the East,* 2005.

———. *Blood at the Crossroads: Making the Case for a Global Arms Trade Treaty,* 2008.

Danssaert, Peter, and Brian Johnson-Thomas. Disarmament Forum. *Illicit Brokering of SALW in Europe: Lacunae in Eastern European Arms Control and Verification Regimes,* 2009.

Finardi, Sergio (TA), Amnesty International. *Dead on Time: Arms Transportation, Brokering and the Threat to Human Rights,* 2006 .

Finardi, Sergio, Brian Johnson-Thomas, and Peter Danssaert. IPIS vzw (21 December 2009): *From Deceit to Discovery: The Strange Flight of 4L-AWA;* and IPIS vzw (8 February 2010): *From Deceit to Discovery: An Update.*

———. IPIS (3 December 2010): *Mapping the Labyrinth: More on the Strange Weapons Flight of 4L-AWA.* Available at ipisresearch.be.

Griffiths, Hugh, and Mark Bromley. SIPRI/SEESAC, *Air Transfers and Destabilizing Commodity Flows*, 2009.

———. *Stemming Destabilizing Arms Transfers: The Impact of European Union Air Safety Bans*, 2008.

Griffiths, Hugh, and Adrian Wilkinson. UNDP, SEESAC, *Guns, Planes and Ships: Identification and Disruption of Clandestine Arms Transfers*.

IPIS vzw: All Party Parliamentary Group on the Great Lakes Region: *Arms flows in Eastern DR Congo*, 2004.

Mercury Public Affairs LLC, on behalf of its foreign principal His Highness Sheikh Khalid bin Saqr Al Qasimi. *Ras Al Khaimah: A Rogue State in the UAE?*, (2010).

———. *Ras Al Khaimah: Gateway to Trade with Iran*.

Reports of the Group of Experts Submitted by the Security Council Committee Established Pursuant to Resolution 1533 (2004) Concerning the Democratic Republic of the Congo, 2004–2010.

Reports of the Monitoring Group and the Panel of Experts on Somalia and Submitted Through the Security Council Committee Established Pursuant to Resolutions 751 (1992) and 1907 (2009) Concerning Somalia, 2002–2010.

Reports of the Security Council Committee Established Pursuant to Resolution 1267 (1999) Concerning Al-Qaida and the Taliban and Associated Individuals and Entities, 1999–2009.

Reports of the Security Council Committee Established Pursuant to Resolution 1521 (2003) Concerning Liberia, 2003–2010.

Reports of the Security Council Committee Established Pursuant to Resolution 1591 (2005) Concerning the Sudan, 2005–2010.

Reports of the Security Council Committee Pursuant to Resolutions 751 (1992) and 1907 (2009) Concerning Somalia and Eritrea, 2005–2008.

SEESAC/UNDP. Western Balkans Parliamentary Forum on Small Arms and Light Weapons. *Analysis of National Legislation on Arms Exports and Transfers in the Western Balkans*, 2006.

Wood, Brian, and Johan Peleman. *The Arms Fixers*. Peace Research Institute, Oslo, 1999.

NEWSPAPERS AND PERIODICALS

I am particularly indebted to Serbia's *Vreme*, whose investigation into the Belgrade crash and its significance laid the foundations for so many subsequent monitoring reports as well as the account here; and *Zyrianskoe*

Zhizn, whose tireless chasing (by activist-reporter Ernest Mezak) of the causes and motivations surrounding the crashes of Russian airmen in Africa, and statements from authorities and airmen, have shaped my understanding of their world. Ernest, thank you for your generous assistance. I also owe a debt of thanks to the *New York Times* for the quality and foresight of the interviews with Damnjanovic and Bout, and *The Guardian* for its arms dealers series. Others: the *Moscow Times*, *Pravda*, *Sovershenno Sekretno*, *Take-Off*, *Current Digest of the Post-Soviet Press*, *Kommersant*, *Moskovsky Komsomolets* (Moscow), *St. Petersburg Times* (St. Petersburg), *Zyrianskoe Zhizn* (Komi), *Vreme*, *Politika*, *VIP* (Belgrade), the *Guardian*, the *Independent*, the *Times*, the *Economist*, *International Who's Who* (UK), the *Independent*, the *Daily Monitor*, *New Vision*, the *Eye* (Kampala), *Foreign Policy*, the *New York Times*, *Washington Monthly*, *An-Novosti/Antonov News* (from the Antonov Aeronautical Scientific/Technical Complex, Ukraine), *Afghan Daily* (Kabul), *Gulf News*, *Gulf Today* (UAE)

ONLINE RESOURCES

Afghan newswire: www.pajhwok.com
Amnesty International: www.amnesty.org
Aviation Safety Network Database of the Flight Safety Foundation: www
       .aviation-safety.net
Ethical Cargo: www.ethicalcargo.org
International Peace Information Service: www.IPISresearch.be
The Professional Pilots' Rumour Network: www.pprune.org
Registan news source in English for Central Asia: www.registan.net
The South Eastern and Eastern Europe Clearinghouse for the Control of
       Small Arms and Light Weapons (SEESAC): www.seesac.org
Stockholm International Peace Research Institute: www.sipri.org

SOME OF THE PEOPLE IN THE BOOK

Air Cess: www.aircess.com
Viktor Bout: www.viktorbout.com
Richard Chichakli: www.chichakli.com

Adam Curtis: adamcurtisfilms.blogspot.com
Mark Galeotti's excellent blog: www.inmoscowsshadows.wordpress.com
Arthur Kent's documentary news channel: www.skyreporter.com
Doug McKinlay: www.dougmckinlay.com
Amb. Dmitry Rogozin: www.rogozin.ru
Andrei Soldatov's index on Russia's secret state: www.agentura.ru
The Yorkshire Ranter: www.yorkshire-ranter.blogspot.com
Evgeny Zakharov's Soviet Air Charter: www.sovietaircharter.com

Index

A Note on the Author

Matt Potter is a British journalist, editor, and broadcaster. He has reported for BBC Radio from Eastern Europe, Afghanistan, and Southeast Asia, and copresented its award-winning global travel shows. As a journalist, his nose for the unusual has seen his writing appear in places as diverse as the *Daily Telegraph*, *Golf Monthly*, *Sunday Telegraph*, *Jack*, *Maxim*, and the *Irish Examiner*, and his stories on cocaine trafficking in Latin America have been translated into Russian, German, and Spanish. As a journalist in Belgrade, he broke the story of the NATO "spy" giving away secrets to Serb forces on the Web. He speaks a handful of languages to wildly varying degrees, but attempts to speak at least twenty more. Find out more on *Outlaws Inc.* and Matt Potter at www.mattpotterbooks.com.